GAY AND LESBIAN
STUDENTS

GAY AND LESBIAN STUDENTS
Understanding Their Needs

Hilda F. Besner
Clinical Psychologist
Fort Lauderdale, Florida

Charlotte I. Spungin
Education Specialist
Fort Lauderdale, Florida

Taylor & Francis
Publishers since 1798

USA	Publishing Office:	Taylor & Francis
		1101 Vermont Ave., N.W., Suite 200
		Washington, DC 20005
		Tel: (202) 289-2174
		Fax: (202) 289-3665
	Distribution Center:	Taylor & Francis
		1900 Frost Road, Suite 101
		Bristol, PA 19007-1598
		Tel: (215) 785-5800
		Fax: (215) 785-5515
UK		Taylor & Francis, Ltd.
		4 John Street
		London WC1N 2ET
		Tel: 071 405 2237
		Fax: 071 831 2035

GAY AND LESBIAN STUDENTS: Understanding Their Needs

1 2 3 4 5 6 7 8 9 0 BRBR 0 9 8 7 6 5

This book was set in Times Roman by Christine Winter. The editors were Christine Williams and Christine Winter. Cover design by Michelle Fleitz. Printing and binding by Braun-Brumfield, Inc.

A CIP catalog record for this book is available from the British Library.

∞ The paper in this publication meets the requirements of the ANSI Standard Z39.48-1984 (Permanence of Paper)

Library of Congress Cataloging-in-Publication Data
Besner, Hilda, F.
    Gay and lesbian students: understanding their needs/Hilda F. Besner and Charlotte I. Spungin.
        p. cm.
    Includes bibliographical references and index.

    1. Homosexuality and education—United States. 2. Gay students—United States. 3. Lesbian students—United States. I. Spungin, Charlotte, I. II. Title.
LC192.6.B47 1995
370.19'345—dc20   95-12727
                                                     CIP

ISBN 1-56032-337-X (cloth)
ISBN 1-56032-338-8 (paper)

For Mark, Adriana, Hanna, Mom, Dad, Adele, Allyson, Jason, Tyler, Eleanor, and in memory of Sharon.

Contents

Preface

If a school you attended had an enrollment of 1,500 students, were you aware that at least 150 of them were gay and lesbian? Probably not, and you were not alone. Generally, school personnel are unaware of the 10% statistic. Many people have been educated to believe gays and lesbians are easily identifiable, although most of them are not. The truth is, there is an invisible gay and lesbian minority in every school, and the needs of these students within the educational setting are often unknown and unmet.

Historically, when the nation's school systems have been made aware of minority needs, there have been positive responses to address these needs through changes in policies, curricula, and staff development. So far, only a small number of American school districts have taken positive steps to address the problems associated with gay and lesbian students in the educational setting.

In New York City, the Harvey Milk school was established in 1985 for gay and lesbian students who were not succeeding in the New York public schools.

> Many young people—especially those who were cross dressers, or young men who were effeminate, or young women who were "too butch" (tough, independent, and "masculine")—found their peers hostile, often to the point of violence. For gay youth who could "pass" and remain undetected in the school system, advocates found the hiding process robbed students of much of their energy and vitality. Whether lesbian and gay youth were open about their identities or were closeted, societal prejudice took its toll; young gay people were often anti-social, alcohol- and drug-abusing, and/or depressed to the point of suicide. (Rofes, 1989, p. 449)

Although this school addresses some of the needs of gay and lesbian students, it also fosters isolation from the real world. There is some debate among educators about separating the education of gay and lesbian students from the mainstream culture. The focus of this book is on gay and lesbian students in a predominantly heterosexual school context.

This book is directed to all school-related personnel and the educators who provide their training:

- Inservice and preservice teachers
- Counselors
- School psychologists
- Administrators
- Social workers
- Curriculum directors
- Media specialists
- School board members
- School nurses
- Visiting teachers
- Undergraduate and graduate professors
- Human resource development personnel
- Noninstructional personnel

The purpose of this book is to promote awareness of the problems encountered by gay and lesbian adolescents in the educational setting and the effects of these problems on the school dropout rate, academic achievement, substance abuse, teenage pregnancy, AIDS, school violence, and the epidemic of suicide and suicide attempts by young gays and lesbians as revealed in the 1989 federal report on youth suicide (Gibson, 1989).

The book is designed to:

- Promote an understanding of the needs and problems of gay and lesbian teenagers
- Dispel the myths associated with the lives of students who have diverse sexual orientations
- Present various theories concerning the origins of sexual development
- Explain how institutional homophobia has affected the belief system and behavior of a large segment of the nation's population
- Make curriculum suggestions that will promote self-acceptance among gay and lesbian students and reduce homophobia among heterosexual students
- Provide information concerning students who are children of gay and lesbian parents

Because *inservice teachers* have daily contact with students, it is important for them to know and understand the needs of the gay and lesbian students who make up approximately 10% of the total number of students assigned to them for instruction. In addition, these teachers are in a position to reduce homophobia by dispelling myths about gays and lesbians, presenting information about gay and lesbian role models within the appropriate curricula, and helping gay and lesbian students who approach them for counseling.

It is essential for the *preservice teacher* to acquire information about diverse sexual orientations to understand the needs of these students and assist them in their emotional and social development. *Undergraduate and graduate professors* play a key role in training teachers for this professional responsibility.

This book can be instrumental in planning for a vital part of the preservice teacher's training.

Counselors, school psychologists, social workers, and *visiting teachers* whose trainers may have neglected instruction concerning diverse sexual orientations will benefit from reading this book. It will assist them in understanding the needs of gay and lesbian students and provide special insights into some of the related issues, such as suicide, dropouts, poor academic achievement, low self-esteem, runaways, family conflicts, substance abuse, poor attendance, and behavior problems.

Administrators and *school board members,* who are responsible for policy decisions and their implementation, will find the information helpful in understanding the needs of gay and lesbian students as well as the importance of providing positive adult role models within the school setting and establishing a safe learning environment for these students. The information in this book adds a dimension to the search for prevention and resolution of the numerous problems that challenge present-day school systems, such as student violence, substance abuse, dropouts, low achievement, poor attendance, and discipline problems.

For the *curriculum director,* who has the primary responsibility of developing and facilitating curriculum innovations, this book addresses human development education, AIDS issues in health education, sexual orientation biases within the existing curriculum areas, and integration of the concept of diversity in sexual orientation within appropriate curricula.

This book supplies information for *school nurses* regarding the physical symptoms that may be experienced by gay and lesbian students who are attempting to deal with their sexual orientation. Problems that may be directly or indirectly related to sexual orientation may include eating disorders, alcohol and other substance abuse, AIDS, sleep disorders, depression, sexually transmitted diseases, and promiscuity. In addition, school nurses are frequently called on to speak in health education courses; this book can be a resource for answering questions posed by heterosexual, gay, lesbian, and bisexual students. Appendix C may be especially helpful in referring gay and lesbian students to national agencies and hotlines staffed with people who are trained in dealing with the needs of gay and lesbian adolescents.

As teenagers struggle to understand their sexual orientation they need accessible accurate information and they quite often turn to the school media center as a resource. *Media specialists* can play a key role in the selection and maintenance of periodicals, books, and audiovisual materials that deal with gay and lesbian issues. These resources not only help gay and lesbian students, but also provide information that will increase the level of awareness among all students and the school staff. Appendix A includes a list of books and periodicals coded to help media specialists choose appropriate materials for teenagers, younger readers, educators and other professionals, and parents. Appendix C provides a list of national agencies that will send pertinent information to media centers. Resources for videotapes are also listed.

Human resource development personnel have the ability, through inservice programs, to help all school-related personnel understand the needs of gay and lesbian students. This book supplies information to assist trainers in their preparation for structured workshops. One of the initial steps to increasing awareness of gay and lesbian student needs is training about homophobia. Appendix B provides a detailed model workshop for inservice on this topic. It is advisable for *noninstructional personnel* who have daily contact with students to also participate in this type of inservice training.

Chapter 1 of *Gay and Lesbian Students* sets the stage for the rest of the book through a presentation of the significant theories and research findings concerning the origins of homosexuality, including the biological, psychological, and social approaches.

Chapter 2 is a discussion of the all too familiar myths about homosexuality that are believed by a large segment of society. The perpetuation of these myths impedes understanding, promotes ignorance, feeds prejudice, and results in discrimination, violence, and death.

Chapters 3 and 4 focus on the concept of homophobia and how it manifests itself in societal institutions, such as education, the military, religion, and the workplace. Chapter 3 emphasizes the devastating effects of homophobia on gay and lesbian educators and teenagers and includes a heterosexual questionnaire, designed by Dr. Martin Rochlin, that delivers a subtle message. Chapter 4 includes a list of school policy recommendations to help combat homophobia, made by the Massachusetts Governor's Commission on Gay and Lesbian Youth.

Featured in Chapter 5 is a discussion of gay and lesbian youth suicide and an extensive list of risk factors involved. Chapter 5 also deals with a number of related issues, such as the process of gays and lesbians *coming out* to their families, friends, and school personnel; the importance of support within the school setting; the special problems experienced by gay and lesbian youth who belong to various ethnic minorities; gay fathers; lesbian mothers; bisexuality; and AIDS. All of these issues affect involved students in a variety of ways; educational professionals need to be informed as to how these issues may be impacting particular students. Also included in this chapter is a practical list of guidelines to consider in response to gay and lesbian students who disclose their sexual orientation to educational professionals.

Chapter 6 consists of a number of case studies of gays and lesbians that will help readers understand and become aware of the needs of these students. In many of the case studies someone within the educational setting was instrumental in helping these young people deal with their confusion, anxiety, emotional pain, struggle for self-identity, isolation, depression, and lack of information.

Chapter 7 concerns the lack of identification and acceptance of one's sexuality and how it contributes to other problems, such as the abuse of alcohol and other substances. We present several case studies that demonstrate the dynamics involved.

Chapter 8 answers the question we hope educational professionals will be asking themselves: "What can we do to help?" Included in this chapter are recommendations from the National Education Association (NEA) and the Association for Supervision and Curriculum Development (ASCD), both of which have taken an active role to help school districts develop policies that will protect the rights of gay and lesbian students, provide equal opportunity and a safe school environment, and initiate counseling programs for gay and lesbian students. School-based programs are discussed in this chapter, the most notable of which is Project 10 in the Los Angeles school district. The chapter includes specific advice for school districts and educational and related professionals to assist gay and lesbian students.

Appendix A consists of a selected list of books and periodicals coded for the following groups of readers: educators and other professionals, younger readers, teenagers, and parents. The list is also coded to distinguish fiction from nonfiction.

Appendix B is a detailed model workshop on homophobia for educators and other school-related personnel. The workshop is designed to be administered in 6 1/4 hours.

Appendix C is a resource list of the following:

1 National organizations that provide information and support to professionals and students
2 Short summaries of audio and video materials including information on how to order them
3 National hotlines that address specific gay and lesbian needs, such as an AIDS hotline for the deaf and an AIDS hotline for those who speak Spanish

Appendix D provides a list of famous gays and lesbians who have contributed significantly to our world from early history through contemporary times.

As a service to the reader, the male pronoun is used throughout the text where it improves readability. This is not meant to diminish the importance of the female gender.

We were motivated to write this book after years of counseling desperate gay and lesbian adolescents and adults who suffered from intellectual and emotional debilitation caused by hiding their sexual orientation or by experiencing discrimination, rejection, and abuse from their families, peers, and the community when their sexual orientation was disclosed. The case studies cited are based on our personal experiences with these people. The names have been changed to maintain confidentiality. Some of the cases presented are of young adults who were first able to address their feelings when they could access professional assistance. Many of these adults would have sought counseling earlier if it had been more easily available.

The psychological crippling and loss of potential endured by so many gay and lesbian young people can be dramatically reduced through an awareness by the nation's educators and school-related professionals, who have assumed the enormous responsibility for the intellectual, emotional, physical, social, and vocational development of all students.

We wish to express our gratitude to the following people for their contributions: Elaine Pirrone, Acquisitions Editor, Taylor & Francis, for recognizing and appreciating the need for this book; Bernadette Capelle, Development Editor, Taylor & Francis, for her guidance and assistance in helping to bring a complete and publishable manuscript to the production department; Christine E. Williams, Production Editor, Taylor & Francis, for her expertise and keeping us on task; Christine L. Winter, our copy editor, for her tenacity and superb detective work; Mark Colin, Eleanor Barton, and Iris Bass for the time and energy spent reviewing the manuscript and making valuable editorial comments and suggestions; Hugh Wilburn, Librarian, Frances Loeb Library, Harvard University, for sharing his bibliographical expertise; Adriana and Hanna for sharing their mother with the computer for countless hours each night throughout this project. They were an inspiration and motivation to help other children in need. Special thanks to Mark Colin and Adele Besner for helping to make free time so that this manuscript could be completed, and to Allyson, Tyler, and Jason for all their help. Thank you to Robert Schulman of Shared Technologies, Inc., for his computer assistance. Finally, this book would not have been a reality were it not for the encouragement and support of the late Sharon Solomon, who was catalytic in inspiring us to address this issue years before it became socially acceptable. We hope that, through this effort, we have been able to emulate her love and care for young people in need.

Chapter 1

The Origins of Homosexuality

The issue of homosexuality evokes passionate responses from individuals, yet people do not have a strong concept of its origin. Some individuals view homosexuality as a negative developmental process that results from familial or environmental factors. Although the sexual revolution resulted in greater awareness and acceptance of gays and lesbians, many individuals continue to believe old stereotypes and myths about homosexuality. And although many individuals express acceptance of homosexuals as a legitimate part of society, they believe that it should be regarded as deviant behavior when examined in the context of heterosexual relationships.

In *Symposium*, Plato wrote that humanity once consisted of three sexes instead of two: its partners were joined in pairs of two men, two women, or a man and a woman. Zeus cut each pair apart to diminish their power and to teach them to fear the gods. Humans spend their time on earth searching for their other half, with whom they can find more love (Byne, 1994).

Homosexuality has been present since the beginning of civilization. It is present in most cultures, and in some cultures it is considered to be the dominant sexual behavior. Tripp (1987) has reported that societies that tend to suppress homosexuality do so based on moral tenets. These moral beliefs usually have a greater impact on the behavior of heterosexuals than homosexuals. Societies that are lenient toward and accepting of homosexuality tend to have high birth rates and thus serious problems with overpopulation. Therefore, acceptance of homosexuality does not increase its incidence in society.

In his analysis of cultures with low rates of homosexuality, Tripp has found that there are several factors involved. Some of these societies advocate and provide opportunities for nonerotic forms of body contact between men. In other societies, heterosexuality is quite rigorously programmed (such as through arranged marriages), and there is strong pressure for social conformity. However, even in these societies, if homosexuality were permitted it might take off like wildfire. In some tribes of North American Indians, when effeminate behavior is recognized in a young boy he is trained to take on the role and behavior of a female. The Cheyenne Indians allowed married men to take on *berdaches*, or male transvestites, as second wives. These marriages were socially approved unions and did not necessarily involve sexual union. The berdache training program was built on the characteristics evidenced by some young children. Sometimes, when the number of berdaches needed to satisfy the community became low, a greater number of boys was selected to be raised as women (Hoebel, 1960).

HORMONAL EFFECTS

Biological sex is determined before the 12th week of fetal development by a process of successive differentiation. The presence or absence of prenatal hormones determines the genital structure of the fetus. Endocrinological studies have attempted to determine the role of hormones in controlling sexual behavior (Money & Tucker, 1975). Some researchers have suggested that prenatal hormones influence which sex the person will be attracted to and that improper hormone exposure before birth results in greater same-sex attraction (Ellis, 1936). Other researchers have proposed that sex hormones play an important part in the power of human sexual expression but that they do not determine sexual orientation. For example, in reported cases of infants who were assigned the wrong sex at birth, all have developed same-sex attractions (i.e., males who were incorrectly identified as females developed an attraction to males) (Money, 1970; Money, 1988; Money & Ehrhardt, 1972). Thus, there is no definitive answer as to whether hormones directly influence one's attraction to members of the same sex. There comes a point in the developmental process when an individual's sexual value system, based on internal and external factors, will determine which sexual behavior will be predominant.

In 1978, Gorski, Gordon, Shryne, and Southam examined a rat's hypothalamus and found that one group of cells was several times larger in male than in female rats. This finding was noteworthy because the area in which Gorski found these differences was related to the generation of sexual behavior, particularly male sexual behavior. Gorski and his colleagues felt that androgens (male hormones) were influential in bringing about dimorphism during development. Although male and female rats have similar neurons in this area, a surge of the androgen testosterone secreted by the testes of male fetuses around the time of birth seems to stabilize the neuronal population. In females, the lack of a surge results in the death of neurons, which results in a smaller structure. The neurons that are sensitive to the androgen testosterone are affected for a few only days before and after birth. Removing the androgens in an adult rat by castration did not reduce the number of neurons. This research piqued the interest of scientists who felt there might be a similar response in humans and thus a genetic basis for homosexuality.

CHROMOSOMES

Hamer, Hu, Magnuson, Hu, and Pattatucci (1993; Pool, 1993) identified a link between some cases of male homosexuality and a small segment of DNA on the X chromosome. First they identified 76 homosexual men and investigated how many of their family members were homosexual. They found that 13.5% of the brothers were homosexual, significantly higher than the 2% found in the general population. In examining the family history, they found that there were more gay relatives on the maternal side than the paternal side; they found that homosexuality occurred more among maternal uncles of gay men and cousins who were sons of maternal aunts than in the general population. These findings led them to suspect that the trait for male homosexuality might be passed on through the female. If there is one gay male in the family, there is a greater likelihood of there being another gay family member. Hamer et al.'s research confirmed the results of a sibling study by Pillard and Weinrich (1986), who found that brothers of gay men have a 14% likelihood of being gay compared with 2% for men without gay brothers. Maternal uncles had a 7% chance of being gay; sons of maternal aunts had an 8% chance. Fathers, paternal uncles, and other cousins had little chance.

Bailey and Pillard (1991) studied 161 homosexual males and their twin or adoptive brothers and found that 52% of their subjects' identical twin brothers, 22% of the fraternal twin brothers, and 11% of the adoptive brothers were homosexual. This supports a biological link theory. A study of lesbian twin sisters revealed that identical twins of lesbians were three times more likely than fraternal twins to be lesbians or bisexuals (Bailey, 1993).

As a second phase of their research, Hamer et al. recruited 40 pairs of homosexual brothers and analyzed their DNA with genetic linkage analysis using gene markers. Of the 40 pairs of brothers, 33 pairs shared a set of five markers located near the end of the long arm of the X chromosome in a region designated Xq28. Statistical analysis revealed a 99.5% level of certainty that there is genetic material on the X chromosome that predisposes a male to become homosexual.

BRAIN

Allen, Hines, Shryne, and Gorski (1986) also found dimorphic structures in the human brain. They reported that the cell group called INAH3 in the hypothalamic region was three times larger in men than in women. LeVay (1991) studied the brains of 19 homosexual men, 16 heterosexual men, and 6 women whose sexual orientation was unknown, all of whom died before age 60. He found that one tiny region within the hypothalamus (the INAH3 area) of homosexual men was more like that in women than in heterosexual men. He concluded that the INAH3 area of most of the women and homosexual men was about the same size. In heterosexual men this region was, on average, twice as large. This supported the research by Allen et al. In some homosexual men this cell group was found to be absent; statistical analysis indicated that the probability of this happening was one in a thousand.

Allen et al. (1986) have also stated that the anterior commissure is smallest in heterosexual men, larger in women, and largest in gay men. After correcting for overall brain size, the anterior commissure in women and in gay men were found to be comparable in size.

These studies raise the issue of the connection between sexual orientation and brain structure. Several hypotheses have been presented: the structural differences were present early in life, perhaps even before birth, and helped to establish sexual orientation; differences arose in adult life because of sexual feelings or behavior; or there may have been some developmental event during uterine or early post-natal life (LeVay & Hamer, 1994). The direct model of biological causation theory states that genes, hormones, and other factors act directly on the developing brain, probably before birth, to wire it for sexual orientation. The social learning model theory states that biology provides a blank slate of neural circuitry which then responds to the experiences of an individual. The indirect model states that biological factors do not wire the brain for orientation but predispose individuals toward personality traits that influence the relationships and experiences that shape sexuality. To date, there is no definitive answer (Byne, 1994).

GENDER IDENTIFICATION

Gender identification is not necessarily with one's biological sex. A child identifies his gender by learning at an early age whether he is labeled a boy or a girl. He becomes aware that there are two different sexes and that a boy will always be a boy and a girl will always be a girl. By the age of three, most children have a strong sense of their gender identity. Once children have identified themselves as boys or girls, it is very difficult to change this concept. Gender identity is a psychological rather than an anatomic reality. Individuals who have tremendous conflict between their biological sex and gender identity may opt for surgical intervention to modify their biological sex (DeVries, 1969; Slaby & Frey, 1975).

Children

As children become aware of their gender identity they begin to recognize behavioral differences between the two sexes. They look to their parents and other significant adults to determine which behaviors are associated with boys or girls. They may mimic some of these behaviors in their play: girls tend to play house and with their kitchens whereas boys play with tools. They may ask why some boys wear earrings or have long hair, or comment on the short hair cut of a woman. In preschool and grade school, social pressure from their peers may modify their choice of toys and behavior. This further solidifies feelings of belonging and a recognition of the differences between the genders. It is not until children get older that they begin to feel comfortable modifying their initial perceptions and behavior (Mussen, 1969; Thornton & Nardi, 1975).

Although a young child may feel different, he may not be able to concretely identify why and may not fully understand his feelings. It is during adolescence that the potential to label oneself as a homosexual begins to emerge. This awareness may evoke anxiety and confusion. It becomes important for the adolescent to engage in experimental behavior to further clarify his feelings and learn the roles and experiences in which he will be most comfortable. It is during this period that the ego identity is formed; social involvement, interpersonal relationships, and friendships with peers develop; and independent thinking and autonomous behavior begin.

Adolescents

For many gay and lesbian adolescents this developmental period is a time of great apprehension. They do not know how to confront their feelings and express their needs. A number of behaviors may result: they may deny or try to repress their true feelings; they may suppress their homosexual desires and adapt a heterosexual orientation; or they may self-disclose. Whichever path they choose, they encounter obstacles that are difficult to overcome.

Adolescents who try to repress their homosexual feelings find this difficult to accomplish. Often, the feelings emerge with greater frequency, and the adolescent feels less control over his feelings. These adolescents may be anxious, have few close relationships with peers, tend to isolate themselves and withdraw from social situations, and have difficulty with overall coping strategies.

Suppressing feelings and redirecting energies toward heterosexual behavior sometimes seems the easiest choice for the adolescent. However, it may not be as easy as adolescents might like to believe. They may place a strong emphasis on their appearance and engage in heterosexual experimentation to win peer approval and acceptance. Although this allows them to develop peer relationships and gain some acceptance within the heterosexual culture, frequently there is a feeling of alienation and deceit. Self-image and self-respect are questioned and often there is fear of discovery. These adolescents may feel they are always putting on an act and that they cannot relax and be themselves. They are also concerned that if the truth was known, they would not be accepted.

Some adolescents make the decision to disclose their identity. This may be a difficult choice for several reasons:

1 They may find little acceptance and understanding from their parents, who may tell them that they do not understand these feelings. Parents may advocate therapeutic intervention to try to modify their child's feelings.

2 They may have few peer associations because they feel ostracized from their heterosexual friends. Although there are numerous support groups for

gay and lesbian adults, generally there are limited support groups for gay and lesbian adolescents. Guidance counselors, school psychologists, and administrators are in positions to initiate the formation of these support groups in school settings.

   3   The disclosed adolescents may have to confront societal prejudices at a time when they may not have a strongly developed coping strategy for dealing with these attitudes. Adolescence is a difficult time for most teenagers, but it is especially complicated for the gay or lesbian adolescent.

PSYCHOLOGICAL THEORIES

There are many theories about the psychological development of homosexuality. Perhaps one of the earliest theories was set forth by Freud, who viewed homosexuality as a developmental interruption of the child's relationship with his parents. He believed that homosexuality occurred because of the child's strong incestuous desires for the parent of the opposite sex. For example, in the absence of a strong male figure a boy might fall in love with his mother and wish to become her lover. Because this is not possible, he might respond emotionally by suppressing his desire for women and developing an attraction for men. This intense conflict may be the basis for castration anxiety and the fear of penis loss (Freud, 1963b).

   Another possible explanation is the child's strong identification with the same-sex parent. Because the adolescent cannot have the relationship he desires with this same-sex parent, he seeks out a same-sex partner with whom he can establish a relationship. Freud acknowledged that, developmentally, most adolescents experience a homosexual attraction. His explanation of homosexuality is that, for some individuals at this point, development becomes arrested (Freud, 1963b).

   Another psychological theory is that some cases of homosexuality develop because of an antisex Puritanism present in the home. If a young boy is told that it is vile and sinful to defile women he may develop a repugnance or fear of sex. As he approaches adolescence he may channel his sexual desires toward other men so that he will not have to defile women.

   In clinical case studies, Isay (1985, 1986, 1987) found that adult gay men reported a lack of close bonds with their fathers in childhood. He believed this stemmed from the defensiveness the gay men felt about their early erotic attachments to their fathers. He believed that cross-gender behavioral characteristics in these boys were manifested in order to acquire and maintain the attraction and attention of their fathers. Furthermore, Isay (1987) believed that sexual orientation needs to occur before gender identity can be developed.

   Adolescence is an extremely challenging time in the sexual development of most children. School transitions and new social relationships can have a strong impact on these adolescents (Clausen, 1975; Peterson & Crockett, 1985). Kinsey, Pomeroy, and Martin (1948) felt that the onset of puberty and adolescence was particularly challenging for male homosexuals. They reported a high positive correlation between the earlier onset of puberty and the frequency of homosexuality during adolescence and later life. Kinsey looks to an environmental conditioning hypothesis to explain this (Gebhard, 1965; Tripp, 1987). This theory states that boys who masturbate early form a strong connection between maleness and male genitalia and that these result in sexually arousing and stimulating feelings. According to Tripp (1987), these associations may get generalized and transferred to other male attributes and to same-sex partners, with heterosexual interests being derailed.

Social learning theory suggests that multiple role models affect the sexual acquisition of children. Observing various male and female models, both in and outside the home, helps children become more comfortable with their sexuality and acquire less stereotypic sex-role behavior. Sexual scripts help direct and focus sexual conduct by providing affective and cognitive boundaries for sexuality (Gagnon & Simon, 1973). Children and adolescents learn about appropriate and inappropriate sexual partners, proper sexual behavior, permissible settings for sex, why people have sex, and acceptable sexual techniques. People learn to identify and label their sexual feelings through experiences with gender roles and their related sexual scripts.

To identify themselves in terms of a social condition or category, homosexual adolescents need to learn that their feelings are legitimate and that there are others who feel as they do. They can then identify with that group of people. Once they form that identification, they need to be able to label themselves as gay or lesbian and feel adequate and accept themselves as homosexuals (Lofland, 1969).

LIFE HISTORY THEORISTS

Life history theorists perceive gender as a life course whose social construction revolves around the reproductively relevant aspects of role and identity, whether or not that gender includes reproduction (Adam, 1986; Blackwood, 1985). Life is a series of sequential steps that involve decisions about major life parameters that affect survival and reproduction. Some of these decisions revolve around sex, rate of growth, age at maturity, length of reproductive life, level of fertility, degree of investment of energy and resources in offspring, and longevity. Life history theory purports that birth order can have a significant impact on the sexual roles and behavior that are adopted by various siblings. Sexual behavior and responsibility are determined by the role the individual plays in the family system. In European history and in other cultures where patrilineal succession was important there was a strong preference for male children. The birth order of the male child had a great impact on the familial expectations for that child and the behavior and belief system that the child eventually adopted for himself. These theorists believe that environmental and familial expectations shape sexual orientation.

Life history theorists believe that all sexuality is in part situational—the product of the interaction of familial and social pressures, social opportunities, and individual temperament and experience. Therefore, homosexual contacts are a component, either mandatory or optional, of that gender or life course definition. Gender rules always dictate the circumstances in which homosexual contact is appropriate.

> The ultimate guarantee of safety for an openly gay or lesbian lifestyle is only superficially paradoxical: a stable industrial social system providing the most adequate, most egalitarian support (social, economic, medical and educational) for reproducing adults, will provide us, as well, the environment of greatest personal freedom in all relations of sex and love. (Dickemann, 1993, p. 66)

BOYHOOD INFLUENCES

Some people still believe that young males are seduced to homosexuality by older males. Although many males have early homosexual activities, what seems to be important is not the sexual act itself but the feelings associated with the experience. This probably determines why heterosexual men may have homosexual experiences but are not homosexual.

In a 25-year analysis of longitudinal data from the Fels Institute, Kagan and Moss (1962) found a strong relationship between boys' childhoods and adult gender role behaviors and interests. Other researchers have stated that the influences within families are bidirectional (Bell & Harper, 1977; Boxer, Cook, & Cohler, 1986; Cohler & Geyer, 1982; Cook, 1988; Hagestad, 1981); children may influence parents in as many ways as parents influence children.

IDENTITY FORMATION

Troiden (1989) identified a four-stage model of homosexual identity formation: sensitization, identity confusion, identity assumption, and commitment. He believes that sensitization occurs before puberty but that most gays and lesbians at this stage do not see homosexuality as being personally relevant because they believe they are heterosexual. Research by Bell, Weinberg, and Hammersmith (1981) showed that homosexual males were almost two times more likely than heterosexual controls to report feeling "very much or somewhat" different from other boys during grades 1 to 8. Lesbians also were more likely than heterosexual controls to have felt "somewhat or very much" different from other girls during these grades.

Troiden believes it is during adolescence that lesbians and gay males begin to personalize homosexuality. It is at this stage that they recognize how they are feeling and identify their feelings and behaviors as possibly being homosexual. Because they do not quite understand their feelings, they may not be certain about their homosexuality. This stage is very confusing for adolescents, especially when they have limited information and knowledge about homosexuality and recognize that there is a stigma associated with being gay or lesbian. Research has indicated that lesbians and gay males may respond to their identity confusion by denying their feelings (Goode, 1984; Troiden, 1979); avoiding their feelings; redefining their feelings; or accepting their feelings (Cass, 1979; Troiden, 1979).

Identity assumption generally occurs in late adolescence. During this phase the individual's homosexuality becomes more comfortable for him and he may present this self to other homosexuals. This may be the early stages of coming out, especially in safe environments (Coleman, 1982b; Lee, 1977). Retrospective studies of adult homosexuals report that gay males arrive at homosexual self-definitions between the ages of 19 and 21 (Dank, 1971; Harry & DeVall, 1978; Kooden et al., 1979; McDonald, 1982; Troiden, 1979). Retrospective studies of small samples of adolescent gay males indicate that they began to identify themselves as such at 14 (Remafedi, 1987). Adult lesbians recalled first thinking of themselves as homosexual between the ages of 21 and 23 (Califia, 1979; Riddle & Morin, 1977; Schafer, 1976).

The final stage, commitment, is when the individual adopts his homosexuality as a way of life. He accepts himself and is comfortable with the homosexual identity. Over time this identity formation often leads to an increasing desire to disclose this identity to heterosexuals (Cass, 1984). Few individuals disclose to everyone in their social environment, and they have many degrees of openness with others (deMonteflores & Schultz, 1978).

Although there are many interesting perspectives on the origins of homosexuality, there is no single definitive explanation. Because many of the studies to date have been based on retrospective recollections, there may have been valuable information lost in establishing how children and adolescents discover they are homosexual. It may be safe to say, however, that essentially every type of human homosexual behavior also occurs in some animal species. Human homosexuality may have as strong a biologically natural component as does heterosexuality. Biological models involving an interaction between genetic and environmental factors are promising and may eventually provide an explanation as to how homosexuality develops.

School personnel assist children and adolescents in various aspects of developmental progress throughout their learning experience, including academics, emotional and physical maturation, and social skills adjustment. If sexuality and identity formation are also developmental processes, then perhaps school personnel should adopt a more proactive role in assisting youth through this developmental stage as well.

Chapter 2

Debunking Myths About Homosexuality

A myth is a traditional story of unknown origins that becomes accepted as fact. Although the belief may initially be based on some partial truths, as the story is retold it can be embellished to the point that it has little resemblance to the actual events or situation. In modern American society, despite instant access to information, many myths persist about homosexuality that are not only inaccurate but harmful.

ORIGINS OF MYTHS

Most myths are perpetuated by word of mouth and frequently develop unchallenged. They are handed down from generation to generation, with each generation adding its own perspective to the story. Myths typically develop out of fear and ignorance. When individuals have little knowledge about something they tend to rely on past experience or what they have been taught. This knowledge frequently goes unchallenged and these belief systems then become generalized to other areas. Because many gays and lesbians remain in the closet about their identity as they interact with mainstream society, the group that has chosen to come out publicly does not necessarily reflect the mainstream gay and lesbian community. Therefore, society bases its assumptions about the gay and lesbian community on inaccurate and incomplete knowledge of members of the mainstream but closeted gay and lesbian community.

Sometimes myths arise as a sense of cultural solidarity. Cultural solidarity occurs when a group embraces certain myths and encourages others to adopt this belief system in order to recruit them into their group. This allows them to rationalize their point of view. The North American Man/Boy Love Association (NAMBLA) perpetuates the myth that all gay men want to molest young children. This group advocates that it is okay for gay men to have sexual relationships with young boys. Antigay groups tend to adopt this myth to reinforce their discriminatory attitudes toward the gay and lesbian community.

The media perpetuate many societal myths. They generally focus on the unusual and stereotypical behaviors, which encourages the general population to believe that these are common or accepted behaviors. When the media show pictures of Gay Pride marches, they frequently focus on individuals who are attired in unusual or bizarre clothing or who are acting atypically and fail to note that the majority of the gays and lesbians attending these marches act and look as normal as mainstream America (Bawer, 1993).

Religious institutions often contribute to the negative attitudes and stereotypes. By teaching that homosexuality is a sin, religious leaders promote homosexuality as unhealthy and unnatural; this helps magnify fears and misperceptions that may already exist in their congregations (Wagner, Serafini, Rabin, Remien, & Williams, 1994). In addition to teaching from the pulpit, many religious leaders perpetuate these myths by purchasing radio and television time and newspaper and magazine space, and by distributing printed materials in their congregations.

Individuals in positions of power may contribute to the stereotyping of homosexuals and to the escalation of the general population's insecurities and misbeliefs. If a leader is a charismatic and effective communicator, he can help mold others' thinking. Adolf Hitler used his power and influence in the 1930s to direct an entire country against certain sectors of the German population in the pursuit of what he believed was a pure race. Plant (1986) has reported that during 1933 and 1934 the Nazis convicted more than 50,000 males of homosexuality and placed them in concentration camps. Many of them were executed; most of the survivors were subjected to gruesome "scientific" experiments. In the concentration camps all gay men were required to wear pink triangles on their shirts and on a pant leg. The pink triangle has been adopted by modern-day gays and lesbians as a symbol of gay pride and the oppression, prejudice, and discrimination they continue to endure (Plant, 1986).

Books, magazines, and periodicals that misinform help perpetuate destructive myths. This has been seen recently in the misperception that AIDS is a disease of gay men and intravenous drug users. Although it was initially correct that these two populations were impacted the most by AIDS, in more recent years the rate of new cases of AIDS has been much lower within the gay population than in the general population. According to the World Health Organization, 75% of the people infected with HIV worldwide have been infected through heterosexual sex ("Gay Men's Health Crisis," 1993). In 1993, 48% of all new AIDS cases in the United States were accounted for by men who had sex with other men. This was down from 53% in 1992 (Neergaard, 1993).

Parents also perpetuate myths, although they may often be unaware of the messages and stereotypical thinking they convey to their children. Because of the special relationship between parent and child, children pick up both overt and subtle messages regarding parents' feelings toward homosexuality. Parents may communicate these messages nonverbally (e.g., through facial expressions and/or gestures). Verbal messages can include statements such as "You ride that bike like a girl" or "Stop being such a sissy—big boys don't cry." Sometimes, unintentionally, strong sexual-orientation messages are sent by the parent when conveying accepting versus nonaccepting attitudes toward certain behavior.

After parents, the most influential adults in a young child's life are teachers, administrators, and other school personnel, who may inadvertently reinforce myths and stereotypes regarding gays and lesbians. They may make derogatory remarks that they consider harmless around children or remain silent when children make derogatory remarks about gays and lesbians; this silence may be interpreted by students as agreement. When they perceive that others have a lax or negative attitude toward certain individuals or groups of people, they may interpret this as permission to act out on their own feelings of nonacceptance.

Gangs are empowered by having a target group on which to focus their energies, aggressive frustrations, and behavior. Gays and lesbians are often a focus of gangs. According to the U.S. Department of Justice (1987), homosexuals are among the most frequent victims of hate violence, along with African Americans, Latinos, Southeast Asians, and Jews. Typically, gang members will identify targets they fear or hate and scapegoat these individuals or groups of individuals as deviant and socially undesirable. Gang members feel superior and powerful by physically displaying their aggressiveness.

MYTHS

The following are some of the most commonly held myths:

1 All Gays and Lesbians Are Easily Identifiable, Because Gay Men Are Effeminate and Lesbian Women Are Masculine

If this were true, homosexuals could not stay in the closet because they would be easily identified. Just as there are effeminate gay men and masculine lesbian women, there are macho gay men and feminine lesbian women. If parents, educators, and other significant adults use masculine and feminine traits as criteria for judging whether a person is gay or lesbian, it will be difficult for them to help young people deal with their sexual orientation. If young gays and lesbians do not fit the stereotypes, they may be dismissed from any assistance and told their suspicions are unfounded. In Chapter 7 we will further explore through case studies some examples of the impact this myth can have on others.

In a 1987 study by Berger, Hank, Rauzi, and Simkins, 71% of gay men and 44% of lesbians believed they could look at someone they do not know and identify that individual's sexual orientation. When tested, only 20% exceeded chance levels of correct detection.

The majority of the gay and lesbian population is indistinguishable from the rest of the general population. They do not dress differently or have mannerisms that make them easily identifiable. Quite the contrary, many gays and lesbians go to great lengths to ensure they fit in with mainstream society. Because they have to be discrete and cautious in order to maintain their jobs and community status, most gay and lesbian individuals are not discernible. They look and act like everyone else.

2 In Homosexual Relationships One Partner Plays the Male Role and the Other Plays the Female Role

Saghir and Robbins (1973) and Harry and DeVall (1978), as well as other researchers (Bem, 1974, 1975; Block, 1973; Heilbrun, 1976; Spence & Helmreich, 1978), have found that there tends to be an egalitarian relationship between homosexual partners rather than a dichotomization of male and female behavior.

As we will discuss later in greater detail, the Gay Liberation movement that began in the late 1960s gained momentum in the 1970s and 1980s when many gays and lesbians representing a cross-section of occupations, socioeconomic levels, races, religions, and so forth came out of the closet to help dispel the masculinity–femininity myth. It was a great shock to the American public to see popular male athletes, macho romantic movie actors, high-level politicians, and sexy female movie stars acknowledge their homosexuality.

3 Homosexuality Is an Emotional Illness

The respected American Psychiatric and American Psychological Associations both formally rejected this idea in the early 1970s (American Psychological Association, 1975; Morin & Schultz, 1978). They said mental health professionals should be instrumental in removing the perception that homosexuality is a mental illness. It is true that many gays and lesbians may become emotionally ill from being persecuted or being forced to hide their sexual orientation from a hostile society. Many gay or lesbian children learn to feel guilty about their differences at an early age and discover their only safety is in pretense, which can take its emotional toll. Not being able to express feelings within the family, worrying about not fitting in or being accepted among their peers, and forcing themselves to play acceptable social roles causes emotional problems. Inability to seek adult support increases the problem because young people are frequently unaware of why they feel different. Homosexual adults who have come to terms with their homosexuality, who do not regret their sexual orientation, and who can function effectively sexually and socially, are no more depressed psychologically than are heterosexual men and women (Bell & Weinberg, 1978).

Before the 1970s, much of the psychological literature promoted the idea that gays had passive or absent fathers and overly protective or possessive mothers. Lesbians were assumed to have disinterested fathers whose affections they tried to earn through overidentification with the masculine role. In psychological literature, these ideas were substantiated by actual case studies from clinical practices (Boxer & Cohler, 1989). During the early days of the Gay Liberation movement in the 1970s, researchers had access to gays and lesbians within the general population and it became apparent that making generalizations concerning gay and lesbian family relationships had been the result of poor or inadequate application of the scientific method. (The scientific method is a research methodology involving three steps: selection of a problem, systematic observation of important variables, and organization and interpretation of emerging facts.) Studies carried out by Bell and Weinberg (1978) of the Kinsey Institute have shown that gays and lesbians come from families with diverse family relationships, just as do heterosexuals. There are gays and lesbians who come from well-organized, warm, loving, supportive, sensitive families, just as there are those who come from families with the opposite characteristics. So the parent–child relationship answer has turned out to be of little or no significance.

The research of the past two decades has been unable to verify any substantiative psychological, genetic, or hormonal uniformity among gay men and lesbians or among heterosexuals. As discussed in the previous chapter, further research is being conducted to search for a biological component (Pillard & Weinrich, 1986).

4   Gays and Lesbians Can Change to Become Heterosexuals

This myth has been particularly destructive. Ironically, much of this destruction has been guided by mental health professionals who have used various techniques in good faith, based on what they believe to be true about the causes of homosexuality. These techniques include aversive conditioning (which involves a mild electrical stimulation); psychoanalysis (guided by the theory that parent–child relationships are responsible); and antiandrogen drugs (altering sex hormones, which may cause asexuality). Scientific evidence is lacking to support the view that gays and lesbians can change their sexual orientation. A person's behavior may change to avoid punitive therapies or the wrath of a hostile society, but the sexual orientation does not seem to change. Today, mental health professionals who try to cure adolescents of homosexuality against their will can be prosecuted. According to the American Psychiatric Association, there is no public scientific evidence that supports the effectiveness of therapy to modify one's sexual orientation ("Attempts to Cure Homosexuality," 1994).

Despite the change in philosophy by the American Psychological and the American Psychiatric Associations, there are professional therapists who continue to hold the belief that homosexuality is abnormal and amoral. Even some homosexuals agree with this thought. The Evergreen Foundation is a nonprofit organization of former homosexuals and their friends who believe that homosexuality can be cured through sports and therapy. Their premise is that homosexuality is caused by a "gender-inferiority complex originating in early childhood" and that this attitude can be changed. Another organization, Exodus Ex-Gay Ministries, also claims to be able to change homosexuals to heterosexuals. This thinking further confuses the homosexual into believing that there is something wrong with him and helps perpetuate the myth that homosexuals can become straight. Although there may be isolated instances of individuals participating in a homosexual relationship and then feeling comfortable with a heterosexual relationship, it remains unclear whether this is due to an individual being bisexual and then feeling more socially and sexually comfortable in a straight relationship, or to other factors. For the majority of homosexuals, psychotherapy or other types of intervention have not been successful in modifying their sexual orientation.

Being gay or lesbian, for the majority of homosexuals, is not a matter of choice. Their sexual orientation is determined from an early age despite efforts to modify their behavior. Although some individuals are comfortable with both the homosexual and heterosexual lifestyles, these individuals may be bisexual. There are not just two ends of the spectrum to sexuality. If we accept the view that there is a genetic component to sexuality and that this is determined by the influence of hormones and other factors, there may be a wide range of sexual feelings and behaviors. Therefore, we will find individuals who are homosexual, heterosexual, bisexual, asexual, or somewhere else along this spectrum.

Individuals cannot be seduced into one sexual orientation or another. They may test certain behaviors and experiment with different lifestyles to determine who they are and how they feel most comfortable. After self-examination, an individual may become aware that what he feels is actually homosexual in nature. He may then decide that he wishes to continue to pursue a homosexual relationship. This is not a seduction. It is a choice based on exploration of feelings, and a gravitation to a way of life that feels comfortable. Lesbians do not become lesbians because they are failures at being female or because they have not found the right man. Neither do lesbians want to become men. Lesbians are lesbians because they feel attracted to women and are most comfortable emotionally and sexually in the company of other women. Likewise, gay men do not want to become women. Gay men are attracted to other men and want to be in their company. For the most part, homosexuals are no different from anyone else in their desires and needs, except that they want to experience their feelings with someone of the same sex, rather then someone of the opposite sex.

There is a small segment of the population whose core identity is different from their physical sex. These transsexuals are different from homosexuals in that they feel they are trapped in the wrong physical body. Some of these individuals may seek sex change operations, which often makes their body image consistent with their sexual orientation. According to Blumenfeld and Raymond (1993), many transsexuals are heterosexuals.

5 Acting Like a "Sissy" Or a "Tomboy" Causes Homosexuality

Both heterosexuals and homosexuals may act like "sissies" or "tomboys." This type of behavior does not necessarily result in homosexual behavior. Green (1987) found that for some of the boys he studied over a 15-year period, feminine behavior was an indicator of, but not an exclusive predictor of homosexuality. He believes that although there may be a genetic and hormonal basis for homosexuality, environmental factors may play a role in the development of some homosexual behavior. In following 44 "feminine" boys from childhood to adulthood, Green found that "sissy" boys frequently expressed wishes to be girls throughout their childhood, played with girls exclusively, played girl-type games, and often dressed in girl's clothing. Many of the parents of the boys in Green's study encouraged their sons' behaviors in subtle ways. They may have unknowingly reinforced cross dressing, doll play, or female role-playing in a positive manner through laughter, frivolously sharing this information with family members and friends, or memorializing it through photographs and videotapes. Although these responses do not cause homosexuality, they can lead to the development of feelings of inadequacy, low self-esteem, and confusion regarding one's sexual identity.

Because of the work of Kinsey et al. (1948) less attention is focused on the dichotomy between masculinity and femininity. Instead, there is emphasis on a continuum of sexual behaviors and responsiveness from exclusive heterosexuality to bisexuality to exclusive homosexuality.

Sexual orientations may be established before birth (Bell et al., 1981), evolve from gender role preferences between the ages of three and nine (Henry, 1982), or be developed out of gender role experiences at a later stage (Gagnon & Simon, 1973). Troiden (1989) believes that sexual feelings evolve from the interpretation and definition of an individual's feelings from the sexual meanings articulated by one's culture. People learn to identify and label their sexual feelings through their experiences with gender roles and their related sexual scripts.

6 Gays and Lesbians Are Oversexed and Indiscriminately Promiscuous

There are no known statistics to support the belief that homosexuals are oversexed or are any more promiscuous than the heterosexual community. This myth may have been perpetuated recently because of the publicity associated with the AIDS epidemic and the closing of many bath houses, which were believed to be contributing to the spread of AIDS. (A bath house is a facility that some gay individuals frequent to meet other gay individuals sometimes for the purpose of finding sex partners.) Although there may have been a great amount of unsafe sex practiced in these settings, the gay community has been at the forefront of trying to prevent the spread of AIDS, and statistics indicate a decline in the percentage of new cases within the gay community (and an increase primarily in the young heterosexual female population).

7 Gay Men and Lesbians Gravitate to Particular Occupations

It is a common belief that all gay men work as hairdressers, clothing designers, interior decorators, or table-waiters, or are involved in the theater. Lesbians are associated with athletics and the military. The population at large has been willing to accept gay men and lesbians in these occupations and has found comfort in believing they are safely identified and categorized. What seems to be less known is that the vast majority of gay men and lesbian women are members of every profession or job description and do not fit the perpetuated stereotypes. More likely to be overlooked are the gay and lesbian doctors, lawyers, stock brokers, accountants, educators, policemen/women, nurses, entrepreneurs, dentists, secretaries, repair workers, football players, chemists, psychologists, physicists, engineers, politicians, postal employees, truck drivers, officers and noncommissioned personnel in the military, and others. Considering that gays and lesbians make up 10% of the general population, it is unrealistic to believe that they all work within only a few occupations. In our society, most gays and lesbians feel they must remain closeted in order to function in their jobs and maintain their invisible status in the community. Disclosure in a hostile society can be disastrous, as will be evidenced by some of the case studies in Chapters 5, 7, and 8.

8   Gays and Lesbians Tend to Hang Out in Seedy Bars and Restaurants, and Gay Men Frequent Bath Houses

Although some homosexuals frequent bars and bath houses, most do not because they feel uncomfortable in these places and do not feel they have the potential to develop a long-term relationship with individuals they meet in these settings. The majority of homosexuals want to settle down and develop a mutually satisfying, long-term relationship. In this regard, most homosexuals are no different from heterosexuals. They look for companionship, similar values/belief systems, and a partner for life. Many homosexuals are very family oriented and want to have close relationships with their partners and their families. Some homosexuals want to have children and may go to great lengths to try to achieve this. There are numerous cases in the court system involving gays and lesbians who want permission to adopt children or to become foster parents. Some lesbians take steps to become pregnant and have their own children.

The laws of many states permit an unmarried person to be an adoptive parent; however, Florida and New Hampshire have enacted legislation prohibiting lesbians and gay men from adopting. The Florida statute was recently declared unconstitutional by a state trial court. Most gay and lesbian adoptions appear to involve adoption by a single parent to avoid calling attention to their relationship. There are few mechanisms in most states for joint or coparent adoptions by same-sex couples. California, Alaska, and Oregon have allowed for same-sex coparenting without terminating the partner's parental rights (Hunter, Michaelson, & Stoddard, 1992).

9   Gay and Lesbian Parents Will Raise Gay and Lesbian Children

In *Gay and Lesbian Parents*, Bozett (1987) stated that he found no evidence to support this belief. A review of more than 30 studies comparing the children of gay or lesbian parents with those of heterosexual parents showed no significant differences in terms of gender identity or sexual orientation (Patterson, 1992). According to Schulenburg (1985), children of gay or lesbian parents have about the same chance of being homosexual as the children of heterosexuals.

10   Gays and Lesbians Cannot Maintain Long-Term Relationships

In a study of 979 gays and lesbians, Bell and Weinberg (1978) concluded that many homosexual men and women lead stable lives without frenetic sexual activity and that some are considerably happier and better adjusted than heterosexuals as a whole.

A study by Peplau (1983/1984) showed that approximately 60% of lesbians and 40% of gay men were involved in a long-term relationship. Additionally, gay couples are forming unions and having ceremonies where they exchange vows, although, as of 1993, all 50 states deny gays and lesbians the right to marry (National Gay and Lesbian Task Force, 1993). Gay and lesbian couples are requesting and demanding that their partners be included on their health insurance policies and that they be given the same benefits that married spouses enjoy. Gay couples are actively involved with attorneys in structuring legal documents to protect their assets and make sure their partners will be protected should something happen to them. They are active participants in couples counseling and go to great lengths to preserve their union. In 1981, there was no public or private jurisdiction in the United States that recognized lesbian or gay relationships (Rubenstein, 1993). By September 1993, 25 jurisdictions recognized some type of domestic partnership for lesbians and gay men. And at least 20 private-sector companies and organizations recognize same-sex domestic partnerships in employee benefits (National Gay and Lesbian Task Force, 1993).

11   Homosexuality and Religion Are Antithetical

In Greek there are words for same-sex sexual activities that never appear in the original text of the New Testament. As recently as 1946, the word *homosexual* first appeared in a translation of the Christian Bible. There is no mention in the Bible of homosexuality per se as a sexual orientation, although the Bible does refer to specific acts, primarily homosexual temple prostitution (Blumenfeld & Raymond, 1993). Depending on which version is cited and how the Hebrew and Greek words are translated, eight references to homosexuality are commonly cited in Judeo-Christian scripture: Genesis 19; Leviticus 18:22, 20:13; Romans 1:18–32; 1 Corinthians 6:9; 1 Timothy 1:10; and Revelations 21:8, 22:15 (Comstock, 1991).

Both the Old Testament and the New Testament contain numerous references to homosexuality as a serious offense worthy of punishment (Genesis 19:4,5,24; 1 Corinthians 6:9; Leviticus 20:13), although there is much disagreement within the clergy regarding the acceptance and interpretation of this attitude. In 1985, a leading New York Reform rabbi criticized Orthodox Jewish leaders for their hostile attitudes toward gay and lesbian Jews. The charge was made in an article in *Reform Judaism*, the scholarly publication of the Union of American Hebrew Congregations, the association of Reform Synagogues (Mason, 1994).

On October 30, 1986, the Vatican issued a directive to the Catholic bishops to withdraw support from any organization that is either "ambiguous" or opposed to the church's teaching that gay and lesbian behavior is sinful. The main target of this directive was Dignity, an organization for gay Catholics that had been allowed to hold special masses in numerous dioceses. Despite the directive, Dignity chapters around the country have managed to find priests willing to celebrate mass in churches and in non-Catholic buildings. From 1986 to 1991, 50 chapters of Dignity were expelled from Roman Catholic Church property (Harding, 1991). As of 1992, Dignity had 6,000 dues-paying members (Fletcher, 1992).

Protestant denominations in the United States vary in their attitudes concerning homosexuality and sin. Some adhere to the literal interpretation of the Bible and others take a more liberal view. Many denominations, including Presbyterians, the United Church of Christ, and Unitarians, have made public announcements supporting gay and lesbian causes.

12   Gays and Lesbians Have Abandoned Organized Religion

Because gays and lesbians are a cross-section of the general population, it is reasonable to believe that they have been brought up in homes where organized religion played a variety of roles in the family, similar to the religious experiences of heterosexuals. When gays and lesbians turn away from institutional religion, it is usually because they feel rejected or are made to feel guilty due to religious doctrines, but the need for religious affiliation does not disappear, nor does it become less intense.

There are various religious organizations that provide affiliation for gays and lesbians. The most popular international denomination is the Universal Fellowship of Metropolitan Community Churches (MCC), founded in 1968 by Reverend Troy Perry. MCC's 291 churches in 17 countries reach out primarily to Christian gays and lesbians.

Jewish gays and lesbians have found spiritual connection through a movement called Jewish Gays. Gay synagogues have been established in New York and Los Angeles, and in other major cities Jewish gay and lesbian groups have organized and hold services in private homes or in a variety of facilities. Beth Simchat Torah, one of the largest congregations, is located in New York City, and has approximately 1,000 members (Bull, 1992).

Many gays and lesbians have organized other religious groups that correspond to the mainstream denominations in which they were raised. These groups include the United Gay and Lesbian Christian Scientists, Integrity (gay and lesbian Episcopals), Sovereignty (gay and lesbian Jehovah's Witnesses), and

Affirmation (a name taken by the gay and lesbian Mormon and Methodist groups) (Fletcher, 1992).

The current trend is for organized religions to examine their attitudes toward the issue of homosexuality, prompted by the efforts of gay and lesbian organizations across the nation.

13 Gays and Lesbians Contribute Little to Society and Are Not Part of Mainstream America

The list of talented gay and lesbian artists, composers, writers, doctors, scientists, lawyers, architects, politicians, activists, and others in Appendix D clearly refutes this myth. Gays and lesbians have made and continue to make significant contributions, especially in the judicial and military arenas. Because most gay and lesbian couples are working partners who have a serious commitment to their work and tend to be financially successful at their career endeavors, they have a greater amount of discretionary income than most heterosexuals and therefore have a great impact on the economy of our society. A survey cited in the *New York Times* (Elliott, 1994) reported the average annual household income of gays and lesbians as $63,100 compared with the national average of $36,500 for heterosexuals.

Gays and lesbians feel they are similar in their thoughts and actions to mainstream American society and want to feel more a part of it. In 1994, in Miami Beach, Florida, gays and lesbians organized a conference called Pathways to Pride. The focus of this conference was a discussion of some of the same day-to-day issues that heterosexuals experience: parenting, the stresses of being a working parent, love, the law, and financial planning. Approximately 600 gays, lesbians, and bisexuals came together to celebrate their ordinariness. The sponsors of the conference hope to make this an annual event (Smith, 1994).

The gay and lesbian community is an increasingly vocal element of the public and is having a great influence on political and social events. The 1996 summer Olympics were scheduled to be held in Atlanta, Georgia. One of the events was to be completed in Marietta, Georgia, where there was an ordinance discriminatory to gays and lesbians. Because of pressure from the gay and lesbian community, the Olympic Committee told the Marietta City Council that unless they rescinded the ordinance the site of the Olympic event would be changed. The Marietta City Council revoked the ordinance (Henry, 1994).

In 1991, Cracker Barrel Old Country Store, Inc., fired at least 11 employees because they were, or were perceived to be, gay or lesbian. A shareholder resolution sponsored by the New York City comptroller's office to reinstate the fired employees was unsuccessful in its attempt to make Cracker Barrel drop its stance of discrimination. Although they did not accomplish their stated goal, some shareholders believe Cracker Barrel's stock was adversely affected (Mickens, 1994).

Courting the gay community during the 1992 presidential election, Bill Clinton promised that if he were elected he would push for equal rights for gays and lesbians. He received a large portion of the gay and lesbian popular vote because of these statements. Once elected President, he nominated known gays and lesbians for political office and attempted to rescind the ban on gays in the military. Although his placement of several gay and lesbian individuals in high public office was accepted, his desire to allow gays and lesbians to be open about their sexuality in the military created much controversy. The Joint Chiefs of Staff came out strongly against his plan and members of Congress threatened legislative action. It was finally agreed that gays and lesbians could remain in the military as long as they did not openly declare their orientation or have same-sex relationships while serving in the military. Raising this issue as part of a presidential campaign helped increase public awareness of gay and lesbian rights. Clinton's "don't ask, don't tell" policy is discussed in greater length in Chapter 4.

Although it is well known that there are gays and lesbians in the military, disclosure of their sexuality has resulted in their dismissal. The belief is that gays and lesbians in the military are a threat to American security; if their sexuality is uncovered, it could be used to blackmail them. It is also believed that gays and lesbians cannot serve in close quarters with heterosexuals without making sexual advances. Furthermore, some individuals believe that gay men could not respond well in combat circumstances because they are sissies.

In *Conduct Unbecoming: Gays and Lesbians in the U.S. Military*, Randy Shilts (1993) refuted many of these beliefs. He emphasized that the presence of gays and lesbians in the ranks was not destructive to order and discipline. It was the antigay probes and actions taken by the military that contributed to low morale and insecurity among gays and lesbians. He pointed out how the suspicions about sexual orientation resulted in investigations of private lives that led to discharge and/or imprisonment. Several discharged servicemen and women have been reinstated by the armed forces because of district court rulings that such discharges were based solely on prejudice and are a clear violation of the equal protection clause of the 14th Amendment of the Constitution.

There is a segment of society that believes gays and lesbians should be who they are and be open about their sexual orientation. This sounds good in theory, but in reality it is not always feasible and may result in discrimination or dismissal. Although many corporations espouse an equal opportunity employment policy, the reality is that if their employees were open in the expression of their sexuality, they feel their job opportunities would suffer. Therefore, many employees lead a double life at work. They may decline to attend social functions or attend alone for brief periods. Other individuals handle this problem by having a friend of the opposite sex, who is often also gay, to attend with them as their cover.

14 All Gays and Lesbians Think Alike and Tend to "Stick Together"

It is often assumed that because homosexuals share a sexual orientation, there is an added camaraderie and empathy to the problems fellow homosexuals may be experiencing. Although in many cases this is true, there are individuals who, despite their homosexuality, are antigay. They may be antagonistic, hostile, and at times destructive to the well-being of others. For example, a psychiatrist who was particularly hostile toward his homosexual clients would make them wait an inordinate length of time for appointments, was unusually cruel in his demeanor, and had a negative attitude toward gays and lesbians, despite the fact that he himself was gay. Eventually, he was ostracized from the gay professional community, but not before he had done an enormous amount of harm to his gay and lesbian clients.

There are groups of activists, such as Queer Nation, who use unusual and sometimes outlandish approaches to heighten gay visibility. They may organize a "queers' night out," public displays of affection, and other radical events to make strong statements about their sexuality. These public demonstrations are uncomfortable not only for many heterosexuals but also for mainstream gays and lesbians.

The fallacy of the myth that all gays and lesbians think alike is further evident in the actions of individuals who believe in *outing* gay and lesbian individuals, that is, exposing closeted prominent members of the gay and lesbian community. In 1993, Scott Peck was contacted by Queer Nation and told that his homosexuality would be exposed. Scott Peck's father, a colonel in the Army, was preparing to testify before the Senate Armed Forces Committee hearings on the subject of gays and lesbians in the military. The group told Scott they would embarrass his father by publicizing Scott's homosexuality. Until then, Scott's father was unaware that his son was gay. This situation forced Scott to tell his father that he was gay, which his father publicly announced in the Senate hearing. Scott's family was supportive of his revelation; however, many other people's families are not as receptive (Bawer, 1993).

The process of outing fellow homosexuals creates added turmoil in the lives of those individuals who are outed, and can have destructive and long-lasting consequences. In some cases, however, once the initial trauma has subsided, some gays and lesbians are relieved about not having to remain closeted.

15 Having One or a Few Homosexual Experiences Designates a Person as a Homosexual

It is not uncommon for adolescents, particularly males, to experiment sexually with one another, but these early sexual experiences do not necessarily mean a person is homosexual. Kinsey et al. (1948) developed a seven-point scale that measured sexual orientation. In their study they reported that approximately one third of all males have had at least one postpubertal orgasmic experience with another male. They concluded that this did not constitute sexual orientation. According to Mathis (1972), when adults discover and mishandle this sexual experimentation among their teenagers, the results are frequently disastrous.

16   Gay Men Molest Children

Child molesters are primarily heterosexual and the victims generally are female. According to Paul et al. (1982), recognized researchers in the fields of child abuse and law enforcement concur almost unanimously that homosexuals are less likely to approach children. Child molesters, instead, are generally hostile toward homosexuals (Groth & Birnbaum, 1978). In a study by Freund, Langevin, Cibiri, and Zajac (1973) where they measured actual sexual arousal in response to various erotic displays, they found that heterosexual males were more likely to be sexually aroused by photos of little girls than were homosexuals viewing photos of boys.

CONCLUSIONS

The impact of these myths is far reaching. They have led to suicide, depression, alcoholism, substance abuse, and numerous mental conditions. Many individuals experience social isolation and guilt because they feel different and rejected by society. They frequently do not perform up to their potential because they are preoccupied; this preoccupation can also lead to poor emotional and/or physical health and behavior.

In an effort to conform to mainstream society, some homosexuals marry and have children; thus, their spouses, children, and other family members become affected by the inability of these gays and lesbians to accept their sexual orientation. When they finally publicly come to terms with their sexuality, family members may experience great anger, pain, and confusion. Strained interpersonal relationships as well as failures in school, business, and social situations are common. Sometimes individuals will strive to achieve in order to feel a greater acceptance. These individuals may be superior in one area of life at the expense of other areas. There may be spiritual disappointment because they are looking for comfort from a higher power and feel they have been abandoned by their traditional religious training.

The perpetuation of myths has a tremendous impact on families. It can create tension and schisms among family members if they believe the myths and therefore have a hard time accepting the homosexuality of their loved one. Parents may be ashamed or harbor guilt because they feel responsible for their child's sexual orientation. They may feel they have lost their hopes and dreams for the future, such as being grandparents or handing down the family business. Consequently, the family may feel isolated, disappointed, and very hurt. Closeted gay parents may experience a tremendous amount of turmoil because they feel there is a barrier between them and their child that is difficult to overcome. They may also feel they cannot discuss their child with others. This will be exemplified in the story of George in Chapter 6.

Belief in the myths described here takes a great toll on society in various ways. Individuals who are not free to be who they are live under great pressure, and there is a tremendous loss of potential as they struggle to successfully live their lives. Crimes against gays and lesbians cost society in terms of economic resources to deal with such crimes. Homophobia has taken its toll by stifling gays and lesbians and inhibiting their creativity, thus undermining the development of potential.

This toll is especially great for gay and lesbian adolescents because they are struggling with many competing issues during their formative years. Having to adjust to society's negative attitudes and misperceptions toward gays and lesbians further compounds their development and contributes to the high truancy rate, substance abuse, suicide, mental illness, academic underachievement, and drop-out rate, which will be discussed later in greater depth.

Therefore, it is important to dispel the myths that people hold about gays and lesbians. The deleterious effects on self-concepts and levels of functioning, the disruption in families, and the financial and emotional strain that the perpetuation of these beliefs has on society has impacted all Americans. These myths must be addressed and dispelled through education and personal experience.

The first step in helping school personnel dispel these myths is to provide inservice education on homophobia for teachers, administrators, counselors, school psychologists, social workers, and all other school professionals who have direct contact with teenagers. As the inservice education is applied on the job it will have positive effects on the gay and lesbian students and on curriculum and instruction (see Appendix B and Chapter 8).

Chapter 3

Understanding Homophobia

It is natural for individuals to have fears and insecurities in life. No one is without some type of unfounded anxiety. These fears develop in a number of ways. Some fears are learned through first-hand experience. Others are passed on through what has been read or heard from others. How individuals react to these experiences and information determines whether these beliefs become magnified. This is true for homophobia. As discussed in Chapter 2, many fallacies about homosexuality have been perpetuated throughout society, creating many problems, including verbal and physical violence.

PREJUDICE

Prejudice is a universal phenomenon that has been around since the earliest existence of man. For prejudice to continue to survive, it needs to satisfy a purpose. Wurzel (1986) has identified four basic functions of prejudice: the utilitarian function, self-esteem (the protective function), the value-expressive function, and the cognitive function. The utilitarian function theorizes that by maintaining the prejudice or belief one gains certain rewards and avoids negative consequences. By maintaining the prejudice, the individuals consolidate their own personal and social relationships and enhance their own self-concepts. The self-esteem of individuals may be enhanced because, by projecting prejudice onto other people, they protect themselves from having to face and confront their own limitations and weaknesses. Those who maintain the prejudice may strengthen their values when their values are different from those of the targeted group. Frequently this results in giving those who are prejudiced a false sense of superiority. Attempting to gain a sense of order and understanding in the world, prejudiced people tend to stereotype others. This stereotyping intensifies the prejudices.

Homophobia can be described as a dislike, fear, or hatred of individuals who are attracted to members of the same sex. This attitude frequently leads to acts of discrimination against gays, lesbians, and bisexuals. Gays and lesbians become natural targets for people who may be consciously or unconsciously looking for a group to hold accountable for the social or personal ills that they are experiencing. History has repeatedly reflected this phenomenon.

SCAPEGOATING

Allport (1983) defined scapegoating as a phenomenon wherein some of the aggressive energies of a person or group are focused on another individual, group, or object, the amount of aggression and blame being either partly or wholly unwarranted. Allport further defined a number of stages or degrees of hostile relationships: predilection, prejudice, discrimination, and scapegoating. Predilection is the preference for a particular culture, skin color, language, etc. This may be a natural, or even subconscious, preference, but when it becomes a more active bias it may be termed a prejudice. Prejudice is a rigid, inflexible, and often exaggerated attitude. Individuals who are prejudiced maintain their thinking even when confronted with evidence contrary to their views, and they tend to project their belief systems on others. When prejudice becomes so intense that it leads to acting out, it is discrimination, which is an act of exclusion prompted by prejudice. Scapegoating is full-fledged aggression in word or deed where individuals or groups are verbally or physically attacked and abused. Sometimes the line between discrimination and scapegoating is very thin.

People who have been deprived of love, recognition, or acceptance feel angry and resentful. Frequently, rather then looking at themselves and what they may have done to contribute to the situation, they turn their feelings of frustration toward someone else whom they perceive as responsible for their deprivation. There is an even greater tendency to scapegoat during times of social and economic difficulty.

Scapegoating may also result from fear and anxiety, which stem from the anticipation of real or imaginary danger. When individuals feel threatened, it is not uncommon for them to develop a defensive posture and at times even an offensive posture to protect themselves from the perceived threat. This is especially true with homophobia, where misinformation, stereotypical thinking, and uncertainty of one's own sexual identity promotes the tendency for individuals and groups to act on their fears. They may respond to their fears by withdrawing and becoming more isolated and insecure, by joining groups that harbor similar thoughts for consensual support, or by acting out through aggressive behaviors.

Feelings of inferiority can also lead to scapegoating. Bullying another group or person enhances the self-images of the perpetrators and makes them feel more powerful. By being able to assume control over another person's feelings or actions, an individual or group that espouses certain thinking can then be in a position to influence an even broader audience. The poor and other minority groups have frequently been the targets of efforts to influence and control them. These groups have responded with great resistance, but have not always been successful in combating the discrimination and prejudice they have encountered. Gays and lesbians are one of the last minority groups trying to challenge and modify this type of thinking.

During periods of social stress and economic hardship discrimination and scapegoating reach their peak. As different groups rise to combat this prejudice, it is natural for weaker, less vocal groups to become the focus of the discrimination and scapegoating. Children and adolescents can be particularly cruel and frequently form opinions based on little or no information. Because of their desire to belong to the group and their own ego development, they may look to peers to help them establish their belief system and feelings of belonging. For gay and lesbian students, or students who are shy and uncertain of their own feelings, school and growing up can be exceptionally difficult. They may be inhibited and unable to express their true feelings or ask questions because of fear that they will be prejudged or subject to discrimination. This may cause further isolation from teachers or school counselors. In a 1987 study conducted by the South Carolina Guidance Counselors' Association (Sears, 1991), 8 of 10 prospective teachers and nearly two thirds of guidance counselors expressed negative feelings about homosexuality. In some schools there may be a few vocal gay and lesbian students who emulate some of the stereotyped myths. This creates more anxiety and apprehension for closeted students. Many students learn to be secretive about their identities because they believe they are less likely to be bullied and singled out for negative attention or acts of aggression.

In 1982, James Price gave 300 11th- and 12th-grade students enrolled in health classes an attitude survey instrument. Students were first asked to write a brief definition of homosexuality and then given a modification of the Attitudes Toward Homosexuality Scale (ATHS), Form G. The most common responses to what defined a homosexual were "a person who has sex with a person of the same sex" or is "attracted physically and mentally to a person of the same sex." Analysis of the data indicated that males had a significantly more negative attitude toward homosexuality than did females. Both males and females agreed that "homosexuality is a sin" and that "homosexuality is unnatural." They also held to the stereotype that "homosexual males are generally more feminine than other males." Price concluded that homosexuals needed to be treated as a legitimate minority like other minority groups subjected to injustices.

Coles and Stokes (1985) surveyed the sexual attitudes of more than 1000 American teenagers and found that 75% considered sex between two females "disgusting" and more than 80% felt this way about two males. Thirty-two percent of the males and 16% of the females reported they would sever ties with same-sex friends if they learned they were homosexual.

VIOLENCE

Most of the violence against gays and lesbians is committed by teenage males motivated by homophobic attitudes. The National Gay and Lesbian Task Force surveys involving antigay and antilesbian violence conducted during the past three decades report incidents of verbal harassment, vandalism, physical assaults, threats of violence, and assaults with a weapon. In 1992, the National Gay and Lesbian Task Force tracked 1001 hate crimes against gays and lesbians in five major American cities. From 1988 to 1992, in these same cities, the antigay and antilesbian incidents increased 72% (National Gay and Lesbian Task Force, 1993). Many additional acts of violence against gays and lesbians go unreported because gays and lesbians fear disclosure of their sexual orientation.

Millions of Americans who watched the *Oprah Winfrey Show* on November 13, 1986, witnessed testimonies by two victims of homophobia, one victim had been stabbed and the other beaten and raped. Viewers heard a *gay basher* describe how, as a teenager, he and his friends hunted gay men and beat them with baseball bats. A more recent *Oprah Winfrey Show* episode (1994) in which teenagers were interviewed revealed that little had changed over the past eight years.

On April 30, 1994, the *New York Times* (Lewin, 1994) reported an antigay murder of a 44-year-old musician from a small Pennsylvania town; a 17-year-old 11th grader had beaten him to death. Homophobic acts of harassment and aggression take place everywhere, in big cities, small towns, schools, college campuses, the workplace, and the military.

Homosexuals have been oppressed in the same manner as other minority groups. Boswell (1980) argued that throughout European history the treatment of homosexuals has paralleled the treatment of Jews. The same laws the Nazis applied to Jews were also used against homosexuals. The tremendous hostility and violence toward homosexuals led to their persecution and extermination.

EUROPEAN PERSPECTIVE

During the classical Greek civilization homosexual love was accepted; however, by the ninth century it had been made a felony punishable by banishment or death, a policy instituted by Lycurgus, a Spartan lawmaker (Day, 1980). In 346 A.D., Greek law forbade male prostitution out of concern that if a man sold his body he might also be willing to sell out other community interests (Dover, 1980).

The early Roman civilization was tolerant of homosexual practices, but during the fourth century attitudes began to change. When Constantine I came to power he adopted Christianity as the state religion. Because Christianity prohibited same-sex relationships, many laws prohibiting homosexuality were enacted, and many edicts were passed that prescribed death to men engaging in homosexual activity. Some of these laws would later form the basis for the canon and secular doctrines of Europe.

With the fall of the Roman empire came a change in the treatment of homosexuals. From the seventh to the middle of the 12th century homosexuals lived in a climate of tolerance. During the late 12th century, when the edicts of the Catholic Church became more powerful, legislation was again implemented against homosexuality (Boswell, 1980).

In the 13th century in Spain, homosexuality was not tolerated. Homosexuals were subjected to castration and execution by stoning. This attitude pervaded English law, under which homosexuality was considered a felony. The death penalty for homosexual behavior was not repealed in England until 1861 (Bray, 1982). In reviewing the literature (Crompton, 1978; Gilbert, 1976; Lea, 1907; Ruggerio, 1975; Taylor, 1978), there are many documented deaths of individuals sentenced because they were homosexuals.

Change did not occur in France until the 18th century, when penalties for consensual adult sexual activities were eliminated from the criminal code. Many of the European countries followed in modifying their penal code; however, Russia continued to imprison homosexuals for up to five years, and England and Germany did not rescind their codes until the 20th century (Bullough, 1979).

THE UNITED STATES

The early American settlers left England because they wished to escape religious persecution and intolerance. However, the settlers were not tolerant of homosexuality, and the laws and attitudes toward homosexuals held in England prevailed in the original colonies. In the early 1620s Richard Cornish, a ship's master, was the first man to be executed in the Virginia colony for alleged homosexual acts with one of his stewards (Katz, 1976). In 1637 there was another documented case in which two men were found guilty of engaging in lewd behavior with one another (Shurtleff, 1898).

During the writing of the Declaration of Independence, there were minor reforms regarding the death penalty for homosexuality. Thomas Jefferson proposed that the death penalty be dropped and that individuals convicted for homosexual acts should be punished instead with castration (Katz, 1976).

Currently, in the United States the laws are varied. Some cities have passed legislation to protect the rights of homosexuals; other legislation restricts homosexual activity. Until 1961, every state in the Union had a sodomy law prohibiting oral and anal sex between homosexuals and, in most states, between heterosexuals (Rubenstein, 1993). The first state to decriminalize homosexuality was Illinois, in 1961 (Fletcher, 1992). As of 1993, there were still 20 states in which one could be imprisoned for same-sex sexual relations, described as "sodomy," "unnatural intercourse," "deviant sexual conduct," "sexual misconduct," and "crimes against nature": Alabama, Arizona, Arkansas, Florida, Georgia, Idaho, Kansas, Maryland, Massachusetts, Minnesota, Mississippi, Missouri, Montana, North Carolina, Oklahoma, Rhode Island, South Carolina, Tennessee, Utah, and Virginia. Four states—Arkansas, Kansas, Missouri, and Tennessee—currently have laws that prohibit oral and anal sex only between persons of the same sex (*Lambda Legal Defense and Education Fund,* 1993). Maximum penalties for sodomy convictions range from 10 years in Oklahoma, North Carolina, Montana, Mississippi, and Maryland and 20 years in Georgia, Rhode Island, and Virginia, to life imprisonment in Idaho (National Gay and Lesbian Task Force, 1993).

As of September 1993, there were 140 ordinances, laws, and executive orders nationwide protecting the civil rights of lesbians and gay men (National Gay and Lesbian Task Force, 1993). The first city to ban discrimination against gay men and lesbians was East Lansing, Michigan, in 1972. In 1982, Wisconsin was the first state to pass a civil rights law (Fletcher, 1992). Eight states have passed laws protecting gay and lesbian rights: California, Connecticut, Hawaii, Massachusetts, Minnesota, New Jersey, Vermont, and Wisconsin (National Gay and Lesbian Task Force, 1993). Nine states placed antigay and antilesbian initiatives on the November 1994 ballot: Arizona, California, Florida, Idaho, Maine, Michigan, Missouri, Oregon, and Washington; in seven of these states national or religious right groups made attempts to limit or avoid these proposals (People For the American Way, 1993).

CHARACTERISTICS OF HOMOPHOBIC THINKING

Homophobia is perpetuated through ignorance and untruths. Herek (1985) identified several predominant characteristics of people who have strong homophobic beliefs:

1   They have limited personal contact with lesbians and gay men.
2   They have limited homosexual activity or are less likely to consider themselves lesbian or gay.
3   They perceive their peers as negative—especially males.
4   They live in areas where being negative toward gays and lesbians is the norm, especially during the teenage years.
5   They are more likely to be older and have a limited education.
6   They tend to be religious and are frequent churchgoers with a conservative religious perspective.
7   They hold traditional, restrictive views about sex roles.
8   They are less permissive sexually or feel more negative and guilty about sex.
9   They are more authoritarian in their personality characteristics.

Herek further defined three basic causes of antigay bias: experiential attitudes, defensive attitudes, and symbolic attitudes. Experiential attitudes develop from an individual's personal experience. If an experience with a homosexual is in some way negative, that perception then becomes generalized to all individuals of this subgroup. Defensive attitudes develop when individuals feel personally threatened by homosexuality. These individuals may be insecure regarding their own sexuality, and therefore may become threatened by a feeling or behavior that is different from their own. This is especially true of high school students, who are going through a developmentally insecure time in their lives, when peer pressure and conformity are very important. When teenagers are confronted with difference, many react with fear and hatred. Gay and lesbian teenagers tend to isolate themselves and feel they will never grow up to be normal and enjoy the same things that their heterosexual friends will, such as long-term relationships, a family, and success in life. Symbolic attitudes develop when antigay belief systems are incorporated into the philosophy of an organization. This thinking may be a standard belief that is necessary in order to join or maintain membership in an organization.

Tinney (1983) proposed a *cultural homophobia* theory, which suggests a large conspiracy of silence toward homosexuality. When a society does not allow certain individuals to express their feelings and manifest their behavior, it is a covert denial of individuals' identities, implying that there is something wrong with them. Information is thus suppressed and there is a shortage of social role models. Earlier in American history this was true of blacks, but in the 1990s much of this has changed as a result of education and legislation. However, present society is not tolerant of gay and lesbian individuals, especially of teenagers (Herek & Berrill, 1992). Because a large percentage of the population is heterosexual, the cultural assumption is that everyone is heterosexual, which creates insensitivity to those who are not. Epithets and other derogatory labels are directed toward every target group. Many of the terms that are used against gays and lesbian are symbols of great hurt and bigotry. Even tolerance and acceptance can be a form of homophobia for some individuals. According to Dorothy Riddle (1985), tolerance can be a mask for an underlying fear or even hatred. Acceptance assumes that there is indeed something to accept. Intolerance becomes eradicated only through education and experience. It becomes modified through familiarity and trust in relationships that are developed over time, sometimes one person at a time. The heterosexual questionnaire that follows allows individuals to further explore their attitudes about both heterosexuality and homosexuality.

Heterosexual Questionnaire
by Martin Rochlin, Ph.D.

1 What do you think caused your heterosexuality?
2 When and how did you first decide you were a heterosexual?
3 Is it possible that your heterosexuality is just a phase you may grow out of?
4 Is it possible that your heterosexuality stems from a neurotic fear of members of the same sex?
5 Isn't it possible that all you need is a good gay lover?

6   If heterosexuality is normal, why are a disproportionate number of mental patients heterosexual?

7   To whom have you disclosed your heterosexuality? How did they react?

8   The great majority of child molesters are heterosexuals (95%). Do you really consider it safe to expose your children to heterosexual teachers?

9   Heterosexuals are noted for assigning themselves and each other to narrowly restricted, stereotyped sex roles. Why do you cling to such an unhealthy form of role playing?

10   Why do heterosexuals place so much emphasis on sex?

11   There seem to be very few happy heterosexuals. Techniques have been developed that you might be able to use to change your sexual orientation. Have you considered aversion therapy to treat your sexual orientation?

12   Why are heterosexuals so promiscuous?

13   Why do you make a point of attributing heterosexuality to famous people? Is it to justify your own heterosexuality?

14   If you've never slept with a person of the same sex, how do you know you wouldn't prefer that?

15   Why do you insist on being so obvious and making a public spectacle of your heterosexuality? Can't you just be what you are and keep it quiet? (Rochlin, 1992, pp. 203–204)

MEDIA IMPACT

Television and Film

The media contribute to the attitudes and stereotypes toward homosexuals. Gay or lesbian characters presented on television shows or in films frequently fit the stereotypes of effeminate men as hair dressers, interior designers, or in some other creative profession, and masculine women who are "tough" and participate in traditionally male jobs, hobbies, and sports. In addition, when a gay or lesbian character is introduced to a sitcom there is a lot of media attention. There are few examples of gay or lesbian relationships that are warm, stable, and nurturing. Yet most mainstream gays and lesbians have relationships very similar to the relationship experiences of heterosexuals.

There have been some positive films on television and in the movies that have attempted to modify some of this thinking, including *Longtime Companion*, *Philadelphia, And the Band Played On,* and *Tales of the City*. Unfortunately, there have also been documentaries on homosexuality presented on Public Television that have inadvertently reinforced some of the mainstream stereotypes and prejudices. This issue has commanded much national attention.

Programs such as the *Phil Donahue Show* and the *Oprah Winfrey Show* produce numerous shows about homosexuality and have done much to heighten the public's awareness and provide a forum for education. However, many times the representatives who appear on these shows are not good spokespersons for modifying stereotypical ideas. Many of these individuals are highly politicized, sexually obsessed, promiscuous, or uncharacteristic of the majority of gays and lesbians. Thus, rather than making others more comfortable with homosexuality, the message that is communicated to the general public is sensational, counterproductive, and misleading. When this sensationalism occurs with heterosexual topics it is often viewed as being representative of a small minority. With homosexuality, it is often viewed by the largely heterosexual population as the norm.

Another example of the media's reinforcement of gay and lesbian stereotyping is the reporting of Gay Pride Day. This event is held once a year in New York and other major cities across the nation. At this event gays and lesbians are openly proud of who they are and deliver a political statement to the heterosexual community, demanding such things as equal rights and more money for AIDS research. Although the majority of marchers are individuals who blend in with mainstream and corporate America, the people who are typically shown on national television are the people attired in the most bizarre outfits and who fit the stereotype. The people shown are generally the most extreme elements of the gay community. For every individual who participates in the Gay Pride marches, there are many at home who are living a mainstream lifestyle and are rarely represented when homosexuality is discussed or viewed. The cameras are more likely to focus on the more outrageous marchers, reinforcing the attitudes of already prejudiced viewers.

Music and Video

Homophobia is also reinforced through music sold to adolescents. Groups such as Guns 'n Roses have been criticized for using lyrics that make it acceptable to have negative attitudes about homosexuals and that encourage antigay and antilesbian aggression.

Student homophobia toward fellow gay and lesbian students can have a negative impact. Forty-five percent of gay males and 20% of lesbians experience physical or verbal assault in high school. Twenty-eight percent of these students feel forced to drop out of school because of harassment based on their sexual orientation (Remafedi, 1987). Surveys conducted from 1985 to 1989 at Yale, Rutgers, Pennsylvania State, the University of Massachusetts at Amherst, and the University of Illinois found that between 45 and 76% of gay and lesbian students reported being verbally threatened or harassed, with 90% of these incidents being unreported (Harbeck, 1992).

The insufficient number of visible role models for gay and lesbian adolescents perpetuates the myth for them that their future looks bleak. None of the social institutions (schools, religious institutions, community organizations) to which adolescents are most frequently exposed provide gay and lesbian adults with whom they can identify and form relationships. Because they have little opportunity to develop a comfort level with their true identities, they resort to secrecy, denial, and deception, rather than self-disclosure. When gay and lesbian school personnel and religious and community leaders feel safe about disclosing their sexual orientation, they will become role models for gay and lesbian adolescents. Until then, gay and lesbian adolescents are likely to emulate the closeted lifestyle of adults they admire and suspect of being gay or lesbian, which reinforces gay secrecy, denial, and deception. Thus, homophobia in society is responsible for the silence among adult gays and lesbians, who are fearful of public disclosure and are thus prevented from becoming role models for young gays and lesbians.

The more homosexuality is treated as a taboo topic and not discussed openly, the greater the risk of homophobia and misinformation. Stereotypical thinking about gays and lesbians will continue so long as it is unacceptable for them to discuss their sexual orientations with families and peers. If gay and lesbian relationships were taken for granted by everyone and gay and lesbian adolescents were taught to be as comfortable with their sexuality as straight adolescents, much of the stereotypical thinking and behavior that has developed around homosexuality would subside and disappear. Therefore, it is urgent that social institutions that deal with adolescents be at the forefront in modifying this attitude of silence.

A prime example of this was the Los Angeles citywide prom entitled "Live to Tell" that was held in May 1994 for 100 homosexual couples. Because these gay high school students felt they could not attend their individual high school proms because of slurs, threats, and risk of violence, they were given the opportunity to attend a function designed exclusively for homosexuals. The prom was sponsored by school administrators, paid for by private donations, chaperoned by 25 adults, and protected by eight off-duty police officers. This enabled the gay students to experience a common rite-of-passage event in a safe and nonthreatening atmosphere (Roane, 1994).

Teachers, counselors, administrators, and parents need to be more outspoken in their desire to teach their children about developing positive self-esteem and greater acceptance of differences. Although most individuals would agree with this on a case-by-case basis, everyone seems to have his or her area of difficulty in acceptance of diversity. Educators and school boards in particular have been reluctant to approach the subject of homosexuality because it is an emotionally charged issue with strong opinions on both sides. Prior to 1940, homosexuality was considered innately evil and educators were required to be role models of exemplary behavior. Administrators would be quick to terminate individuals who did not maintain this exemplary behavior. This will be explored in greater detail in the next chapter.

Chapter 4

Homophobia in Society

Homophobia permeates each of society's major institutions: the family, religion, education, the economy, and government. Homophobia affects not just gays and lesbians, but the entire society. Prejudice and discrimination have enormous costs, the greatest cost being the immeasurable loss of human life and potential. In this chapter we examine the impact of homophobia on education, the workplace, the military, religion, and the Boy Scouts.

EDUCATION

According to Harbeck (1992), in 1992 there were 3,600,000 teachers in the United States in public and private elementary and secondary settings. If we accept Kinsey et al.'s (1948) estimate of 10% of the general population being homosexual, we can assume that there are approximately 360,000 homosexual teachers in the United States. Harbeck believes that because of the gay rights movement and because teaching is an occupation that attracts single women and nontraditional men, this estimate might be higher. In 1992, Harbeck reviewed the literature, trying to reference notable American homosexual teachers in history. She identified several mid-19th century Americans teachers with strong same-sex affiliations, among them Margaret Fuller, Ralph Waldo Emerson, Elizabeth Peabody, Henry David Thoreau, Amos Bronson Alcott, Herman Melville, and Walt Whitman.

With the recommendation of the American Law Institute's 1955 Model Penal Code that all forms of sexual activity between consenting adults be legalized, it became difficult for school administrators to gather information on the personal behavior of their teachers. Administrators could no longer rely on the courts to provide them with a basis for dismissing their teachers. In response to these changes, new legislation was sponsored in California that required police officers to notify local boards of education whenever a teacher was detained or arrested in a criminal matter and that allowed for the immediate suspension of teaching credentials if an educator were convicted of any one of several statutes pertaining to sex and morality (Harbeck, 1991).

The climate in Florida for homosexuals was not much better. In 1956, the Florida Legislative Investigative Committee, also known as the Johns Committee, was formed. The initial purpose of this group was to concentrate on race relations. Over the following several years, however, it received resistance from the NAACP and became mired in legal battles. Consequently, in 1959 the Johns Committee turned its attention from blacks to focus on gays and lesbians. The committee issued the following statement:

> The practicing homosexual is, almost entirely, the product of environment and practice. The homosexual who is one because of organic or bodily reasons, glandular or otherwise, is almost a medical rarity. In other words, homosexuals are made by training rather than born. The greatest danger of a homosexual is his or her recruitment of other people into such practices. (McGarrahan, 1991, pp. 10, 12)

The Johns Committee felt that homosexuals were more dangerous than child molesters. They employed a network of informants who went undercover anywhere and everywhere they felt homosexuals were known to socialize. They would then compile a register of people they felt were suspected of being homosexual and use strategies to have many of these individuals fired.

At Florida State University the Johns Committee used subversive techniques to lure suspected homosexual educators into situations where their homosexuality would be revealed. They would then photograph these individuals in homosexual acts or record conversations that alluded to their homosexuality. After this information was compiled, the suspected homosexual would be summoned by the head of security for the campus and, after questioning, would be expelled.

In 1963, the Johns Committee's exposé extended to the classroom at the University of South Florida in Tampa. The committee objected to what it labeled "beatnik" literature being presented in the classroom. J. D. Salinger's "Pretty Mouth" and "Green Eyes" were considered offensive because there was a section that referred to two individuals being like "two goddamn peas in a pod." Any reference to homosexuality, whether discrete or overt, was considered inappropriate and unacceptable and therefore should not be taught. The Johns Committee was responsible for the firing of a professor because of the literature he taught.

In 1964, the Johns Committee issued a report entitled *Homosexuality and Citizenship in Florida*. In the pamphlet they included a glossary of homosexual terms ("deviant acts"), a history of sexual orientation, a section against recruitment, and a discussion of recommendations for action. They encouraged the creation of a central records repository for information on homosexuals, which should be open to all publicly funded agencies for use in screening job applicants.

The pamphlet backfired on the Johns Committee because the public was not receptive to their inclusion of photographs of two men kissing and of young boys in their underwear. The photos created instant public outrage. The governor of Florida, Farris Bryant, quickly withdrew his support of the pamphlet, and the Johns Committee lost its credibility.

By 1969, the law in California had changed, with the recognition that homosexuality was not sufficient reason for dismissal. The California Supreme Court's decision in *Morrison v. State Board of Education* stated that extensive analysis of an individual's behavior in relation to his or her job responsibilities was necessary before employment dismissal. Being homosexual was not sufficient grounds for dismissal unless it were coupled with some related misbehavior (Harbeck, 1991).

As previously discussed, throughout the 1950s and 1960s discrimination and harassment of gays and lesbians was common. On June 28, 1969, a landmark event occurred at the Stonewall Inn, a gay bar in the Greenwich Village section of New York City, marking the beginning of the modern Gay Rights movement. On the evening of June 28, 1969, the New York police raided the Stonewall Inn, rounding up patrons for not carrying identification, for dancing, and for not wearing "gender appropriate" clothing. The raid led to a fierce riot followed by five days of civil disobedience in the streets. Shortly after this uprising, gay and lesbian political activist organizations were formed to fight for gay and lesbian rights (L. Martin, 1994). The past 25 years of organization and political activism have resulted in various legislative victories to protect gays and lesbians from discrimination on the basis of their sexual orientation. According to the National Gay and Lesbian Task Force, in 1969 there were 50 lesbian and gay organizations in the United States. In the 1990s the statistic has grown to 2,500 (*Gay Yellowpages,* 1993).

As a result of various educational and legislative reform efforts, changes began to occur in the educational community as well. In 1974, the National Education Association amended their nondiscrimination statement to include protection for sexual orientation. This statement was designed to prevent discrimination against gay and lesbian teachers because of their sexual orientation. To date, the NEA has been instrumental in funding gay and lesbian teacher litigation for its union members (National Education Association, 1974).

In 1974, a case was brought before the court dealing with a gay or lesbian person's right to be a teacher. While a student at Penn State, Joseph Acanfora III was treasurer of the Homophiles, a gay activist group on campus; he was co-plaintiff in the lawsuit that won official status for the group. Six weeks into student teaching, the Dean of the College of Education suspended him because of his membership in Homophiles. Another lawsuit followed and he was reinstated and finished his student teaching. After graduation he was hired as a middle school teacher in Montgomery, Maryland. He applied for teacher certification in Pennsylvania because that was where he had done his student teaching. During the certification process, the Pennsylvania Secretary of Education revealed Acanfora's homosexuality through a press conference, and the story appeared in the *New York Times* and the *Washington Post.*

Acanfora was transferred in Montgomery, Maryland, to a nonteaching position and he sued to be reinstated to the classroom. His transfer to a nonteaching position became a media event (e.g., radio and television, including an appearance on *60 Minutes*). During a *60 Minutes* interview, Acanfora stated he had every right to be gay and be a teacher. The district court did not agree with him (*Acanfora v. Board of Education of Montgomery County,* 1974). Expert testimony by psychiatrists and child development researchers in the case of *Acanfora v. Board of Education of Montgomery County* revealed that the role modeling influence of lesbian or gay teachers was minimal because a child's sexual orientation is probably determined by age five or six. The judge ruled in favor of the teacher because the rights of gays and lesbians and of teachers were protected by doctrines such as the equal protection, privacy, and First Amendment rights; ultimately, the judge permitted the dismissal of Acanfora because he had lied about his political activities as a homosexual on his job application (Harbeck, 1991; Paul, Weinrich, Gonsiorek, & Hotvedt, 1982).

During 1977 and 1978 Anita Bryant, former Miss America finalist and popular singer, was very successful in getting many communities to repeal their homosexual rights ordinances. Appealing to conservative America and to the fundamentalist religious positions, Bryant influenced legislation in Florida, Oregon, Minnesota, Oklahoma, and Kansas. The issue was brought to the ballot in California in Proposition 6 in 1978. One of the candidates for governor, John Briggs, called for the passage of a proposition whereby any school employee could be fired for advocating, soliciting, imposing, encouraging, or promoting private or public homosexual activity directed at, or likely to come to the attention of, school children and/or other employees. This proposition was defeated partly because of the opposition expressed by former governor Ronald Reagan, who felt innocent lives could be ruined and that enforcement would be very expensive. He also argued that the prevailing opinion of professionals was that an individual's sexuality is determined at an earlier age than school age and thus was not under teachers' influence (Harbeck, 1991).

In 1993, the Massachusetts Governor's Commission on Gay and Lesbian Youth published a document recommending the following:

School policies which protect gay and lesbian students by:
 1 Anti-discrimination policies which includes sexual orientation for students and teachers, including teacher contracts.
 2 Policies which guarantee equal access to education and school activities.
 3 Anti-harassment policies and guidelines which deal with handling incidents of anti-gay language, harassment or violence.
 4 Multi-cultural and diversity policies.
Training teachers in suicide prevention and violence prevention as well as changing teacher certification requirements and school accreditation to include this training.

School based support groups for gay and straight students.

Curriculum which includes gay and lesbian issues.

Information in school libraries for gay and lesbian adolescents. (Governor's Commission on Gay and Lesbian Youth, 1993, p. 3)

Subsequently, the Massachusetts Board of Education unanimously adopted the nation's first state educational policy prohibiting discrimination against gay and lesbian elementary and secondary students and teachers.

In 1980, after much reflection and consideration of the consequences, Aaron Fricke, a gay student, decided to invite a male date to his high school senior prom in Cumberland, Rhode Island. He was motivated by his desire to make a statement about his sexual orientation and his human rights. When he met with administrative opposition he sued the school for the right to take his same-sex date to the prom. The judge ruled in Fricke's favor; he was allowed to take a male date to the prom (Fricke, 1981).

Although the law states that governmental employers are subject to constitutional requirements providing for fair treatment of all individuals, the reality is that care and discretion need to be exhibited in revealing one's sexual orientation.

> The general legal standard is that while a teacher's right to freedom of speech may be balanced against the importance the state attaches to the education of its youth, a teacher's comments on public issues that are knowingly false or made with reckless regard of the truth afford no ground for dismissal when they do not impair the teacher's performance of his or her duties or interfere with the operation of the school. (Hunter et al., 1992, p. 7)

THE WORKPLACE

Gays and lesbians who are concerned about what will happen to them if they reveal themselves at work are generally less productive at work than people who do not have those concerns. Closeted gays and lesbians expend a great deal of energy masking their private lives and their innermost feelings. Many gay and lesbian educators have been dealing with these issues for years. Gay and lesbian teenagers need to be aware of the potential discrimination in the workplace. More than 100 major companies have stated they do not discriminate on the basis of sexual orientation (National Gay and Lesbian Task Force, 1993). Yet, according to a *Wall Street Journal* survey, 66% of major company chief executive officers said they would be reluctant to put a homosexual on a management committee (Stewart, 1991).

As previously stated, in 1991 Cracker Barrel Old Country Store fired at least 11 employees because they were gay or perceived to be gay (Mickens, 1994). There is no federal law that prevents private employers, regardless of size or incorporation, from refusing to hire, firing, or undercompensating a gay or lesbian employee solely because of that person's sexual orientation and regardless of aptitude or work record. Five states—Connecticut, Hawaii, Massachusetts, New Jersey, and Wisconsin—forbid discrimination based on sexual orientation. Some large cities such as New York, Los Angeles, Chicago, Detroit, Boston, Philadelphia, San Francisco, and Atlanta also ban such discrimination (Hunter et al., 1992).

THE MILITARY

A ban on gays and lesbians in the military was instituted in 1943 and has since resulted in the discharge of 100,000 men and women for alleged homosexuality (Bérubé, 1990). Reports prepared by the Pentagon show that gays and lesbians have served in the military honorably and have not been a threat to security, morale, or the functioning of military units. In 1957, the Crittenden Committee (a government committee) reached the conclusion that there was no sound basis to assume gays and lesbians were a security risk; yet, for 20 years the Pentagon would not admit to the existence of the report (Shilts, 1993).

Two high-profile cases concerning military discharges for homosexuality appeared in the media prior to the 1992 presidential election. One case involved Petty Officer Keith Meinhold, a 14-year veteran Navy antisubmarine warfare instructor, who was discharged from the Navy in August 1992 after revealing his sexual orientation. He went to court and, in November 1992, a federal judge ruled the ban on gays and lesbians unconstitutional and ordered Meinhold reinstated. The U.S. Justice Department has appealed the case; meanwhile, Meinhold reenlisted for two years (Long, 1994). The second high-profile case dealt with the discharge of Margarethe Cammermeyer, a National Guard colonel, who has an exemplary military record and received the Bronze Star for her service in Vietnam. She was discharged in 1992 because she is a lesbian. She had revealed her sexual orientation to an investigator in 1989 while being interviewed for a top security clearance job. Cammermeyer filed a lawsuit challenging her discharge and in an April 1994 hearing before a U.S. District Court judge, her lawyers argued the discharge violated the constitutional guarantee of equal protection. Two months later the district court judge ruled that Cammermeyer be reinstated ("Judge Orders That Lesbian Be Reinstated," 1994).

In June 1992, a congressional report indicated that the ban on homosexuals in the armed forces costs the Pentagon at least $27 million a year and perpetuates a policy unsupported by science and sociology. One of President Clinton's first efforts was to try to rescind the ban on gays and lesbians in the military. Military leaders were not pleased with this suggestion and lobbied hard against it. The Joint Chiefs of Staff were strongly opposed to the change and Congress threatened legislative action. National support for gays and lesbians in the military dropped to below 50%. The belief was that having openly gay and lesbian people in the military would lower morale, increase anxiety, and lead to destruction of the order and discipline of the military. After much discussion, a compromise known as "don't ask, don't tell" was established to allow gays and lesbians to remain in the armed forces as long as they did not reveal their sexual orientation or have same-sex relationships on or off the base. A *Wall Street Journal/NBC News* poll in April 1993 revealed that 47% of Americans opposed allowing gays and lesbians in the military and 43% supported it as long as gays and lesbians did not openly declare their sexual orientation (Bawer, 1993). Recently, a suit has been filed on behalf of some gay and lesbian members of the armed forces, claiming violation of free speech.

RELIGION

Religious leaders were very vocal in their opposition to gays and lesbians openly serving in the military. Despite Christian teachings that one should love and accept one's fellow man, very little sensitivity, tolerance, or acceptance for homosexuals has been shown by organized religion.

From the early roots of Christianity, it appears that Paul advocated celibacy and stressed that sex was for procreation. Sex for pleasure was consistently condemned. "Interestingly, Jesus himself never condemns same-sex sexual relations" (Blumenfeld & Raymond, 1993, p. 195). It has been suggested by some authors (e.g., Blumenfeld & Raymond, 1993) that early Christianity paid little attention to the issue of homosexuality. It was the writings of Thomas Aquinas in the late 13th century that profoundly affected the Christian Church's views on sexuality. Aquinas felt that homosexuality was a sin against nature that represented a defect in the person. He believed that such acts were morally repugnant, and attitudes such as his were incorporated into some of the basic beliefs of the Catholic Church at that time. "Sodomites" were classified in the same category as individuals who were greedy in their pursuit of material wealth or who were traitors. Blumenfeld and Raymond report that between the years 1250 and 1300 A.D. homosexual activity went from being completely legal in most of Europe to meriting the death penalty.

Today there are some Christian religions that continue to hold strongly to Aquinas's position on homosexuality viewing it as sinful and immoral; however, there are many sects that are teaching other perspectives. One approach advocates an official church position stating that homosexuality is not a sin; however, it continues to publicly affirm that heterosexual marriage is the ideal and that the homosexual may not be responsible for his condition. This divergent opinion creates schisms in some churches. Other religious leaders promote the concept that homosexuality is a sin and deteriorates the morals of those who participate. Many of these members of the clergy preach intolerance of homosexuals to their congregations and believe that homosexuals can change if they turn their faith to the Lord.

Most churches have taken a position on homosexuality. Of the 47 religious bodies examined by Melton (1991), 8 have released statements supporting lesbian and gay rights; 4 have stated that homosexuality and traditional Christian moral precepts are compatible; 9 have distinguished between homosexual *behavior*, which they consider to be a sin, and a homosexual *orientation*; and 34 condemn homosexuals and homosexuality.

Among world religions, Buddhism does not condemn homosexuality (Dynes, 1990). Although the Koran does not condemn homosexuality, Islamic law punishes men and women found guilty of public homosexual behavior that is witnessed by four adult males (Blumenfeld & Raymond, 1993).

Southern Baptists believe in a literal interpretation of the Bible and consider homosexuality to be a learned behavior that is a "perversion." Although the Presbyterian Church prohibits the ordination of gays and lesbians, they do not interpret the Bible literally; they love gays but hate their "sin." The United Methodists speak out against discrimination of gays and lesbians, whereas the Episcopal Church feels that any physical sexual expression is appropriate only within the institution of marriage. The Catholic Church believes the homosexual can be changed and believes homosexual sex violates the moral law of God (Landers, 1993). Certain sects of Judaism are more accepting of gays and lesbians; however, Orthodox Judaism believes that homosexuality is an abomination (Mason, 1994).

There continues to be the fear among many gay and lesbian clerics that if their sexual orientation were known, they would be stripped of their power and licenses. They fear being excommunicated, ostracized, or denied their participation in religious ceremonies. In 1992, this became a rather controversial issue at Harvard University. Reverend Peter John Gnomes had served as minister of the university's Memorial Church and as Plummer Professor of Christian Morals since 1974. In 1991, he publicly stated he was a Christian who also happens to be gay. There was a tremendous public furor at the university, with people calling for his resignation. He received the support of Harvard's well-organized gay and lesbian community and was able to maintain his position (Ostling, 1992).

Mel White is a Christian who was a speechwriter for and trusted colleague of several Christian megastars. When he came out of the closet, he was ignored by the very religious leaders who once sought his assistance and counsel. He felt devastated by this rejection by people who once trusted him implicitly (Hecker, 1994).

Despite the greater openness of gays and lesbians in society and in the workplace, there continues to be reluctance in society to accept them. In a 1994 *Time Magazine* poll, 47% of the respondents supported giving gays and lesbians the same civil rights protection as racial and religious minorities; 57% of the respondents believed that gays could not be good role models for children; and 21% would not buy anything from a gay or lesbian salesperson. Furthermore, 65% of those polled believed that too much attention is being paid to gay and lesbian rights (Henry, 1994).

According to a poll of New Yorkers published in *New York Magazine* in June 1994 ("Will All the Homophobes Please Stand Up?" 1994), acceptance of gays and lesbians is greatest among young people (58%), people who have advanced degrees (59%), single people (54%), and Jews (51%). Those who were not accepting of gays and lesbians and thought homosexuality was wrong were predominantly Protestants (49%), blacks (49%), conservatives (68%), and Catholics (39%). Most respondents who were accepting of gays and lesbians also believed that they have a right to privacy.

Many adolescents are confused about homosexuality and religion. If they have been taught by the religious community that homosexuality is sinful and immoral, it is difficult for them to reconcile this belief system when they learn they are gay or lesbian. It is next to impossible for them to seek the support of their parents or the clergy when they realize disclosure will probably result in agonizing conflict and rejection. As a defense mechanism, some of these adolescents turn to self-rejection or castigation of others, and often, ironically, they try to find an answer to their problems by delving further into religion.

In April 1994, the Christian Action Network, a pro-family group based near Lynchburg, Virginia, placed an ad in the *Washington Times* stating that money from a United Way organization went to support two gay groups in the San Francisco area. The advertisement claimed that the United Way was allowing its good name to be used by a gay group to distribute gay and lesbian textbooks to the public schools and that money went to a group that was promoting homosexuality among teenagers. The Christian Action Network wanted the United Way to issue a policy statement stating that financing gay-related programs is not within the goals of the United Way. The Christian Action Network was trying to influence policy it disagreed with and was trying to garner public support ("Thou Shalt Not Lie," 1994). To date they have not been successful in attaining their desired goals.

Boswell, in his book entitled *Christianity, Social Tolerance and Homosexuality* (1980), stated that there is no definitive scriptural basis for the condemnation of homosexual relationships. In fact, many of the beliefs to which mainstream homosexuals ascribe are identical to teachings of Christianity: love and acceptance of humankind.

Sometimes gay bashing is carried out in the guise of standing up for the moral sanctity of the community. If the notion of homosexuality is sinful and immoral, then bashers can hide behind the cloak of religious teaching. Religious institutions need to be cautious in order not to appear to condone and sanction this violence perpetuated against people who are viewed as sinners.

Violence against gays and lesbians is a major concern. In 1992, the FBI, which had begun keeping statistics on hate crimes, reported there were at least 750 cases of assault and intimidation against homosexual men and women. This is a small number when compared with the data gathered by the National Gay and Lesbian Task Force; for 1992, it reported 2,103 episodes in six cities (Boston, Chicago, Denver, Minneapolis–St. Paul, New York, and San Francisco). Statistical data is inconclusive because many incidents go unreported so that the victim's sexual orientation can remain a secret (Henry, 1994).

THE BOY SCOUTS

The Boy Scouts has not been very tolerant of gay adolescents. A spokesman for the Boy Scouts stated that a homosexual is not a role model consistent with the expectations of mainstream American families. In 1992, James Dale, a gay, highly decorated Eagle Scout, was expelled from his position as an assistant scoutmaster when he disclosed his sexual orientation. In his Boy Scout oath he vowed he would be trustworthy, so he told the truth about being gay. Although the Boy Scouts teaches a creed of being honest and trustworthy, Dale was penalized for upholding the creed. Instead of becoming a role model for other individuals, both gay and straight, he was expelled from the organization (Bawer, 1993).

CONCLUSION

Although society has made strides toward greater acceptance of gays and lesbians, many negative attitudes and misbeliefs perpetuate and contribute to homophobia. Institutional change is helpful in modifying society's attitudes and beliefs; but, gay and lesbian students need to be prepared for what they may encounter. By reaching out to teenagers and helping them get the tools they need to better handle prejudicial and discriminatory thinking, educators can increase the self-esteem and coping abilities of their students. Educating children about the deleterious effects of prejudice and discrimination can be beneficial to everyone. Those responsible for working with children and adolescents should take the lead in trying to help foster an atmosphere of greater tolerance and acceptance of all individuals.

Chapter 5

Relevant Issues

KIDS AT RISK

Families often teach homophobic attitudes in subtle ways, such as through persistent derogatory jokes and homophobic conversations. The one-in-ten gay and lesbian children who absorb these attitudes and realize their sexual orientation during preadolescent and adolescent years become victims of their parents' homophobia. These teenagers may respond to the confusion in a number of ways as they try to deal with their homosexual feelings. Some respond by denying their sexual orientation and dating and engaging in sexual activities with members of the opposite sex, trying to pass as heterosexual. Others respond by developing a strong contempt for those gay and lesbians who are more open and obvious. They may take out their own sexual frustrations through varying degrees of aggression toward gay and lesbian members of the community. Other gay and lesbian teenagers respond by withdrawing from society and becoming shy and isolated. They are reluctant to join in social activities with friends or family and live in a world all their own. Some of these teenagers are so filled with self-hatred they cannot find anything acceptable or positive to say about themselves. Some seek out groups that believe their homosexual orientation can be changed. These individuals will go to great extremes and will be highly motivated to do whatever it takes to be straight. Internalizing homophobia and self-hatred has many devastating effects on adolescents' self-concept; their personal, academic, and emotional development; the quality of their future same- and opposite-sex relationships; the development of future life plans; and the well-being of their families.

In a recent series of studies of self-identified gay male adolescents, Remafedi (1987) found these adolescents to be at high risk for physical and psychosocial dysfunction as a result of experiencing strong negative attitudes from parents and peers. Additionally, some of these teenagers reported verbal abuse, physical assaults, and discrimination.

Impact of Homophobia

Homophobia hurts everyone. It serves the dominant group by establishing and maintaining power and superiority over the minority. It causes inhibition of creativity and self-expression. It defines specific sex roles and leads to false assumptions about one's sexuality. It interferes with the development of close relationships with members of one's own sex. It limits family interactions and closeness. It causes isolation and lack of close relationships. Homophobia can contribute to premature sexual involvement, which in turn can lead to unwanted pregnancy and sexually transmitted diseases. Homophobia contributed to the slow public response to the AIDS crisis (Feldman, 1989).

For gay and lesbian teenagers, in addition to the above problems, there are increased academic problems. Because they are preoccupied with their social discomfort and trying to find out where they fit in, teenagers encounter difficulty concentrating and do not feel as comfortable participating in their classrooms or in school activities. This has a great impact on society in general, because many of these individuals do not realize their potential. In a 1987 study of gay male youths, 69% reported a history of school problems related to sexual identity (Remafedi, 1987).

Girls may be likely to develop some type of eating disorder. "Anorexia nervosa characteristically begins in the years between adolescence and young adulthood, approximately ninety percent of patients are females, most commonly from the middle and upper socio-economic strata" (Tierney, McPhee, & Papadakis, 1995, p. 1066). Anorexia or overeating can be a means of denying one's sexuality and not having to confront the issue of growing up. If a girl is concerned about being a lesbian and does not want to attract anyone, she may either undereat or overeat and develop a distorted body image.

For some gay and lesbian teenagers their sexual orientation is the primary motivation for running away from home. One in four gay and lesbian youths is forced to leave home because of conflicts with their families about their sexual orientation (Remafedi, 1987). Because many gays and lesbians do not have any other support system, they feel they have few options other than leaving the family home. Gay and lesbian teenagers constitute up to 25% of all youths living on the streets in the United States (U.S. Department of Health and Human Services, 1989). Approximately half of the gay and bisexual males forced out of their homes engage in prostitution to support themselves (Savin-Williams, 1988). These teenagers have few job skills and, not having completed their formal education, find that obtaining employment sufficient to maintain the basic necessities of life becomes prohibitive. Prostitution seems to be the most expedient way to do so. However, engaging in this type of behavior contributes further to the development of self-hate and the destruction of their self-images.

Suicide

Every day, 13 Americans ages 15 to 24 commit suicide. In 1989, suicide was the leading cause of death among gay, lesbian, bisexual, and transgendered youths. Lesbian and gay youths are two to three times more likely to attempt suicide than their heterosexual peers, and they account for up to 30% of all completed suicides among youths (U.S. Department of Health and Human Services, 1989). A 1991 study of 137 gay and bisexual male youths found that 30% had attempted suicide once and 13% had made multiple attempts. The mean age of those attempting suicide was 15.5. Three quarters of first attempts came after the teenagers had labeled themselves as homosexual (Remafedi, Farrow, & Deisher, 1991).

Although young gays and lesbians face the same risk factors for suicide as heterosexual youths, those risks are magnified by issues of sexual orientation. The U.S. Department of Health and Human Services listed the following risk factors for gay and lesbian youth suicide:

General
  Awareness/identification of homosexual orientation at an early age
  Self acceptance of homosexual orientation
  Conflicts with others related to homosexual orientation
  Problems in homosexual relationships

Society
  Discrimination/oppression of homosexuals by society
  Portrayal of homosexuals as self destructive by society

Poor Self-Esteem
  Internalization of image of homosexuals as sick and bad
  Internalization of image of homosexuals as helpless and self destructive

Identity Conflicts
  Denial of homosexual orientation
  Despair in a recognition of a homosexual orientation

Family
  Rejection of child due to homosexual orientation
  Abuse/harassment of child due to homosexual orientation
  Failure of child to meet parental/societal expectation
  Perceived rejection of child due to homosexual orientation

Religion
  Child's homosexual orientation seen as incompatible with family religious beliefs
  Youth feels sinful, condemned to hell due to homosexual orientation

School
  Abuse/harassment of homosexual youth by peers
  Lack of accurate information about homosexuality

Social Isolation
  Rejection of homosexual youth by friends and peers
  Social withdrawal of homosexual youth
  Loneliness and inability to meet others like themselves

Substance Abuse
Substance use to relieve pain of oppression
Substance use to reduce inhibitions on homosexual feelings

Professional Help
Refusal to accept homosexual orientation of youth
Refusal to support homosexual orientation of youth
Involuntary treatment to change homosexual orientation of youth
Inability to discuss issues related to homosexuality

Residential Programs
Refusal to accept/support homosexual orientation of youth
Isolation of homosexual youth by staff and residents
Inability to support homosexual youth in conflicts with residents

Relationship Problems
Inability to develop relationship skills like heterosexual youth
Extreme dependency needs due to prior emotional deprivation
Absence of social supports in resolving relationship conflicts

Independent Living
Lack of support from family
Lack of support from adult gay community
Involvement with street life

AIDS (Acquired Immune Deficiency Syndrome)
Unsafe sexual practices
Secrecy/unplanned nature of early sexual experiences

Future Outlook
Despair of life as hard as the present
Absence of positive adult gay/lesbian role models (Gibson, 1989, pp. 137–138)

The reduction of suicide among gay and lesbian youth is directly related to progress in reducing institutionalized homophobia and in providing necessary information, acceptance, and support to gay and lesbian youth.

Homophobia is devastating for gays and lesbians; but it also has a negative influence on the heterosexual community. Straight individuals may feel uncomfortable forming relationships with gays and lesbians because of their concern about what their heterosexual friends and family may think. This is unfortunate because friendships with individuals of the same sex can often lead to greater freedom and intimacy than with straight individuals, because the concern of the development of a sexual relationship is removed. These relationships also help people learn to accept individuals for their strengths and weaknesses and remove people from the stereotypical roles of what defines masculinity and femininity. When we have greater freedom to be who we are, we are more likely to achieve our true potential and to have relationships and friendships with a broader sector of the population. Fighting homophobia is like fighting any other prejudice. Through awareness, education, a commitment to eliminate the problem, and a concerted effort to effect change, homophobia can be eradicated.

COMING OUT

The advent of the Gay Liberation movement created greater visibility for gays and lesbians; however, the process of coming out is still difficult for the majority of teenagers. Coming out is a dual process of first accepting oneself as a homosexual and then disclosing sexual identity to others: family, friends, peers, and strangers. As Gadamer (1965) has stated, there are some presuppositions regarding hetero-sexuality and adolescence. Gadamer believes there is a general assumption that teenagers are going to be heterosexual, so that teenagers who are not heterosexual are stigmatized and face consequences regarding their development and adapta-tion. The perception may be that all gays and lesbians are the same in their coming out process and in their identity. Green (1987) reported that children who manifest nonconformist gender behavior from an early age are most susceptible to parental and peer pressure to change their behavior. Feeling different and alienated can be associated with early aspirations to change identity, which will eventually lead to coming out (Troiden, 1979).

Developmental Stages

Coleman (1982b) identified five stages as part of homosexual development. In the pre–coming out stage the individual becomes aware of same-sex interests and come to terms with himself. The response to this new awareness might be dismissal, repression, or rejection of these feelings. Some individuals respond by becoming depressed, having a poor self-concept, having difficulty in interpersonal relationships, and lacking direction in what to do with themselves or their lives. As individuals begin to come to terms with their sexuality and accept these feelings, they move on to the next stage, coming out.

During the coming out stage, the individual will choose someone with whom he can share his awareness and disclose himself. Acceptance or rejection at this point is critical. If the individual encounters acceptance, he will begin to feel more confident and his self-esteem will increase. If, however, he encounters rejection, self-esteem will be reduced, and he may become depressed and return to the pre–coming out stage. As the individual begins to work through this process and accept his sexual identity, he progresses to the next stage, exploration.

During the process of exploration the individual begins to experiment with the new sexual identity and begins to make contact with the homosexual commu-nity, reaching out to other gays and lesbians to form new relationships. For adolescents this stage can be awkward, intense, and very confusing.

When the individual perceives himself as capable of loving and being loved, he begins the next stage, a first relationship. It is during this period that he begins to work toward intimacy. Frequently, at this stage of a relationship there is much intensity, possessiveness, and insecurity. Because this is a first relationship and the individuals have gone through tremendous developmental growth to arrive at this point, there may be great pressure to succeed. The first relationship stage is similar to that experienced by heterosexuals. It is through the development of self-confidence and success that individuals move into the last stage, integration and viewing themselves as functioning well in society (Coleman, 1982b).

Sophie (1985/1986) similarly defined the coming out process and identified four stages. During the first awareness stage the individual realizes that he is different and that homosexuality may be the relevant issue. During this period there is no disclosure to others, resulting in feelings of alienation. The next stage is testing and exploration, during which there is limited contact with the gay and lesbian community and alienation from heterosexuals. In the third stage of identity acceptance a preference develops for social interactions with other gays and lesbians. Negative identities are replaced by positive ones and it is at this point that disclosure to heterosexuals is likely to occur. The last stage is identity integration, during which individuals view themselves as gay or lesbian with pride and disclose their sexual orientation to many others.

Lesbians and gay males generally come out to siblings and close heterosexual friends rather than to parents, co-workers, or employers. For many gays and lesbians, these seem to be the safest arenas for disclosure. Gays and lesbians who do not reveal their sexual identity to others will try to blend into society through gender-appropriate behavior without disclosing their true identity. Identity disclosure, for most gays and lesbians, brings with it a tremendous amount of personal freedom and a more complete integration of their sexual identity and their environment.

Gay and lesbian teenagers feel torn between two worlds, one represented by the heterosexual lifestyles of their parents and the other represented by the adult gay and lesbian community. Adolescents at first may feel isolated or depressed. Some postpone dealing with these sexual issues until they reach their late teens. However, more and more gay and lesbian teenagers are coming to grips with their sexuality early and feeling more comfortable about coming out. In one of the earliest studies on coming out, Dank (1971) revealed that the mean age for coming out was 19.3. More recently, Coleman (1982b) reported age 15 for males and 20 for females, and Remafedi (1987) reported a mean age of 14 for gay youth. Herdt (1989) believes as the age of coming out lowers, additional developmental age-related pressures may overburden the gay or lesbian teenager. He is concerned that this has greater psychosocial costs for these teenagers and will raise risk factors such as suicide.

de Monteflores and Schultz (1978) believe there are differences between gay males and lesbians. They believe gay males sexually act on their homosexual feelings earlier, after they become aware of same-sex attractions. Homosexual behavior usually occurs for lesbians after an intellectual understanding of the term *homosexual*; gay males act before such an understanding. Lesbians avoid self-identifying as homosexual by emphasizing their feelings; gay males avoid such self-identification by avoiding their feelings. The homosexual self-label is more threatening to males. Coming out is more likely to be a political decision among lesbians.

In a study of gay and lesbian youth, Savin-Williams (1990) found that most of those who had come out could be described as follows:

1 They were politically and socially involved with other gays and lesbians, had numerous homosexual encounters, regularly frequented bars, and described an early onset of homosexual feelings that were beyond their control.

2 They felt acceptance by family members and friends and felt they had more friends.

3 They felt they were accomplished and self-sufficient, but did not feel competitive and forceful or affectionate and compassionate.

4 They were generally older and well educated, coming from wealthy urban families.

5 Possessions and good looks were not important to their sense of well-being. They measured their self-esteem by their friends, career, and academic achievements.

6 They were politically liberal and supportive of the feminist movement.

Attitudes

Males tend to define themselves as gay in contexts of same-sex erotic contact, but females experience lesbian feelings in situations of romantic love and emotional attachment (Troiden, 1979). Females tend to emphasize attachment and personal orientations whereas males stress independence and positional relationships in public. Youth in close proximity to urban centers have more opportunities for making supportive homosexual contacts (Anderson, 1987). What is of primary importance to most young gays and lesbians is the attitude toward homosexuality and the presence of homophobia within their own families. The importance of parental attitudes is a directive force in the daily lives of teenagers. Gaining parental acceptance is very important to teenagers. Fear of being shunned or rejected by their families is greatest at the beginning of the coming out process. Teenagers are also afraid of being thrown out of the home, being forced into psychotherapy, or being physically abused. Some teenagers also struggle with guilt because they fear they will disappoint their parents, who have hopes and plans for them, such as marriage and children.

Coming Out to Parents

Coming out to parents, for most teenagers, is one of the most difficult life situations they will ever face. They are not sure how to begin and what reception they will receive. Fairchild and Hayward (1979) have provided some suggestions that might be helpful for the teenager coming out to parents:

1 Know how you feel about being gay and express this.

2 Share your feelings when things are going well, or during a period when there is relative tranquillity.

3 Don't come out during an argument because this knowledge may then become a weapon that will cause pain to everyone.

4 It is okay to tell only one parent initially if that is easier or more comfortable for you.

5 Begin by telling your parents that you love them. If you don't usually say these things, then find other positive thoughts to share.

6 Be prepared for your parents to be upset and hurt by this news. Your parents may respond with anger. Try not to be defensive and angry also. Give them the time they need to assimilate this information.

7 Tell them that you are still the same person and you hope they will continue to love you.

8 Maintain open lines of communication. Your parents are going to go through a period of adjustment as well—feelings of guilt, lost dreams, and greater uncertainty of the future.

9 Get reading materials and share them with your parents.

10 Don't force the issue if your parents are not ready to discuss this. Be discrete in your friendships and introduce them to your parents if your parents want to meet them.

For parents, Fairchild and Hayward (1979) have advised that when parents suspect or learn their teenager is homosexual, they need to relax. They need to recognize that it is not the end of the world and their gay or lesbian child is not doomed to a life of pain and unhappiness. They need to emphasize all the positive attributes their child has and how this will help him become a successful, well-adjusted individual. Parents need to keep in mind that their child has paid them the compliment of love, trust, and faith by sharing himself with them. Mothers and fathers need to focus on the future by recognizing that their child can still attain many of the parents' dreams and plans, such as successful careers, long-term relationships, and personal fulfillment and satisfaction.

Fairchild and Hayward (1979) further suggest that parents find an accepting confidant who will understand their feelings. Support groups for parents of gays and lesbians are a good place to begin. Gay and lesbian hotlines and organizations are staffed with compassionate and knowledgeable individuals who are receptive to discussing the parents' feelings. Reading about the topic can also be comforting for parents. There are many easily accessible resources available. Books, periodicals, audio cassettes, videos, and other materials are available from local bookstores, libraries, and gay and lesbian organizations (see Appendix C). It is important that parents try to convey positive messages to their child. They need to be aware of their language and know that how they express themselves may convey discomfort in their child. Parents need to be accepting of their child's friends and ask about his friendships as they would if their child were heterosexual.

Parental Relationships

Savin-Williams (1990) has reported that lesbian youth who had positive parental relationships felt comfortable with their sexual orientation. Satisfying parental relationships, maternal knowledge of their homosexuality, and having relatively little contact with fathers predicted positive self-esteem for gay men. Her research revealed that the mother was important for the self-esteem of both gays and lesbians. Lesbians who had satisfying relationships with their mothers and who had relatively young parents were most likely to be "out" to them. Male youths who were out to their mothers had high levels of self-esteem. It appears that mothers are viewed as considerably more supportive, warm, and compassionate than fathers. Early parent–infant interactions, physical affection, childhood rearing practices, and family religious teachings may be good predictors of the state of comfort with children's sexual orientation.

Values and Cultural Influences

Newman and Muzzonigro (1993) found that traditional family values played a key role in predicting coming out experiences. Families with a strong emphasis on traditional values were perceived as less accepting of homosexuality than were the nontraditional families. Traditional values were based on the importance of religion, the emphasis on marriage and children, and whether English was spoken in the home.

In Savin-Williams' (1990) study predicting self-esteem among gay and lesbian youth, the gay teenagers with the highest levels of self-esteem felt accepted by their mothers, male and female friends, and their academic advisors. They also believed they had a large number of heterosexual friends. Those lesbians who viewed themselves in a positive fashion had many bisexual, but few gay friends. Having bisexual friends demonstrates a personal sense of security because this enables the gay and lesbian to have relationships with individuals who have ties to both the gay and straight worlds.

Gay and lesbian individuals who do not gain the acceptance of friends or family experience almost unbearable isolation and loneliness. These feelings impact the entire family. A good example of this was Ellie, a 42-year-old woman who entered therapy because she could no longer cope with her husband's drinking problem. His heavy drinking began about 10 years earlier but did not become excessive until his daughter was picked up by the police for drug abuse; she was imprisoned and then sent to a drug treatment program. Ellie's husband was having great difficulty handling this and refused to discuss any of his children with Ellie. Apparently, 10 years earlier, Don's son, who was 16, committed suicide. Don felt guilty about his son's death and could not talk about him without crying. Eventually, he just stopped talking about him and would change the subject whenever his name was mentioned. The thought that his daughter had problems was too much for him to face. At the age of 13 Don's son told Don that he thought he was gay. Don reacted with disbelief and tried to convince his son otherwise. Don told him he needed more experience with women, that he did not know how he felt, and that he was a confused teenager. Don also would make belittling remarks about gays. Don sent his son for several visits with a therapist, but this did not help. When Don read the suicide note his son left, he was devastated. His son wrote that, because he knew he was a disappointment to his father and could never live up to his expectations, he felt it would be better for everyone if he just ended his life. Don never dealt fully with his son's death, and now his daughter's difficulties heightened his feelings of failure as a parent. Don refused to seek help. Therapy helped Ellie better understand Don's feelings, but he continued to deal with his emotions by drinking and later died from complications related to his alcoholism.

For gay youth in ethnic minorities, role conflicts may be much more pronounced and coming out may be much more difficult because homosexuality is considered unacceptable in many of these cultures (Hidalgo & Christensen, 1976–77; Icard, 1986; Tremble, Schneider, & Appathurai, 1989; Wilson, 1986). Tremble et al. found that gay and lesbian teenagers who attempted to integrate a homosexual identity into a preexisting cultural belief system experienced conflicts within themselves, their families, and their communities. These conflicts were strongest when religious beliefs were devout, because family members had high expectations regarding marriage and children and gender roles were polarized and stereotypical.

Minority adolescents need to not only come to terms with their homosexuality but also assimilate this with their ethnic identity. Both the Hispanic (Hetrick & Martin, 1987; Hidalgo & Christiansen, 1976–77) and African-American community (Icard, 1986; Wilson, 1986) consider homosexuality deviant. Homosexuality is viewed as being detrimental to the values of marriage, family, and children. Therefore, gay African-American and Hispanic teenagers encounter further alienation from their culture yet do not feel comfortable relating to the typically white gay and lesbian community.

Newman and Muzzonigro (1993) studied 27 gay males between the ages of 17 and 20. Twelve respondents were Caucasian, seven were African-American, six were Hispanic/Latino, and two were Asian/Eurasian. The results indicated that young males from traditional families recalled feeling different from other boys to a greater degree than did those from less traditional families. Race alone was not significant; however, the degree of traditional values within the family did affect aspects of the respondents' coming out experiences. Adolescents from more traditional families reported having a crush at an earlier age. This might be the result of cultural differences in the experience and recognition of sexual feelings.

We know that coming out in a warm, supportive environment enhances the self-esteem of a gay or lesbian teenager. Unfortunately, the reality persists that for many teenagers coming out is met by rejection and ostracism, which can create many behavioral problems:

- High incidence of acting out in school
- Rebelling against authority
- Abusing alcohol and other substances
- Feeling depressed, isolated, and confused
- Engaging in prostitution
- Attempting suicide (and many times succeeding)

Educators should be at the forefront in reaching these students and addressing the issues of sexuality, both heterosexual and homosexual, in an informed, nonthreatening setting.

BISEXUALITY

With the advent of the Gay Liberation movement there has been a greater tendency to identify individuals as being either homosexual or heterosexual. Bisexuality, however, has not received much attention. Some heterosexual and homosexual individuals dichotomize sexuality and do not believe there is such a thing as bisexuality. According to Zinik (1985), significantly higher percentages of people exhibit bisexual behavior than exclusively homosexual behavior. Bisexuality can be defined as eroticizing or being sexually aroused by both females and males, engaging in or desiring sexual activity with both, or adopting bisexuality as a sexual identity label. It can also include the desire to have intimate emotional relationships with both females and males that may include sexual contact (Bode, 1976; Klein, 1978; MacInnes, 1973; Scott, 1978).

Zinik (1985) has presented two theories of bisexuality. The conflict model purports that an individual is either heterosexual or homosexual. Therefore, people who are bisexual are experiencing identity conflict or confusion, living in an inherently temporary or transitional stage that masks the person's true underlying sexual orientation (presumably homosexual) and employing the label as a method of either consciously denying or unconsciously defending against one's true homosexual preference. This model is based on the notion that homosexual interests eradicate heterosexual responsiveness. The least doubt of heterosexuality is taken as evidence of an underlying homosexual orientation.

The flexibility model of bisexuality portrays the bisexual as being capable of moving easily between both the heterosexual and homosexual worlds. The two can coexist in the form of bisexual eroticism. Unlike the conflict model, which is characterized by either–or thinking, the flexibility model is characterized by both–and thinking. Therefore, one can be both heterosexual and homosexual: individuals can feel comfortable with their bisexuality without experiencing conflict.

Sigmund Freud believed all individuals are born with bisexual potential (Freud, 1901/1953; Stoller, 1972), and this point of view has been shared by Money and Tucker (1975). The conclusions of researchers have promoted greater acceptance of bisexuality within the population and bisexuals now seem to feel more comfortable disclosing their sexual orientation than they have in the past. Celebrities who have identified themselves as bisexuals include Madonna, Mick Jagger, Billy Jean King, Joan Baez, and Janis Joplin (Weiner, 1994).

In 1981, Bell et al. conducted interviews of 979 homosexual and 477 heterosexual men and women. They found most of the homosexual subjects were exclusively homosexual, but a sufficiently large number were identified as bisexual. They learned most bisexuals first eroticize the opposite sex and identify as heterosexual. It is not until their 20s or 30s that they discover their homosexual interests. In a study by Zinik (1985), bisexual males and females reported experiencing similar levels of erotic excitement with female and male sexual partners; however, both males and females reported more emotional satisfaction with their female partners. Both male and female subjects reported falling in love with women more often than with men. In Zinik's study, 79% of the bisexual subjects reported some degree of conflict or confusion due to their bisexuality.

In a study by Masters and Johnson (1979), individuals who were identified as enjoying sexual activities with partners of both sexes were viewed as being well adjusted and having no psychiatric or work problems, but were characterized as detached and lonely. Nurius (1983), however, found that bisexuals scored higher than heterosexuals, but lower than homosexuals, on a measure of dysfunctional depression.

Most of the literature in the area of sexuality deals with either heterosexual development or homosexual identity. Paul (1985) has asserted that part of the decision to adopt a homosexual identity, as opposed to a bisexual or heterosexual identity, involves not only the personal significance one attaches to one's homosexual experience and perceived potential, but also one's simultaneous evaluation of one's heterosexuality. Given that the self-identified bisexual can expect hostility and rejection from the mainstream heterosexuals and homosexuals, there often is tremendous pressure to identify oneself as homosexual. Once the bisexual has identified himself as homosexual there is additional pressure to be exclusively homosexual in order to be accepted. Blumstein and Schwartz (1977) reported that this is especially true among a subgroup of lesbian feminists. Therefore, for those adolescents who are trying to better understand who they are and get a clearer understanding of their sexual orientation, these may be additional factors adding to their already confused state. In addition, while teenagers are grappling with the issues of coming out and establishing relationships, the rampant spread of AIDS has added to their difficulty.

AIDS

In the late 1970s, physicians discovered a patient with a number of unexplained maladies. Soon other doctors in the United States and Europe began seeing patients with similar symptoms. By the end of 1980, at least 50 patients, primarily gay men, were identified as having a new disease called Acquired Immune Deficiency Syndrome (AIDS). Since 1982, more than 69,000 cases of AIDS have been reported to the Centers for Disease Control and estimates are that 40 times more people are infected with human immunodeficiency virus (HIV). Although this disease is believed to have existed for some time in epidemic proportions among heterosexual populations in parts of Africa, its initial entry into the gay community affected people's perceptions of homosexuality.

AIDS is a physical condition that affects the body's immune system, leaving it weak and vulnerable to other infections and illnesses. AIDS is believed to be caused by an infectious agent, probably a retrovirus, that is transmissible through intimate contact (usually sexual) involving the direct exchange of bodily fluids. Following the entry of any virus into the bloodstream, antibodies are produced in the blood to fight off infection. The HIV antibody is ineffective in killing the virus. Experts believe AIDS has an incubation period of 7 to 24 months. General symptoms of AIDS include:

Unexplained increasing and persistent fatigue.

Periodic or regular fevers, shaking chills, drenching night sweats not accompanied by a known illness and lasting longer than several weeks.

Weight loss that is unexpected and greater than approximately ten pounds in less than two months.

Otherwise unexplained swollen glands (enlarging lymph nodes with or without pain, usually in the neck, armpits or groin) lasting for more than two weeks.

Pink to purple flat or raised blotches or bumps, usually painless, occurring on or under the skin, inside the mouth, nose, eyelids, or rectum. Initially they may look like bruises but they do not go away; they usually are harder than the skin around them.

Persistent white spots or unusual blemishes in the mouth.

Persistent dry cough that is not from smoking and has lasted too long to be from a typical respiratory infection.

Persistent diarrhea. (Blumenfeld & Raymond, 1993, p. 322)

With the increasing rate of HIV infection and the tendency for frequent unprotected sexual activity among adolescents, it is imperative that these issues be addressed with adolescents. Cranston (1991) reported that adolescent gay and bisexual males face a higher risk of infection with HIV than most other young people because of their unprotected sexual behaviors and because HIV prevention programs have failed to address the concerns of adolescents. He believes that personal empowerment, in the context of a community of shared values and experiences, is a prerequisite to effective HIV risk education for these teenagers. Cranston found that the rate of heterosexual AIDS transmission among adolescents is twice that of adults (approximately 8% vs. 4%); however, he states that the great majority of sexually infected adolescents were infected as a result of homosexual contact. In a seroprevalence study, the rates of HIV infection of gay and bisexual males ages 20 to 24 ranged from 4 to 47%, with a median rate of 25%, a rate of infection 10 times higher than the study's next highest risk group, young urban black males (Wendell, Onorato, Allen, McCray, & Sweeney, 1990).

Cranston (1991) believes that the increased risk among young gay and bisexual males is because of unprotected anal and oral intercourse and shared injection drug needles and paraphernalia. He reports there are significant levels of infection in the gay and bisexual youth population, so unprotected intercourse and needle sharing with peers are extremely high risk behaviors. The statistics indicate that lesbians as a group have significantly lower levels of infection.

Cranston (1991) further noted that because most young gays, lesbians, and bisexuals have not experienced the death of a close friend or family member to AIDS, the reality of contracting this disease is reduced. Many gay and lesbian adolescents believe they are not susceptible to contracting HIV (Berger, 1982). Cranston believes these young people are at increased risk because of their lower self-esteem. He recommends a comprehensive health education model that will not only provide AIDS prevention education but also address the self-esteem of these individuals to enable them to modify their risk factors. The program also should address the issues of personal health and wellness, including alcohol and substance abuse, the anatomy, and physiological function of human sexuality and sexually transmitted diseases as well as the ability to make decisions, communicate feelings, build relationships, and negotiate or refuse certain unacceptable behaviors. Adolescents should be taught how to correctly use condoms and other barrier forms of disease prevention, how to identify health problems, and how to get help when problems are identified. Adolescents also need access to affordable, confidential, and sensitive health care. Cranston believes the most effective way to reach gay, lesbian, and bisexual youth is through education in safe and supportive environments. School-based programs can educate the entire school population about HIV/AIDS-related issues and can address the myths and surrounding fears that individuals have toward homosexuality.

Adolescents should be taught positive protective measures such as the following:

1   Reduce or eliminate sexual activity in which bodily fluids are exchanged.
2   Limit the number of sexual partners.
3   Avoid sharing needles.
4   Limit sexual contact with those known to use intravenous drugs.
5   Learn the proper use of condoms so the transmission of sexually transmitted diseases can be reduced.

It is important that adolescents know their sex partners and inquire about their health. If they have any doubt, they need to learn to avoid sexual contact. Taking good care of their bodies with adequate rest, good nutrition, reduced stress and use of toxic substances, and increased physical exercise is helpful. It can take only one contact to acquire AIDS, and because of the lengthy incubation period, people who appear healthy may be infectious and capable of spreading AIDS (Blumenfeld & Raymond, 1993).

HIV/AIDS has had a devastating impact on many families. Some family members are more supportive than others in giving the emotional and physical assistance that is needed to handle this illness. Judy and Bill came to therapy at the insistence of their family physician because Judy was extremely depressed and suicidal. Judy was very quiet and withdrawn and Bill was intolerant and demeaning toward Judy's feelings. Attempts at identifying potential sources for Judy's depression were unsuccessful. The underlying problem was revealed when the couple was asked whether they had any children. Judy said *two* and Bill said *one*. Their youngest son had died of AIDS at age 23 approximately one year earlier. The couple did not realize their son was gay or had AIDS until a few weeks before his death, when one of their son's friends called and said that John was very ill and that they should come to town, which was 500 miles away, to see him. Bill sent Judy.

Judy accompanied John to the doctor, who told Judy that John had AIDS. Judy was devastated and called Bill for support. He refused to come and told her that as far as he was concerned his son was already dead. John was crushed by this and felt that his father was ashamed of him and rejected him because he had AIDS. John's last few weeks were especially emotionally painful and he and Judy spent many hours discussing his father's nonacceptance of him. Judy felt crushed because she did not know how to soothe her son's feelings or modify Bill's. Judy remained with John until his death. Bill did not attend the funeral.

When Judy returned she tried to discuss her feelings with Bill. He told her the subject was a closed one and that John's name was never to be mentioned again. As far as their friends knew, John had died of pneumonia. Judy was devastated. In addition to dealing with the loss of her son, she had to confront her feelings alone and felt rejected and abandoned by her husband. During the session Bill refused to acknowledge Judy's feelings and refused to allow her to continue with therapy. The family physician tried to intervene but was unsuccessful. Shortly thereafter Judy experienced an emotional breakdown and was hospitalized for more than a year.

Not all parents are as rejecting as Bill was of John. Steve had been divorced from his wife for 24 years, having left home when his son was quite young. Nonetheless, he believed strongly in family and always had an active role in his son's life. His son was the captain of the football team and president of his student council. Steve was proud of his son's accomplishments. He felt he was a chip off the old block. He was distraught to learn his son was gay and "nearly died" when he was told his son had AIDS. Steve experienced great pain and conflict in accepting his son's homosexuality, but because he believed so strongly in family, he worked hard to understand it. He read every book he could find and had many open discussions with his son. Although he disliked his son's behavior, he tried to be as unconditional in his acceptance of him as possible. When he learned his son had AIDS he spent the next two years of his life pursuing every possible treatment avenue available. He worked for an AIDS hotline and became involved with hospice, which he felt brought him closer to his son. He cherished the time he had with his son and felt he grew tremendously. Steve had great difficulty following his son's death. Because of his intense involvement in his son's care there was a tremendous void once his son died.

Today there are teenagers serving as role models for others experiencing HIV. Pedro Zamora is a good example. He arrived in the United States from Cuba during the 1980 Mariel boatlift when he was eight years old. At age 17 he became HIV positive and made the decision to make a difference with the rest of his life by educating teenagers about safe sex and becoming an AIDS activist. He spent the last five years of his life as a public speaker. He was a hero to millions of teenagers, who listened to his speeches in auditoriums and classrooms and heard his message on national talk shows and on MTV's *Real World* program. On November 11, 1994, Pedro Zamora died at the age of 22 (N. S. Martin, 1994).

Adolescents need to have the confidence to express their feelings and protect their personal rights. Through education and greater awareness adolescents can learn to feel good about themselves.

GAY FATHERS

Bozett (1987) has estimated there are between one and three million gay men who are natural fathers. Schulenburg (1985) has estimated there are six million children of gay men and lesbians. Peterson (1984) believes the number is closer to 14 million. Many gay fathers also go through an identity crisis when reformulating their sexual identity from heterosexual or bisexual to homosexual. During this process, gay fathers need to assimilate their sexual orientation with their fatherhood. Each identity tends to be unacceptable to the larger nongay society. Gay men who are fathers are often also rejected by the gay community (Bozett, 1987). Therefore, gay fathers need to achieve congruence between their two identities and their behavior. Bozett (1982) has found the following:

1 Divorce is the most likely outcome when husbands disclose their homosexuality to their wives.

2 If men disclose their homosexuality to their wives before they marry, wives find it easier to assimilate full disclosure during the marriage.

3 Amicable separations and divorces can occur with partial to complete disclosure.

4 When there is no partial disclosure before the marriage, generally the wives are totally unprepared, nonaccepting, and hostile.

5 If wives give permission to their husbands to have sex with other men, in an effort to preserve the marriage, the marriage rarely succeeds.

6 When wives can accept their husbands' homosexuality they tend to have positive marital relationships.

When men are comfortable in the heterosexual marital lifestyle, except with the physically sexual aspect of the relationship, and their wives disapprove of their homosexuality, they have difficulty accepting themselves as gay. However, to meet their affectional and sexual needs, men seek other homosexuals, which increases their exposure to the gay world and increases their acceptance of their gay identity. Once a husband begins to disclose himself and assume a gay identity, no matter what posture the wife assumes regarding her husband's homosexuality, most wives seem to be enablers of their husbands' self-acceptance and their transition toward a homosexual lifestyle.

Although many gay fathers want their children to know they are gay, they have difficulty telling them. The two most common reasons for disclosure are parental separation or divorce and the development of a lover relationship (Bozett, 1981; Miller, 1978). Disclosure can occur in a number of ways, from the father telling the child directly or the child learning it from either the mother or other sources. Bozett (1980) and Miller (1979) have reported that most children have positive responses to the disclosure that their fathers are gay. Disclosure seems to relieve family tensions because the children may be less likely to blame themselves for problems in the home.

This was true of Sarah. At 11 years old, two years after her parents divorce, Sarah was brought to therapy by her mother. Her parents had been married for 12 years prior to their separation. They had a very argumentative relationship and Sarah's father was hostile and verbally abusive toward her mother. Sarah often overheard her parents' fights, which awakened her in the middle of the night. She would hear her name mentioned and would bury her head in her pillow and cry herself back to sleep. When her parents separated they did so following a huge fight over who would take Sarah to school that morning. Sarah was devastated and felt she was the cause of her parents' argument and subsequent separation. She began to experience academic difficulties and became involved in fights with her friends.

Therapy centered on better understanding Sarah's feelings and behavior. She identified feelings of responsibility and guilt over her parents' divorce. Sarah's parents also received counseling. During these sessions it was revealed that the reason for the separation and divorce was Sarah's father's new boyfriend. Sarah's father had always had homosexual inclinations but thought marriage and children could modify these feelings. After much discussion, Sarah's father felt he should disclose his homosexuality to his daughter. Initially, Sarah reacted with shock and disbelief. She was fearful that she might be a lesbian. With greater communication with her parents and a true understanding that she was not the reason for her parents' divorce, her grades improved and she began enjoying more positive interpersonal relationships. She began dating, found she was interested in boys, and felt more comfortable about her own sexual orientation. Her relationship with her father also improved significantly.

Unfortunately, not all children are as accepting of their parents' homosexuality as Sarah. Ryan was 14 when he discovered his father was gay. He had suspected it for several years because he never saw him socializing with women or expressing any interest in the girls he was talking to. Ryan's parents had divorced when he was seven and his mother remarried a year later. Ryan was close to his step-father but did not feel particularly close to his father. When he learned about his father's sexual orientation, he became angry and bitter. He thought his father was "sick and weird." He no longer felt comfortable spending time with his father and did not want his friends to learn his father was gay. He refused his father's phone calls and wished his father would move away.

The therapist tried to help Ryan reduce his anger and develop a greater tolerance and acceptance of his father. His father was willing to attend a session but Ryan refused. Ryan was ashamed and disgusted by his father and was afraid he would also "become gay." Ryan spent much time with his step-father and began to feel more comfortable with his own sexual orientation. He became more accepting of his father's homosexuality but still did not want to have a relationship with him. Therapy was successful in improving Ryan's self-image and reducing his anger but was unable to help modify the relationship between Ryan and his father.

The overriding concern of children learning their fathers were gay was the fear that others would think they too were gay (Bozett, 1987). Bozett found that children, especially heterosexual children, would use social control strategies to assure that others would not think they were gay. These strategies include controlling the behavior of the fathers in order to control expression of their homosexuality, controlling their own behavior in relation to their fathers', or keeping a distance between themselves and their fathers.

Harris and Turner (1986) and Turner, Scadden, and Harris (1985) report that initial reactions of children to news of their fathers' homosexuality included closeness, confusion, lack of understanding, knowing all along, shame, disbelief, anger, shock, and guilt. Most children are accepting of their fathers as gay (Wyers, 1984). One advantage seems to be that fathers who disclose their homosexuality to their children tend to be more open in their communication with them and may create a closer father–child relationship. Another advantage may be the teaching of greater tolerance of people who are different from themselves. Bozett (1987), however, emphasizes that children who feel close to their fathers and express feelings of love and admiration for them do not necessarily approve of their homosexuality. These children may be able to separate their fathers' sexual orientation from the role of fatherhood.

LESBIAN MOTHERS

Lesbian mothers are more successful than gay fathers in custody battles to attain the legal right to rear their children (Goldstein, 1986). Hotvedt and Mandel (1982) found no evidence of differences between heterosexual single mothers and lesbian mothers with respect to gender identity conflict, poor peer relationships, or neglect. Lewin and Lyons (1982) found that although homosexuality may be a significant aspect of a lesbian mother's identity, her obligations to her children are likely to overshadow its expression and to mitigate the degree to which she sees her homosexuality as distinguishing her from other single mothers. Although a substantial percentage of lesbians are mothers, lesbian lifestyles make it difficult for them to adapt to parenthood and function in a predominately heterosexual society where they have to meet many of the needs of their children.

Barbara had been married for 20 years when her husband announced that he no longer wished to be married to her. She was devastated by this news and was especially angered when she learned that her husband planned to marry someone else as soon as they were divorced. Barbara had not worked outside the home during their marriage because her primary responsibility was to raise their three young children. She did not know how she would support herself and was fearful of being on her own. She consulted her lawyer, who referred her to a displaced homemaker program. Through this program she began to gain some direction and her self-image began to improve. She became involved with some women's groups and was surprised by the degree of support that she received. She felt a closeness and warmth that she had never before experienced. She developed a friendship with a woman from one of her groups who was going through a similar type of situation. They decided to pool their resources and move into a house together, where they shared expenses and child-rearing responsibilities.

Both women began to date men but found these experiences unfulfilling and in many ways boring. Instead, they found themselves spending more time together. One day they started kissing and embracing and found the experience much more satisfying. They began a lesbian relationship but felt extremely guilty. Barbara had been a practicing Catholic and could not reconcile her feelings and behavior with the teachings of the Church. She sought counseling from her priest but was told she must give up her lesbian relationship immediately. She did not want to do this and continued to remain in the relationship but felt more and more guilty. This began to affect the relationship, so Barbara decided to seek therapy.

Therapy focused on Barbara's feelings and the messages she had received from her parents, the Church, her peers, and her community. As she began to explore the relationship she had with her lover and compared it with the messages she had received about what she should look for in a good relationship, she realized she was experiencing something she never believed possible to attain. She began to let go of her guilty feelings and felt a contentment and security that she had never experienced during her marriage. Her children were very accepting of her relationship.

A number of researchers (Golombok, Spencer, & Rutter, 1983; Goodman, 1973, Green, 1978; Hoeffer, 1981; Hotvedt & Mandel, 1982; Kirkpatrick, Smith, & Roy, 1981; Miller, Mucklow, Jacobsen, & Bigner, 1980; Pagelow, 1980;

Riddle, 1978; Weeks, Derdeyn, & Langman, 1975) have found that the children of gay and lesbian parents have no more frequent psychiatric problems and gender dysfunction than do the children of heterosexual parents. Furthermore, the increased likelihood of a child being gay or lesbian because a parent is homosexual is not supported by research. Daughters of lesbian mothers worry more about becoming homosexuals than do sons (Pennington, 1987). This may occur as girls become more aware of their emerging sexuality and experience same-sex attractions. They may believe they will become more like their mothers. Boys generally do not face this issue because they are able to maintain greater distance from their mothers' sexual identification and are not as concerned about their relationships with girls.

In Schulenburg's (1985) research, fewer than 10% of parents indicated their children were unhappy or resentful, whereas more than 30% said their children were happy and proud of their gay and lesbian parents. The majority (41%) appeared to be indifferent to this information. Schulenburg research indicated it is better to tell children when they are young than to risk having them find out from someone else. She found that negative conditioning was fairly well established by the time a child was 11 or 12, with boys being more susceptible to this than girls. She believes that if gay and lesbian parents are comfortable with themselves and their sexuality, their children will be more able to accept their parents' homosexuality. If gay and lesbian parents feel guilty or resentful about their sexuality, the children will be sensitive to this and respond accordingly. Schulenburg offers the following additional tips:

1   Be comfortable with your sexuality before you disclose to your children.

2   Don't wait for your children to discover you are gay or lesbian before you discuss it with them. Decide when you think they are old enough to understand, probably before adolescence because they will then be dealing with their own sexuality and the influence of peers.

3   Share this feeling without overwhelming your children with the details of your sexuality.

4   Make sure your children know that your relationship with them has not changed.

5   Invite them to ask questions and be prepared to answer them honestly.

6   Know the support systems in your community and use them.

7   Maintain a calm presence so that they can feel comfortable having this discussion.

There are a growing number of gay and lesbian homes. Educators are confronted with many family constellations other than the traditional heterosexual two-parent families and single-parent families. Children of gay and lesbian parents, like other children, need to be able to express their feelings and feel they will be accepted for themselves if they are to reach their potential for academic success, acquire positive self-esteem, and adjust well socially.

Chapter 6

Identifying and Understanding the Needs of Gay and Lesbian Teenagers

In this chapter, we examine actual case studies of individuals who did not feel comfortable with their sexual orientation, which led to problems in adolescence and in later adulthood. We examine these case studies in light of the issues that they illustrate.

EARLY DEVELOPMENTAL FEELINGS

Paul was 16 years old when his parents brought him in for therapy. He had been cutting classes and his grades had dropped. He had poor concentration and was not completing assignments. When asked what he was feeling, Paul reported being sad and confused. He stated he did not like school because it was boring and he had few friends. As Paul began to feel more comfortable, he began to reveal his feelings of being different. He was not interested in dating girls, but when he looked at some of the other students he knew were gay, he did not feel comfortable thinking he might be one of them. He was very confused about who he was. He was so preoccupied with these thoughts that he could not study; he felt like dropping out. He felt very alone and did not think anyone could understand how he felt. He was afraid to share his feelings with his peers for fear he would be ridiculed and rejected, and he thought his parents would be angry. He tried talking to his teacher once, but when he sensed that his teacher was uncomfortable, he backed off. Although he was afraid to introduce his true feelings in therapy, he was willing to take a risk because the atmosphere appeared safe and accepting.

As Paul began to express his feelings and gain a better sense of who he was his affect improved and his grades went up. He began to seek out male friends. Although he did not feel comfortable sharing his feelings with his parents, their relationship improved because of his more upbeat attitude. A sensitive, knowledgeable teacher or counselor could have referred Paul long before his parents brought him in for therapy. Truancy and poor grades could have been a signal that some issue of significance was affecting Paul.

Many children are first aware that they may be different as early as four or five years old, but they quickly learn there is no forum for presenting these feelings to others. Their first attempts at discussing sexuality may be dismissed by their parents, who are uncomfortable with any discussion of sexuality, or they may not get the answers they are seeking. Sensing the negative reaction from others can cause children to withhold their feelings and to further withdraw into themselves. They learn to not discuss feelings they have—especially feelings of being different.

Parents often try to impart sexually appropriate behavior to children from the time children are born. Parents may begin by dressing their girls in pink and their boys in blue. Girls are given dolls and stoves to play with, whereas boys are given trucks and guns. Girls are encouraged to put on their mothers' make-up and high heels, and boys are given balls, bats, and tools. Many parents are horrified if they find their little boys of two and three playing with their mothers' lipstick or nail polish. They fear this is an early sign of homosexuality. Frequently, comments are made such as "Only sissy boys play with mommy's make-up" or "Big boys don't do these things. You want to grow up to be a big boy, don't you?" Little girls are generally not subjected to the same comments when they play with boys' toys. Attitudes about what behavior is acceptable and what is not are quickly picked up by children as they are socialized through their early years. These attitudes prevail as the children grow older and continue to be socialized in school.

Children who feel different control their feelings. Questions are not asked for fear of their parents' reaction. If they are criticized for playing with their mothers' make-up at two or three, will they feel comfortable asking questions or expressing feelings of being different as they grow older? By preadolescence, when children are becoming more aware of their sexuality, they fear that sharing these feelings will be met with dismissal, ridicule, or invalidation. Therefore, they suppress how they feel. If they want to share their feelings, what avenues exist for this expression? Children will not discuss how they feel with siblings or friends for fear they will be misunderstood or "found out." Often these insecurities generalize to teachers and other significant adults in their lives. Children find there are few people they can trust with their innermost feelings, which leads to confusion, self-doubt, low self-esteem, isolation, and depression.

Children who wish to express their feelings try to find people to whom they can reach out. They are very cautious about whom they choose to trust. Many of the messages they have learned are that people who feel different are weak, subject to ridicule, sick and unhealthy, abnormal, and generally undesirable. This undermines development of a healthy self-concept. In the formative years, when it is so important to help give children all the building blocks needed for the development of positive self-images, they have additional self-image and self-concept obstacles to overcome. Because much of our self-image comes from the feedback and acceptance we get from our environment (our families, friends, and others in social or school settings), if the feedback is negative it is difficult to feel good about ourselves.

Parents are generally rather vociferous in expressing their opinions to their children. Frequently they do not recognize the impact of their comments. Few parents expect that their child will be gay or lesbian or even entertain the possibility; homosexuality is something that happens to other people's children. By the time parents come to terms with their child's sexuality, it may be very difficult to undo the messages previously delivered. This is true not only with respect to sexual development, but also in every other aspect of children's personalities. If children are taught or receive the message that it is not okay to express feelings of anger or sadness, they will experience difficulty as teenagers or adults in expressing anger or sadness. Consequently, it is extremely important that parents try to convey an open attitude toward their children's behavior.

In the area of sexuality, parents must be particularly aware of the messages they convey to their children from the time they are infants. Messages such as "Be who you are and never be afraid to express your feelings," "I love you for you," and "It's okay to talk about anything with me, even if I do not like what you have to say" can do much to foster closer communication between parents and children and assist children in the development of positive self-images.

Whether children are heterosexual or homosexual is unimportant. What is important is that children grow to feel good about themselves and what they have to offer as contributing members of the family and society. If children feel weak, abnormal, strange or different, they will expend much of their energy trying to cope with these emotions instead of developing their full potential. Most parents want only for their children to be healthy, happy, fulfilled human beings. If individuals have no control over their sexual orientation, why should their lives be complicated further by their parents' negative attitudes? As has been previously discussed, there are enough hurdles and obstacles for gays and lesbians without feeling alienation from the people they love most. If their parents cannot accept them, the fear is that no one else will be able to accept them.

SUPPORT SYSTEMS

Children frequently lack a support system for the expression of their feelings of being different. Many places they wish to turn to for support may not be available to them. For example, if children have questions they would like to ask the family physician, when is that opportunity afforded them? Generally, when children go to the doctor, they are accompanied by a parent. It is hard to ask questions they think might upset their parents in front of them. If they ask their parents to leave, it raises more questions. Then there is the fear of whether the family doctor will tell the parents. What kind of reaction can be expected from the physician? Will he or she respond in a way that will also be rejecting and belittling? Thus, it is much easier to say nothing to the family physician; and one more potential support system is removed.

An example of this circumstance occurred when Greg was 16. During a routine physical exam, Greg's doctor asked him if he were dating and if he had a girlfriend. Greg told his doctor he did not feel comfortable with girls. He tried to ask his doctor about why he was not interested in girls, but before he could get the words out, the doctor began offering advice. He told Greg to give dating a chance and to not be afraid of girls. He attributed Greg's problem to being shy and lacking experience. He believed that if Greg had sex with a woman, he would quickly overcome his problems. Consequently, Greg felt even worse than before his conversation with the doctor, and he decided never to respond that way again when asked if he were dating. His answer would always be a "yes" or some noncommittal statement. If Greg's physician had been more aware and open-minded, Greg would not have felt uncomfortable and he might have been able to disclose his true feelings. Instead Greg learned to repress and mask his feelings even more.

Another potential source of support for gay and lesbian adolescents is the clergy. The message typically conveyed in religious settings is that sex before marriage is not okay and that sex should occur only between husband and wife. Any behavior other than accepted religious doctrine is considered sinful. What are children to do who do not have an attraction or interest in the opposite sex but prefer people of the same sex? They often withhold their feelings and become even more isolated. In addition, they may believe they are going to be condemned by God to a life of misery. They may try to find answers within the church, but realize the need for extreme caution so that they do not reveal the true reason for asking questions.

Jack had his first homosexual encounter at age 14. He was very confused by this experience and felt extreme guilt because he enjoyed this activity and wanted to repeat the behavior. During a confession with his parish priest, Jack mentioned this and asked that he be forgiven. Instead, the priest replied he would be absolved of his sin if he did not repeat the behavior. Jack tried to make a genuine commitment to follow this suggestion; however, it became more and more difficult. He could not forget this homosexual experience and became obsessed with having additional experiences. He became increasingly depressed and frustrated and finally attempted suicide. Through the support and safety of an institutionalized setting, Jack was ultimately able to confront his feelings and gain some acceptance of his homosexual identity. Had Jack's parish priest not been so strict, Jack may not have had such a strong reaction.

Jack's feelings of estrangement from the church are not uncommon. In addition to feeling ostracized from their religious support group, teenagers may also feel further ostracized from their peer group and society in general and again withdraw and isolate themselves. Therefore, this too becomes an unsafe forum for presenting feelings of being different. Many of these teenagers leave organized religion and choose not to return, creating a spiritual vacuum for years to come. When people search for answers that traditionally come from a religious setting, they may ultimately turn to gay churches.

Where can children turn for answers and support? In addition to parents, educators play a primary role in the lives of children and frequently are the most available and reliable source of information and support. It is not uncommon for children to develop an affinity for a special teacher or coach. They feel that perhaps this person understands them or, more importantly, that this person will accept them without judging them. Initially, they may try to communicate their feelings nonverbally, and, when they are more comfortable, verbally. If the educator is sensitive and understanding, children may feel more secure with their feelings of being different and may begin to work on developing a more positive sexual self-concept. If the coach or teacher is not receptive, this becomes yet another rejection, which may cause further withdrawal. A rejection by a teacher is exceptionally painful because of the close relationships and daily encounters it involves. Therefore, it may be a long time before the rejected student shares his or her personal feelings with anyone else.

Maria was a sophomore in high school when she developed a crush on her Spanish instructor. She found herself wanting to spend more and more time with the teacher and looking for opportunities where she could be alone with her. A large part of Maria's school day was devoted to finding excuses so she could see the teacher. She became a terrific student in her class and volunteered for projects where she could assist her teacher. Fortunately for Maria, her teacher was sensitive to what was happening and was able to openly discuss Maria's feelings with her. This early experience was very positive for Maria, and she credits it with helping her begin to feel comfortable with the fact that she was different from her peers.

Maria's story is atypical. More frequently, teachers are not aware of their students' behaviors and feelings, either because of ignorance or fear of becoming involved in a situation they are not qualified to handle. Teenagers can be left feeling more confused and isolated. Instead of understanding and acceptance, they feel rejected.

Zeke was a 13 year old who kept seeking out his coach's approval. He volunteered to do the coach's errands and was willing to take on any team assignment. He sought the coach's advice whenever he could and tried to emulate him. Zeke was crushed when he approached his coach one day to ask him what he thought of a gay athlete's performance and his coach replied "that fag." After this conversation Zeke began to distance himself from his coach and felt he could never trust anyone again.

On occasion, gay and lesbian children and teenagers may want to turn to school counselors. However, they may be reluctant because they may have learned that they can trust few adults and may assume that the counselor will not maintain their confidentiality. Many students do not have a strong relationship with a school counselor because they generally have limited contact with them. Many students' contacts with counselors occur for school-related problems or for college planning. Greater involvement by school counselors in students' lives over their school career can help temper and modify students' misperceptions. The same concern regarding confidentiality extends to family members as well. Therefore, children who suspect they are gay or lesbian do not turn to these individuals for support. Occasionally, when they make an initial effort to try to reach out to them, they are met with evasive remarks.

Jennine, age 16, recalled sitting in the assistant principal's office in her junior year of high school for a discussion of why her grades were poor and being told that because she was so bright there was no reason for such low grades. When Jennine tried to bring up concerns about her sexual orientation and explain why she was having difficulty concentrating on her school work she felt that the assistant principal was either disinterested or uncomfortable. She gave up trying to reach out to her and instead tried to do better in her school work. Perhaps if she had been able to discuss her feelings with someone who understood, not only would Jennine's school grades have improved but she might also have felt better about her educational experience.

It is important that all teenagers, regardless of sexual orientation, have safe outlets for the expression of their feelings and a forum for addressing their concerns. Teachers, counselors, administrators, school psychologists, and other school-related personnel need to be able to provide a safe place for discussion. If students take the time to initiate contact and attempt discussion, then adults should try to be receptive. If students do not follow-up, then possibly these adults can foster the development of a relationship that will enable the student to have a potential support system in the future.

ADDRESSING THE NEEDS

If there is no one available with whom the child feels comfortable discussing these feelings, what are their alternatives? They generally lack information they need to better understand who they are and what they are feeling. In a school setting there usually is not a readily available source of reading material. If they can obtain some of this information, there are additional concerns: What happens if someone else sees it? Once the material is read, with whom can they discuss it? How do they find someone they can trust and feel safe with or who may feel the same way they do? TV talk shows with panels of gay and lesbian teenagers can be helpful in providing resources for information, but too often these programs sensational-ize the issue, promote stereotyping, or frighten gay and lesbian viewers by focusing on audience hostility.

Role Models

Much of the early behavior children exhibit is modeling (or imitating) what they observe in others. Children learn what behaviors they feel comfortable with by trying the behaviors they see in others. Little girls and boys sometimes practice being adults by dressing up in their parents' clothes and pretending to go to work, have tea, or go shopping. These behaviors are either reinforced or criticized by their parents. This is how early socialization skills develop. Some parents get annoyed when their children do not imitate appropriate or desired behaviors. For example, a father may become frustrated because his son does not express an interest in pursuing athletics. Another possible scenario is that the son attempts to pursue athletics but exhibits little ability. This lack of ability may further isolate the young child, causing him to withhold his true feelings. The father who tries to teach his nonathletic son football might inadvertently tell his son "All men play sports. What's with you, son?" If the child is afraid to catch the ball, his father might call him a "sissy." The harder the son tries to please and gain his father's approval, the more frustration he might encounter and the greater he may feel his lack of acceptance. This atmosphere does little to foster close feelings between father and son and less to develop self-esteem in the son.

There are few visible positive gay and lesbian role models for children. Traditionally, most gay and lesbian individuals have been classified as falling into one of several categories:

1 Women who were "old maids" who never married and seemed to reject men.

2 Women who looked very masculine and seemed to dress and act like men. These were commonly referred to as "butches" or "dykes."

3 Men who were effeminate and seemed to be "flaming" and were subject to ridicule and dislike because of their flamboyant mannerisms.

4 Men who always seemed to keep to themselves and were never seen with women.

And of course, you would find gay men in certain stereotypical vocational groups: hairdressers, interior decorators, and artists. Football players certainly could never be gay and a gay professional was unheard of. People identified as gay might be thought of as "strange," "weird," "sick," or "someone to stay away from." These negative stereotypes and associations are not helpful to children and teenagers growing up feeling different. They need positive role models and mentors to assist them in their development. The absence of such models or the negative presentation of models further compounds their struggle to develop positive self-images and strong self-concepts and makes it more difficult for gay and lesbian teens to become healthy adults.

PEER PRESSURE

Among gay and lesbian teens, there is increasing pressure to conform to heterosexual behavior. They believe if they act in a "normal" fashion and do not let others know how they really feel, they will gain acceptance and trust and will fit in. Therefore, most gay and lesbian individuals continue to lead a dual life: the public life and the private, personal life. Rarely do the two meet, and there is considerable anxiety about the impact on their lives if they do.

Because they fear they will be discriminated against, gay and lesbian individuals believe they must suppress their true feelings and conform to what the majority deems acceptable. Therefore, if gay and lesbian individuals are out with their lovers they may suppress the urge to hold hands or display any outward sign of affection; to do so may subject them to negative comments or ridicule. This is not a concern for heterosexual individuals, whose display of affection may elicit quite the opposite response (e.g., "Look at that couple. They appear so much in love."). It is not acceptable for gay and lesbian couples to appear so much in love. Gays and lesbians do not feel free to acknowledge the presence of a lover or the joy they may feel in that lover's presence, let alone to openly demonstrate their caring.

Margie was a 15 year old who had a strong attraction to her best friend Alice. They had many classes together and really enjoyed being with one another. They found themselves attracted to one another in a special way and began to date. As they felt more comfortable, they began to hold hands and did so once in school. Almost immediately they were subjected to ridicule by the other students and found themselves socially isolated. Their grades began to drop and shortly after Margie's 16th birthday she dropped out of school. If someone on the faculty or staff had been aware of the real reason Margie was dropping out of school, some type of intervention might have prevented it.

What happened to Margie at school is not uncommon; it occurs in the workplace as well. Joan was a 27-year-old professional who had successfully advanced to a major managerial position in a large firm. She befriended another executive female in the company. She enjoyed spending time with this person and thought it would be interesting to socialize with her. Joan had been involved in a lesbian relationship for the previous three years and thought her fellow employee would enjoy meeting her lover. One day, when Joan was having lunch with her colleague, the subject of drugs came up and Joan revealed that she had briefly experimented with drugs as a teenager. The colleague asked if she were currently using drugs. Joan replied "no." Her colleague responded by saying "Good. Had you said yes, I would have been required to notify our Vice-President." On hearing this, Joan immediately began to cool her new friendship. She became very concerned about what would happen at work if her sexual orientation were discovered. She dealt with this by beginning to talk about her new boyfriend, and she made arrangements with a male friend to attend work events to further protect herself from being "discovered at work."

Both Margie and Joan found ways of handling disclosure of their sexual orientation by withdrawing from their respective situations. However, sometimes repression of one's feelings is not easy. During adolescence, young men and women typically experience increased hormonal activity that results in a great amount of sexual excitement and tension. Containing this energy is often difficult for them. Among gay and lesbian adolescents, these feelings may be greatly magnified because there are few outlets for their release or expression. These feelings and their concerns about them can interfere with the ability to learn, making it increasingly more difficult to concentrate on school material or homework. They may find themselves easily distracted and may need greater discipline to overcome their feelings. In addition, because gay and lesbian adolescents are afraid of being discovered, they have to be constantly aware of their behavior and the messages they are giving to others. They are cautious about what they say and with whom they allow themselves to become friendly. Every adult and peer becomes a potential danger to them. Heterosexual adolescents are not consumed by these issues. As a matter of fact, they are encouraged by their friends to discuss their feelings and fears among themselves. Boys often enjoy discussing their experiences with their friends; girls talk about the guys they like and their sexual experiences. Gay and lesbian adolescents do not have the same freedom for open discussion. Gay and lesbian teenagers who are able to develop gay and lesbian friendships are able to have a smoother transition through adolescence than those who are not. Adolescents who are not able to establish other relationships are further isolated and feel even more different. Gay and lesbian adolescents who reveal themselves to others may experience the pain and hurt of being ostracized by the other students. They may be subject to ridicule and think they are being discussed behind their backs in derogatory ways. Consequently, they feel there is something wrong with them, which will lessen their self-esteem.

Roberto was a 15-year-old sophomore in a large metropolitan high school. He was a rather outspoken individual who freely expressed his feelings. When his friends began discussing their dating experiences Roberto shared that he was not attracted to or interested in girls and thought he was more attracted to guys. Almost immediately he was dropped from the group he had been part of and was the subject of ridicule. Consequently, he became depressed, began to question himself, and even contemplated suicide. Teachers and coaches who had frequent direct contact with Roberto might have noticed his persistent depression and withdrawal. Discussing Roberto's behavioral changes or referring him to the school's counselor or psychologist might have been helpful.

Because they feel or act different from other teenagers, many gay and lesbian adolescents have trouble with their social lives and with interpersonal relationships. During adolescence, a great deal of teenagers' attention and behavior is focused on dating and trying out new male–female relationships. This behavior is encouraged by their peers and their parents who often inquire about their relationships. To gay and lesbian adolescents, dating becomes extremely uncomfortable and threatening. They may go through the motions to see how it feels, but they feel awkward and ill at ease. Teenage boys who do not want to date girls may go out on dates because they want to belong and be part of the crowd. They feel uncomfortable because they are sexually disinterested and they feel awkward about what the girls might expect. They also feel uncomfortable around other males because they realize they are different and fear they might be discovered. Gay and lesbian teenagers will try to conform to heterosexual dating behavior, but those attempts only increase their tension and isolation. Not only are they questioning who they are, they feel they do not belong and are extremely ostracized and alone. It is at this point that many gay and lesbian adolescents become extremely depressed, do poorly in school, and isolate themselves from others.

SELF-CONCEPT

Experiencing the confusion of who they are, feeling unable to express these feelings, and believing some of the negative stereotypes picked up from others can contribute to the development of a poor self-concept. Because gay and lesbian adolescents do not know where they fit in, they believe something is seriously wrong with them and may generalize these thoughts about their sexuality to other aspects of their lives. Because they feel socially and sexually unsuccessful, they may believe they are worth very little and that if people really knew who they were, they would not like them or want to associate with them. They may think their parents also feel this way, and, if they have a strong religious belief, that they are doomed to a life in hell. Consequently, gay and lesbian teenagers' self-confidence and self-esteem diminishes.

Gay and lesbian teenagers are subject to the same misconceptions and myths as the rest of society. They believe, if these myths are correct, they must not be "nice" or "good" people. They feel guilty about their behavior. They wish they were more "normal" and did not have these feelings or desires. They frequently wish to "make themselves normal." They may put themselves in straight situations in the hope that somehow they will feel differently. When this fails to work, however, they feel even more hopeless about who they are and what the future holds.

Sometimes gay and lesbian children and adolescents can recognize the signals and behaviors of their peers and attempt to reach out to them. Again, great caution is exercised in disclosing oneself for fear that a mistake will lead to discovery. Friendships begin very slowly and take a long time to solidify. With revelation and acceptance generally comes a feeling of security and comfort not previously experienced; the bond and intimacy that is established can be extremely strong. It is comforting to know they are not alone, that others share similar feelings, that there is acceptance for who they are, and that pretense is no longer necessary. Sometimes this confirmation can be confusing because of similarities they have with the individual they have befriended. Consequently, they may reassess all their learned stereotypes, begin to reevaluate themselves, and feel they do not "fit in." This may cause them to reevaluate their belief system and help them begin to develop a more positive psychosexual attitude. If the experience with a friend is negative, this may further confirm the negative stereotypes and cause further confusion and apprehension about getting close to someone else.

Jerry had such an experience. Jerry was a 22-year-old tradesman who was especially shy and withdrawn. He had few friendships. People thought he was a "nice guy once you got to know him," but he always kept his distance. Inwardly Jerry knew he was gay and was petrified that he would be ridiculed and rejected if the "truth were known." In high school Jerry kept to himself and never participated in class activities. In 10th grade he tried to get close to a male teacher by asking for extra help, but he felt rebuffed when the teacher stated he could not give him the time he needed. Consequently, Jerry became more withdrawn and trusted no one. Jerry believed many of the stereotypical myths about gays. He felt because he was gay he would never be able to maintain a long-term, satisfying relationship and he would never meet a person who was as conservative and stable as he seemed to be. Gradually, Jerry established a relationship that he thought could be long lasting. After six months the relationship ended because Jerry's partner did not wish to be monogamous. This confirmed one of his stereotypical beliefs about gay relationships and he vowed never to allow another male to be close to him.

PREJUDICE AND DISCRIMINATION

In the 1970s, with the advent of the Gay Rights movement, many of these attitudes and stereotypes began to change. However, with the appearance of AIDS there has again been a resurgence of homophobia, which has caused some gay individuals to be afraid of disclosing their sexuality so openly. The Gay Rights movement has contributed to teenagers having more positive role models: successful gay individuals in every vocational, economic, and social level have become more open, thereby verifying that gay adolescents can grow to be and do anything they desire. This attitude needs continued reinforcement.

In many sectors of society there remains an overall negative attitude toward gay and lesbian individuals, causing them to be fearful of job discrimination (Stewart, 1991). More specifically, they are afraid that being identified as gay or lesbian will cost them their jobs, or, if they remain employed, they will not be able to obtain the promotions they deserve. They are fearful that some of the myths and stereotypes surrounding their sexual orientation will affect their relationships with others. They feel they may be socially ostracized and subjected to ridicule or pity. With the fear that many people have regarding AIDS and the misinformation on how this illness is transmitted, they are concerned that being labeled as gay or lesbian will infer they are promiscuous and potential carriers, creating greater difficulties with interpersonal relationships and job opportunities. In many instances the fears of homosexuals are realistic and well justified, especially in the fields of teaching, child care, and law enforcement.

Many teachers, counselors, school psychologists, administrators, and other school personnel feel especially uncomfortable responding to gay and lesbian adolescents' needs because of their own professional insecurities. For educators who are gay or lesbian, dealing with the gay or lesbian adolescent becomes more challenging because of the inherent risks that their own sexuality will be disclosed. They may fear loss of their careers. There is also the chance of a strong parental response no matter how they handle the situation. Thus they are in a no win situation because of the strong emotional responses this issue generates within the school and the community.

Joyce was a 23-year-old semiprofessional athlete who entered therapy because the woman she was involved with had recently ended their three-year relationship. It was the first significant relationship Joyce had experienced with anyone. As a teenager, she felt shy and uncomfortable and did not date at all. She tried to engage in male–female friendships, but felt extremely ill at ease. Consequently, she isolated herself and threw herself into sports. Her school performance dropped but her athletic talents soared.

Joyce recalled her teenage years as very difficult; she could not wait to grow up. She looked for outlets to express her feelings but few existed. She tried getting close to her physical education teacher with whom she strongly identified, but she felt the teacher was unapproachable. Secretly, she desired to emulate her. Joyce felt the woman with whom she was involved was similar to this teacher. Therefore, when the woman terminated the relationship, Joyce felt all the pain and confusion she had experienced as a teenager. She was devastated by this breakup. She thought she had made a terrible mistake by being involved in a lesbian relationship and believed that if she had been in a straight relationship, it might have survived. She castigated herself for dating women and made the decision to stop dating them. She blamed herself and thought she was a failure as a person and as a woman. She became extremely depressed and during the next year and a half dated men exclusively. This made her very uncomfortable and she realized her attempts at "making herself heterosexual" were not working. This precipitated even greater suffering.

Her feelings were further compounded by her strained relationship with her mother. Her parents still lived together after 30 years of marriage, but her mother had a close female friend with whom she spent inordinate amounts of time. Joyce was convinced her mother had a lesbian relationship with this woman because her father had once confided in her that he and her mother had not had sex for many years and that her mother was just not interested. The message Joyce received was that women were expected to get married but that it was all right to have female friends on the side. Joyce thought this was the appropriate lifestyle for her to seek, but her attempts at doing this were not successful. At the time she entered therapy she was extremely depressed and suicidal.

Therapy focused on assisting Joyce to better identify her feelings and to feel more comfortable with her sexuality. Considerable time was spent discussing her relationship with her parents and the messages she received as a child and teenager. Her relationship with her physical education teacher was also explored thoroughly. Gradually, Joyce became more comfortable with her gravitation toward women and desired to be involved in another close friendship. Sex with a woman continued to be a problem for her, but with the participation of her new lover she ultimately was able to achieve a fulfilling and complete relationship. In this situation, had the physical education teacher recognized that Joyce's athletic achievements were motivated by her desire to emulate her teacher, a stronger relationship between Joyce and her teacher might have facilitated a referral to the school counselor.

Sometimes, gay and lesbian adolescents seek out counselors or are placed in therapy by their parents; but, if they do not feel comfortable with the counselor or feel the counselor will be nonaccepting, they will not disclose themselves. Therapy becomes a disappointment and gay and lesbian adolescents are reluctant to return. If the therapist views homosexuality as a sexual disorder, then the gay or lesbian adolescents' feelings are further compounded. This may have an impact later in life, when, as gay and lesbian adults, they rule out therapeutic assistance because they feel it will not be helpful.

When Tom first entered therapy, he was distraught and depressed. His first question was whether he would be institutionalized if he disclosed his problems to the therapist. It took a considerable amount of time, trust, and reassurance on the therapist's part before he felt comfortable enough to discuss his real problem. Tom was 19 and living with an older male. He felt guilty about his behavior and thought he must be very "sick." He related he did not know of any other men who were involved in a homosexual relationship and he felt very strange and awkward about himself. He revealed that his father was an alcoholic who divorced his mother when he was a toddler and never remarried. Because his mother was diagnosed as being schizophrenic, his father gained custody of him and his older brother. The father was quite abusive, both physically and mentally, and was in and out of ineffective treatment programs. At the age of 16, Tom ran away from home and became self-sufficient. When he was 18, he met an older gentleman who gave him a place to live. This man was nurturing and supportive and gave Tom the direction and assistance he never received from his father. Tom grew to love this man and, gradually, a sexual relationship developed. At first, Tom did not feel guilty about his behavior and seemed to enjoy himself. However, as time passed, he began to reassess the relationship and felt there must be something seriously wrong with it because he did not know any other couples who were engaging in homosexual activities. He related that he had never dated women and did not have any desire to date them. He reported having no significant female friendships but that he had several close male friends. His lover was expressing a desire to maintain their relationship, but Tom was feeling a strong need to disengage himself.

Over the course of therapy Tom separated from his lover and began to explore relationships with both men and women. He found that he greatly missed his lover and had no sexual interest in women. He began to study the subject of homosexuality and became acquainted with other gay professionals. He explored his anger and resentment toward both his father and mother and began to understand how he might have transferred some of these feelings to his lover. They began to see each other again and, 18 months later, moved in together. Tom felt much more comfortable with his sexuality and the security and stability he had found within this love relationship.

One of the problems gay and lesbian adolescents frequently encounter is rejection by apprehensive adult models. Once adults discover an adolescent is gay or lesbian, attitudes and behavior toward that adolescent may change. Adults may feel uncomfortable and not know how to react. Frequently, if the adults have not fully worked through their own sexuality, homophobia and other unresolved sexual issues may evolve. Gay and lesbian teenagers make adults more aware of their own feelings and make them more apprehensive, possibly causing the adult to avoid the adolescent in hopes of not having to confront their own feelings. Conversely, there are adults who wish to exploit adolescents' insecurities and may seek out gay or lesbian adolescents, befriend them, and take advantage of them.

PARENTAL REACTIONS

Most parents have difficulty dealing with the news that their son or daughter is gay or lesbian. Parents may respond with disbelief or denial and discount their child's feelings. They may make negative comments about homosexuality in an attempt to convince their child they are not really gay or lesbian. For some parents this information is a confirmation of their worst fears. The parents may be so concerned with their own feelings, they may be insensitive to what their child is saying and may be unable to reach out to him. For the parents, the news of the child's homosexuality may be quite shocking, but to the adolescent who has been living and dealing with it for a long time, there is no question about his identity and what it means. Convincing his parents becomes an additional obstacle. If parents cannot accept them, teenagers feel there is definitely something "wrong" with being gay or lesbian. This further contributes to isolation and feelings of rejection. Where can they go to explore their feelings in a nonthreatening and accepting environment?

Some parents are overt in expressing their feelings and will directly tell their child they will not have a gay or lesbian child. They may use all kinds of desperate tactics in their attempts to deny the truth about their child's sexual orientation; they may ridicule, name-call, ostracize, deny association with brothers and sisters, or not allow the child's friends to enter the house. This reaction further destroys the gay teenager's self-concept. The parents, however, may be blaming themselves and holding themselves responsible for their teenager's sexual orientation. They may feel there was something they did or said that contributed to their teenager's orientation. Confronting their child means confronting their own feelings. By ostracizing their teenager they may feel free to deny these emotions. They may offer to send the teenager for counseling to change his sexual orientation. They may offer expensive gifts if their teenager will give up the homosexual behavior. Again, the message they are sending is that the teenager is not okay and that somehow a doctor or counselor will be able to correct the problem and make things right, or if the teenager tries hard enough, maybe the homosexual feelings and behavior will disappear.

While these adolescents are struggling with their own issues and concerns, they have to deal with the rejection and abandonment of their own families. They may feel everything they do is subject to close scrutiny and invalidation and they can never satisfy parental expectations or gain approval. At a time when they are looking for support and acceptance, they frequently encounter the complete opposite.

Generally, it is more difficult for fathers to handle the news that a child is gay or lesbian than it is for mothers. Most of the time siblings know before the parents. It is therefore helpful for gay or lesbian adolescents to feel they have an objective outlet for the safe expression of their feelings. Teachers, school counselors, and school psychologists can frequently fill this need.

Kathy, a 23-year-old of above average intelligence, first entered therapy at the insistence of her parents. She was employed as a case worker with a large social service agency, where she had worked for several years. She was involved in an ongoing lesbian relationship of two years, was deeply committed to her lover, and felt she was building a solid future. She had led an active dating life during high school and was engaged to be married while she was in college; therefore, her parents felt her lesbian relationship was simply an act of rebellion and not what she really wanted to do. They even promised to buy her a new car if she would end her lesbian relationship and begin to date men. Her parents felt personally responsible for their daughter's behavior because she had been molested by a family member when she was a young child. Not wishing to create a family scandal, the parents did not reveal the molestation. They hoped therapy might deal with that issue as well as change her behavior. Kathy's motivation for entering therapy was to explore whether she could have a family and raise a child within a lesbian relationship.

Kathy was very verbal and clearly expressed her feelings to all who cared to listen. Although she admitted she enjoyed being in the company of men, she said she was never sexually satisfied by men and "was disgusted at the sight of a penis." She freely discussed the incestuous relationship she had as a child, but she felt this did not cause her to become a lesbian. When she first met her lover, their relationship began as a close friendship and grew in depth. She stated she never thought of herself as a lesbian, but the relationship evolved and felt natural and honest. She had never had similar feelings for any of the men she dated. This knowledge and feeling of completeness felt so right that Kathy expressed little desire to end the relationship and find a relationship with a man. She especially never wanted to have another sexual experience with a man because she found it totally unsatisfactory.

As Kathy became more aware of her feelings, she realized she virtually had accepted her sexuality and that it was not a problem for her. The difficulty was how to explain the situation to her parents in a way that would lead to their acceptance of her. She identified the major concerns she thought her parents might have, then tried to decide how she could address these concerns and allay their fears and anxieties. Her parents' prime concern was that Kathy have a happy, stable relationship and be able to have a family. Kathy believed she had such a relationship. She and her lover discussed having a family and agreed that in approximately one year Kathy would undergo artificial insemination. She approached her parents, and after much discussion they were able to come to an understanding. She also made it clear to her parents that their behavior was not responsible for her sexual orientation, hoping to allay their feelings of guilt and responsibility. The parents began to accept Kathy's lover and tried to include her in family activities. Although her parents continued to acknowledge they would have preferred a different lifestyle for their daughter, eventually they became comfortable with the fact that she had found someone with whom she could share a loving relationship. Of course, not all parents are as accepting.

Chuck was a 24-year-old professional athlete. His father was a minister in a fundamentalist church and dogmatic in his belief system. He stated on numerous occasions that "gays should be shot and were the work of the devil." Sex was something that should occur only between husband and wife in the context of marriage. As a child, Chuck always felt different but was afraid of expressing any feelings that might be contrary to those of his father. He would occasionally express an opposing belief to his mother, but she would respond by reminding him that his father would be very upset if he knew his son's attitude.

Chuck compensated by being an exceptional student. He received straight A's and excelled in sports, winning several state and national competitions. During high school and college he dated many women and enjoyed their company, but he did not feel sexually compatible with any of them. He attributed this to getting negative sexual messages from his father about sex before marriage. He established a close relationship with a coach whom he trusted and respected, but he never thought much of it, even though he was always seeking his approval.

While in college, Chuck became extremely close to a fellow student who was also an athlete. A satisfying love relationship evolved out of this friendship. Chuck stated it was during this relationship that he came to understand his feelings of being different. Although he was frightened of his feelings, he allowed them to grow and develop. The relationship came to an end after two years because his lover decided to move abroad to pursue his athletic career and no longer wanted to be involved. Chuck was devastated and had a difficult time adjusting to the end of the relationship. At first he felt some guilt and remorse and subsequently decided maybe his father was right about homosexuality. He immersed himself heavily in his father's fundamentalist religion. He attended church regularly and tried hard to believe the philosophical tenets that it espoused. It was during this time that his relationship with his parents grew tremendously. Chuck liked the acceptance that he found from his father, but he felt frustrated and lonely inside. He knew that as hard as he tried to believe, he could not accept some of the principles of the religion, especially those that claimed homosexuality is a sin. As the conflict grew, Chuck realized he was gay and moved to another state so he could be away from his family and prevent their discovery of his sexual orientation. As much as he tried to suppress his true feelings, he learned it was impossible; he missed being involved in a relationship with a man and desired another.

While living in the new location, Chuck tried dating women and realized it was definitely not what he wanted. Again, he became involved in a satisfying relationship with a man. Everything might have been fine had his parents not decided to relocate to the same town, where his father had accepted the ministry of a church. Chuck entered therapy to determine how he should deal with this situation. He did not want to move again and he no longer wanted to date women. His parents began to question him again as to why he never brought any women home and he felt this was going to lead to a confrontation. He thought his mother might be more accepting than his father, and he knew if his father learned the truth he would totally reject him. Chuck was saddened by this because he and his father had developed a rather close relationship during the time Chuck was involved in his father's church. He spent a considerable amount of time exploring how to approach his parents. He told his mother first and was pleased by her acceptance. She said she loved him, was proud of him, and that his sexual orientation made no difference to her. She did say it was sad that such a handsome, bright person would never be a father and would miss out on one of life's wonderful experiences. She also expressed anxiety about what his father's response would be to the news that his son was gay. She agreed, however, to lay some groundwork for Chuck by beginning to look for television shows to watch, finding some literature for her husband to read, and trying to soften the shock. In the meantime, Chuck consulted with a minister from a local gay church and explored with him an approach he could take with his father.

With much apprehension, he finally approached his father. He was afraid the news would sever his relationship with his family. Initially, his father's reaction was one of disbelief and anger. He preached various biblical passages and told Chuck if he prayed and believed enough, he could change. Chuck explained that nothing had changed no matter how much he prayed for it. He appealed to his father to accept all his other good qualities, but his father said he believed homosexuality was sinful and if Chuck did not alter his behavior he would no longer be his son. Chuck experienced much pain and never could accept his father's rejection.

Although some parents may be very liberal and accepting of different lifestyles for others, when it affects them personally they may find they are not so liberal. Some of the questions and concerns many parents have are "Why my child?" "This thing happens to other people, not to me." "My child will have such a difficult future. He will never be able to have a normal family." "Gays do not have stable relationships and he could contract AIDS and die." "He will have to live in the closet because of what other people will think." "How will we tell our family members, our friends, our colleagues?" "What will our children's friends think?"

Parents of teenagers generally do not have a close relationship with their children's educators and are not likely to turn to them for support or assistance. Parents frequently feel isolated and have few people they would trust with their concerns. Educators who are sensitive to the needs of their students and parents facilitate a smoother adjustment for families and an easier school situation.

George grew up in a small town in the deep South. He was eldest and the only son of a large family and left home to attend college with intentions of majoring in business and returning home to manage the family business. During high school, George dated women rather extensively, but he realized early on they had little appeal for him. He was more interested in some of his male friends and, in particular, a male teacher, but he did not explore these feelings at that time. He was cognizant of what it meant to live in a small town and did not do anything that might draw attention to himself. He thought by attending college in a large community he might be able to more fully explore his feelings. While in college he established a successful homosexual relationship he did not want to terminate upon graduation. This was a major dilemma; his parents were expecting him to return home to begin taking over the family business. George and his lover were willing to relocate to George's hometown, but they were concerned with what his family would think and how their relationship might affect the family business. He felt a major commitment to his parents and wanted to operate the family business because it was a dream of his since early childhood. He even entertained the thought of finding a woman and marrying so that the outward appearance might be more acceptable to his family and the community.

After much exploration, George decided he would tell his parents about his sexual orientation and his current relationship. Because it was their business, he would respect whatever decision they made. If they could accept his lover and thought this would not harm their business, he would return home. If, however, they thought they could not accept his sexuality or did not want him to return home, he would remain with his lover and try to identify another career path to pursue.

He had always had a close relationship with his mother and decided he would reveal his homosexuality to her before disclosing it to his father. He believed if he could obtain his mother's acceptance it would be easier for him to tell his father. He also thought his mother's support might help his father accept the news. He went home for a long weekend and spent two days with his mother before he could talk to her about this. Initially she was surprised, but she gradually accepted the news. She told George his happiness was of primary importance. She was not so sure that George's father would respond in such a positive manner. She advised George not to disclose the information to his father until she laid some groundwork.

George decided he would return to visit his parents a few weeks later. One of the activities he had always enjoyed with his father was fishing, so he decided they would go on an overnight fishing trip and he would tell his father some time during the trip. He was very restless and anxious on the trip. His father was aware of his nervousness and asked him what was wrong. Finally, after evading the issue, George blurted out that he was a homosexual and he was afraid his father would no longer accept or love him. His father's reaction was similar to his mother's. George learned much later that his mother had told his father so he had had time to adjust to the news and prepare a response.

It was decided that George's parents would attend his college graduation and at that time would meet his lover. His parents were very accepting of his lover, which reduced much of the tension. During this trip they all discussed whether it would be advisable for George to return to run his father's business. It was mutually agreed that as much as George and his parents would like George and his lover to return home, it might not be advisable because of the prevailing attitudes in the community. Instead, they identified an ancillary business George could operate from another community. They agreed George's ultimate goal would be to return at a later date to manage the family business. In the interim, this arrangement would give George and his lover opportunities to visit George's hometown together for holidays and vacations and observe the community's reaction. All were in agreement that they did not want George's homosexuality to have an adverse affect on the family business.

When parents and others involved in the lives of children and adolescents express a positive attitude of open communication and acceptance of differing viewpoints and beliefs, it results in development of greater self-esteem and fosters an atmosphere of working toward one's potential. It is important for everyone involved with young people to be cognizant of the role and impact their attitudes and behaviors have on others and to respond accordingly.

Chapter 7

Unresolved Issues and Needs

Lack of identification and acceptance of one's sexuality can contribute to problems such as alcohol abuse and drug addiction. The initial use of substances such as alcohol and other drugs usually helps make the adolescent more comfortable in social situations. Substance abuse may help individuals feel more relaxed and gain greater acceptance from their social group. After awhile this behavior may become an addiction requiring professional treatment. A case in point is Sue.

ACCEPTANCE

A 25-year-old recovering alcoholic and drug addict, Sue had used drugs heavily throughout her youth and young adulthood to mask her feelings of guilt and shame over feeling different. During her various treatment programs she never fully discussed her sexuality. She stated she was afraid to bring up the issue because she did not know how others would react. During therapy she was very open in expressing her feelings. She said she had always felt different from her friends and learned quickly to keep her feelings to herself. She grew up in a single-parent home and had no siblings. Her mother was continuously in and out of relationships with men. She never seemed to have a stable relationship. Most of these relationships were tumultuous. Sue thought she was unwanted and in her mother's way. She was a poor student and was unable to concentrate. School offered her little interest or support.

As Sue grew older she spent less and less time at her mother's home. She began to date at an early age. She dropped out of high school at age 16 and turned to prostitution to support herself. She soon began to use drugs and alcohol to mask her feelings. She felt total disgust for the men with whom she was involved and began to turn toward women for support and nurturance. A strong friendship with a woman evolved and developed into a serious relationship. It was this woman who encouraged Sue to give up drugs and alcohol and to finally straighten out her life. What was most disconcerting to Sue was the fact that she and her lover were leading a closeted life. Sue's lover had a job that involved child care and was afraid if she revealed her true sexuality she would be fired. Sue, however, had masked her feelings long enough and no longer wished to remain closeted. Therapy helped point out the realities of the situation and she realized certain limits were necessary for job survival.

Even so, discretion was not easy for Sue. When she and her lover went on a trip to another city, she was physically demonstrative in public. She had taken her lover's hand while they were walking down the street and leaned over to kiss her. A couple with a young child had been walking behind them. The man commented to Sue and her lover that they were disgusting and should have some respect for others by not openly presenting their unhealthy behavior. These comments incensed Sue to the point that she almost became physically violent. After this experience, she knew she had to develop greater tolerance of others and learn to be more discrete in public. However, she still had tremendous resentment toward society for the limitations it imposed regarding the expression of her feelings. She wanted to become active in Gay Rights organizations but decided against it because of her lover's anxieties. She had great difficulty handling a dual life, which eventually led to the end of that relationship.

Because of the early sexual messages that teenagers receive, they have strong feelings about what is socially and morally appropriate. However, some teenagers may not be sure about these messages because they find their attractions to members of their own sex strong and positive and their attractions to members of the opposite sex negative or nonexistent. This may lead to a heightened insecurity and potential aversion to sex. The idea of forming an intimate relationship with someone becomes threatening, because at some point the issue of sexuality must be dealt with. Consequently, individuals will tend to withdraw and further isolate themselves from others. They have few friends and are afraid of being discovered and rejected. They feel awkward, ill at ease, and uncomfortable socializing with others.

SEXUALITY

As a number of our case studies have indicated, many students have limited knowledge about sexuality and interpersonal relationships. Perhaps this topic should receive more attention in the curriculum and be addressed not only by health education, science, psychology, and family living teachers but also by school counselors, school nurses, school psychologists, and outside professionals. Beverly demonstrates how the failure to address these issues in the formative years can emotionally cripple individuals later in life.

Beverly was a 24-year-old secretary who entered therapy at the insistence of her lover. She had been involved in a lesbian relationship for six months and had little or no interest in sex. This upset her lover, who had a great interest in sex.

Aside from sex, both partners felt the relationship was good and they wanted to maintain it. Beverly stated she had never been interested in sex. She was a virgin until her early 20s and had never had a satisfying sexual experience. Her parents, especially her mother, had told her that sex was no good and something you did to satisfy your husband. Her mother also told Beverly it was the only thing men wanted and that it was painful. Consequently, Beverly grew very anxious at the mention of sex and found herself shying away from interpersonal relationships. She did not feel comfortable with men and was ill at ease with women even though she was attracted to them. Her confusion led her to decide to discourage the development of relationships; however, with her current lover she found the closeness so natural that she did not want to lose the relationship.

Therapy focused on helping Beverly explore her childhood messages about sex. Her fears and anxieties were examined, as were her attitude toward intimacy. Much time was spent exploring her adolescent years and her insecurities. With time, she was able to feel much closer to her lover and increased the level of sexual activity.

Other individuals may respond to their feelings by forcing themselves to overcome them. They may feel if they try hard enough, they will be able to change their feelings. As a result, they force themselves to fit in by dating, marrying, and having children. This behavior does not feel fully comfortable, and they feel guilty about what they are doing. They feel dishonest and undeserving of the trust and belief others have placed in them, which places a tremendous burden on them. At some point, when they can no longer act in a way that is not authentic, they find themselves sharing their secrets and having to deal with the consequences of self-revelation. In many cases, these consequences are not as severe as they had imagined, but in other cases they are confronted with a messy and unpleasant divorce during which their privacy about this issue is violated. Visitation rights with their children or their position at work may be jeopardized. If disclosure is met with conflict, self-doubt and isolation result. Diane ended up in just this situation.

Diane was 33 years old, married, and the mother of two young children. She had married her college sweetheart following graduation because that was the "thing to do." She had never dated much in high school or college but fell into a comfortable relationship with her husband. Sex was never satisfying but Diane accepted this as the "way it should be." Attempts at improving her sexual relationship were unsatisfactory, so she tried to accept things as they were. She had a close female friend with whom she spent a great deal of time and with whom she had a lot in common; her friend also had a young child. In discussing sex with her, Diane discovered her friend did not have similar sexual feelings. Out of curiosity Diane began to seek other female friendships. One of these friendships evolved into a brief lesbian relationship. For the first time, Diane enjoyed sex tremendously, but she terminated the relationship out of guilt and fear. It was at this point that she decided to enter therapy.

Therapy focused on Diane's feelings of anxiety and guilt. Initially, she wanted to forget about her lesbian experiences and tried to improve her marriage. Sex with a woman had been so satisfying, she found it increasingly difficult to have a sexual relationship with her husband. She also began to explore her early sexual feelings and experiences and became aware that she had never felt fully comfortable with sex. When she was honest with herself, she recognized she felt "different" as a young adolescent. As a teen she was afraid of these feelings and tried to repress and deny them by becoming involved with the first male who took a serious interest in her. It seemed an easy answer to continue the relationship and eventually marry. Having a family was expected of her, so children naturally followed.

As Diane became more aware of her feelings, she felt the need to separate from her husband and take the children with her. Her husband was shocked by her exit from the marriage. He kept telling her he did not understand why she was "breaking up their home." She decided to tell him the truth. At first he was shocked and thought she was lying. Gradually he came to accept the truth but decided he wanted to have nothing to do with her. Although they initially agreed she would have custody of their two daughters, this news changed everything. Her husband hired a powerful attorney and a rather nasty and lengthy court battle ensued whereby Diane lost custody of her children and had restrictions placed on her visitation rights. This devastated her and she fell into a major depression. Eventually she was able to come to terms with the loss of the custody of her children.

SELF-INDULGENCE

Individuals who do not get the acceptance and support they need from others may become narcissistic in their behavior. Because they do not feel the support they need and do not get the positive feedback and interaction they crave, they attempt to fulfill their own needs by indulging themselves in order to make themselves feel better. Oftentimes this indulgence becomes *over*indulgence and may create additional problems for the individual. Many gay and lesbian individuals face this problem of narcissism, as is evidenced by Gene's story.

Gene was a successful professional who was in the public eye. Although he commanded a very good salary, he was always in debt, buying the latest gadgets and looking as though he had stepped out of a men's fashion magazine. No matter how hard he tried to curb his spending habits, he was unsuccessful. In trying to understand his excessive spending habits he discovered it was a means of feeling loved. Few people knew he was gay, and he was afraid if they knew who he really was, they would not accept him. By spending money on himself, he was trying to provide himself with the care and support he did not receive from others. Gradually, Gene allowed himself to develop a network of friends who knew he was gay and loved him for his authentic self. Consequently, he found he had less of a need to spend so much money and, for the first time, he was able to establish a savings account.

INTERPERSONAL RELATIONSHIPS

Sometimes adult gay and lesbians are unable to form satisfying relationships with peers because they have never fully dealt with and resolved their own issues. They may turn to teenagers to get the respect they need and help them better come to terms with their own sexuality. A good example of the long-term effects of a person's inability to accept his own sexual orientation and of his ability to help others who experience the same confusion is exemplified by Stewart.

Stewart was a 43-year-old professional male who was self-employed. He entered therapy at the suggestion of his physician, who felt he was having an unusually delayed grief reaction he could not complete. He was extremely depressed, had lost a tremendous amount of weight in a brief period of time, was unable to sleep, could not concentrate on his work, and had developed poor personal hygiene. He had experienced a brief sexual relationship with a teenager the previous year. The teenager was a runaway who traveled across the country and, when he was in town, would contact Stewart. Stewart would help him out by providing a place to stay, food to eat, and some spending money. The teenager basically worked as a male prostitute to get the money he needed to travel and do whatever he wanted. Stewart tried to get him to stop the promiscuous behavior and agreed to take him in, help him complete his high school diploma, and enter a vocational school for job training. The teenager was reluctant to do this and over the last few months, when he was in town, he would call at the last minute and demand money from Stewart, who usually complied with the request but gradually grew resentful. It was common for Stewart to befriend young teenagers and try to assist them in obtaining job skills and a more stable lifestyle, but he was frustrated by the difficulty he was having with this teenager. Stewart stated he wanted to help teenagers accept their sexuality because he believed that if he had had assistance as a teenager he might have experienced an easier sexual and personal adjustment. He almost made a crusade of helping runaway or delinquent gay teenagers.

Several months before Stewart came for therapy the teenager came to town and called Stewart. He said he was at a phone booth and asked Stewart to pick him up immediately. Stewart refused because he was in the middle of a meeting, but he agreed to pick him up approximately two hours later. When Stewart arrived, the teenager was not there. He figured he would hear from him again soon. Approximately one week later Stewart received a phone call from the police. The teenager had hitchhiked across country with someone he met, went to a fancy place on a lake, wrote a suicide note, and hanged himself. In the note he gave Stewart's name and number and asked that Stewart be notified. Stewart had extreme difficulty accepting his death. He felt personally responsible for the teenager leaving on a cross-country journey and believed if he had responded differently when he received his phone call the teenager would still be alive. Convinced the teenager was murdered, Stewart hired private detectives to investigate. He could not accept his death. He wanted to contact the teenager's family but did not feel comfortable doing this, not knowing how to present himself to his family or how he would be received. Because he felt ashamed of his behavior and his lack of quick response to the phone call, he suppressed his feelings and did not confide in anyone.

It took months for Stewart to come to terms with the teenager's death and accept that he was not personally responsible. This situation caused him to question his homosexual lifestyle and his preference for young men. It made him assess what types of relationships he was looking for and his dissatisfaction with transient, unstable friendships. Much time was spent exploring Stewart's need to take in young male teenagers. Part of his difficulty in establishing a relationship was that he did not feel comfortable with men his own age. He sought someone younger because he felt less vulnerable and less likely to be rejected. Also, he hoped he would be able to serve as a role model for younger males and help them feel more comfortable with their sexuality. As Stewart became more comfortable with his own sexuality, he began to open up and develop more age-appropriate relationships. He found other ways to serve as a role model to teenagers and young adults.

When people are looking for acceptance from others, they may engage in behavior that will call attention to themselves—even if this behavior is outlandish or perceived as negative. *Flaming behavior* may develop because an individual believes this stereotypical behavior is what being gay is about. Acting in this manner may give them the attention and acceptance they are seeking. They may resort to becoming the class clown, because it is easier to cope with acting wildly than it is to conceal and hide their true feelings. Many individuals who exhibit clownish or flaming behavior are truly not comfortable with this role and hate feeling this way. They adapt this method of responding because it helps them interact with others. They would prefer to be themselves but are afraid if they dropped this façade they would either be unaccepted or further ridiculed. By acting stereotypically they promote disparagement that is purposefully encouraged and is much easier to accept than unintentional ridicule. This is especially true of teenagers.

Carey was a 17-year-old high school senior who dressed outlandishly and acted in socially inappropriate ways. He had a high-pitched voice, was tall and lanky, and appeared effeminate, so he decided to act and dress the part. But inwardly he was very depressed and contemplating suicide. Since his early teenage years, Carey had been teased about being different and others had often asked if he were gay. He was ridiculed and had few friends. This upset him greatly. He discovered if he acted silly or dressed flamboyantly, people were more likely to accept him and he did not find their comments as belittling.

Therapy focused on helping Carey identify his real feelings and become aware of how he could begin to accept his true identity. He began to tone down his dress and modify some of his inappropriate behavior. Consequently, he found he was getting a different message from others. He liked this, and for the first time he began to feel more confident and secure. By the time he was a sophomore in college he was able to establish his first significant relationship and feel comfortable with his homosexuality.

Carey had emitted many signals during his high school years that indicated he needed assistance. His appearance, unusual mannerisms, and inappropriate social behaviors were areas that could have been addressed by teachers or school counselors, which may have minimized his feelings.

ISOLATION

Some gay and lesbian individuals may be so afraid others will discover their true identity that they become even more closeted and isolated. They may hide themselves in their apartments with the drapes drawn, fearful of what would happen if the neighbors found out they were gay. They might hide behind sunglasses to avoid eye contact, thinking if people looked them in the eye, they would discover who they were. The fear of rejection causes them to discourage friendships. They know people fear contracting AIDS from them. These are the individuals at greatest risk for suicide. As previously discussed, studies indicate the suicide rate among homosexuals is higher than that of heterosexuals.

Joshua was referred for therapy by his family physician. He had been seeing a male psychiatrist for years, but the family physician felt Joshua was not making any progress; he suggested trying another therapist. Joshua was 34 years old and was an engineer for a rather large firm, where he had been employed for 12 years and had advanced to a level of great responsibility. He entered therapy because he was thinking of suicide, was unable to eat or sleep, experienced extreme anxiousness resulting in uncontrollable tremors, and was extremely fearful that he would be fired from his job. During his first appointment Joshua could not sit without his entire body shaking. He maintained poor eye contact and cried uncontrollably. He said he was afraid he would kill himself. He did not like himself or his life and he felt hopeless. Although he had the respect of his co-workers, he said he had no friends and felt extremely lonely and isolated. He enjoyed his work, but was fearful and anxious. Consequently, he began taking more and more sick time and was afraid his employers would no longer accept his illness. He knew he needed help but felt no one could help him.

Two years earlier Joshua had entered therapy because he was drinking excessively and was afraid it would affect his job. He related that he was proud he had not had a drink in almost two years and that he had done this on his own, without the assistance of a treatment facility or Alcoholics Anonymous. He felt good about being able to control this major problem in his life. He said that his current problems were more difficult and severe than a drinking problem could ever be. When asked to identify some of these problems, Joshua stated that it was too horrible to discuss. The therapist tabled the issue because Joshua did not feel comfortable discussing it. It took several visits before he was able to reveal his homosexuality. After the disclosure, he immediately bombarded the therapist with a series of questions and statements: "Now you know I'm really crazy, so will you still work with me?" "Things are hopeless now, so I might as well kill myself." "Gay people are really bizarre and sick, right?" The therapist spent a considerable amount of time trying to point out that being gay did not mean a person was bizarre, sick, or crazy. He believed many of the negative stereotypes about gays and had much misinformation about how one develops one's sexuality. Some of this misinformation had come from the male psychiatrist with whom he had been working previously, who had told Joshua that homosexuality was a deviant behavior that needed to be changed. Joshua knew he could not change this behavior and felt he was destined to a life of deviancy and unhappiness. He refused to return to the psychiatrist because he knew he would never be able to reveal his true self for fear the doctor would tell him that he was a hopeless case.

The first task, therefore, was to give Joshua some basic information to debunk many of his misperceptions about the meaning of being gay. As he began to read and modify his views he calmed down and stopped the physical tremoring. He began to feel better about himself and returned to work on a more regular and consistent basis. He no longer discussed wanting to kill himself. He and the therapist began to explore his feelings of loneliness and isolation. Joshua explained he did not have any friends because he was afraid if others found out about his sexual orientation, he would not be accepted by them and would be ridiculed. He and the therapist discussed this issue at length and he began to see that he was not the only gay individual in the community. The therapist identified several gay organizations and support groups and suggested that he attend a group meeting when he felt more comfortable. He wanted to reach out, but continued to be fearful. One day, in the grocery store, someone approached him and invited him to a lecture that was being given at a local high school. He attended the lecture and enjoyed the group meeting. It felt good to get out and be among other homosexuals. This experience gave Joshua greater courage and confidence, which motivated him to seek similar opportunities.

As he felt better about himself, it became important for him to disclose his true identity to his family. He wanted them to know and understand who he was. He believed that although they might be shocked, ultimately they would be able to accept him for himself. He disclosed his homosexuality to his mother and sister and was surprised by their responses. His mother reacted by stating she always suspected he was gay and that his admission confirmed her worst fears. She told him he must do everything in his power to change his behavior and feelings. His sister reacted with disbelief and told him she no longer wanted to have anything to do with him. Two days later Joshua's mother had a severe and debilitating stroke.

These family reactions were too much for Joshua to handle and he returned to drinking. He wanted to quit therapy because he felt personally responsible for his mother's stroke. Attempts by his physician and his mother's physician to allay his feelings of responsibility were unsuccessful. Because of his drinking and his nonattendance at work, Joshua was terminated from his position. He felt his world was coming to an end. He was later hospitalized because he was considered a danger to himself, and it took years of intensive therapy to help him overcome his feelings of responsibility and resentment over being gay.

As discussed previously, because of the prevailing negative attitudes society holds toward gay and lesbian individuals, homophobia continues to be rampant in large segments of this country. Consequently, homosexuals remain well closeted and are afraid of identifying themselves. This is especially true of people in professions such as education, child care, law enforcement, and politics. They may have only a few close friends and withdraw from many activities. This isolation has escalated with the current fears concerning AIDS. Threatened by old and new myths, many gay individuals refuse to disclose their sexual orientation or participate in mainstream activities. Therefore, the need for identifying and reaching out to gay youth is even more critical. A good example of a closeted, lonely professional is Jennifer.

Jennifer was a bright, dynamic woman who was politically involved in the community. Because she was in the public eye she felt it of utmost importance that she maintain her public image of being heterosexual. Therefore, she always had a male companion at her side in public affairs. Everyone thought they were engaged but were afraid of making that ultimate commitment. Jennifer felt emotionally isolated and alone. She longed for a satisfying love relationship, but was extremely concerned about someone discovering her sexual orientation, which would damage her career. She suspected that a female friend was a lesbian, but she was afraid to make any overtures for fear, if she were wrong, her identity would be exposed and that the woman might not maintain the confidentiality of the disclosure. Instead, Jennifer began to travel out of town a lot, hoping she could meet someone else. Interestingly enough, it was on one of these trips that Jennifer met someone from her community who was doing the same thing. At first she was surprised and embarrassed at discovering that this woman was a lesbian, but as she overcame her initial discomfort, it gradually led to a close friendship. Although this did not satisfy her need to be in a primary relationship with someone she loved, this friendship enabled her to feel more comfortable with her identity and to have someone else with whom she could discuss her feelings and fears.

It is essential that education take the lead in a movement to help gay and lesbian youth feel more comfortable and accepting of their identity. Intervention at an early age may help prevent or minimize some of the many difficulties that otherwise will be experienced later in life. For many of the above examples, life might have been much less traumatic and more positive had there been accessible individuals able to provide accurate information and guidance. Educators have a critical role in reaching out to gay and lesbian students.

Chapter 8

Ways Help Can Be Provided

Our democratic society is structured to provide help for the gay and lesbian minority, but so far there is little evidence that we have used the structure to successfully accomplish this goal. The fact that gays and lesbians are at risk for suicide, alcoholism, substance abuse, academic difficulties, poor peer relationships, and lowered self-esteem heightens the importance of addressing these issues within the school system. One of the first places gay and lesbian teenagers may turn for information and support is their schools: teachers, guidance counselors, administrators, school psychologists, and other school personnel. Educators need to be prepared for effectively dealing with these issues and their students' feelings.

TEACHER ATTITUDES

Sears (1991) conducted a two-year survey of the perceptions of lesbian and gay youth regarding the attitudes of school personnel toward homosexuality. According to the students, teachers, counselors, and administrators generally avoided the subject of homosexuality. For the most part, they viewed guidance counselors as academic and not personal advisors. There were a few students who reported some supportive educators who had made a difference in their lives. As discussed in Chapter 4, some educators harbor negative perspectives toward gays and lesbians. According to Sears, three-fourths of the participants reported that their teachers had negative attitudes about homosexuality and more than 80% reported that few or none of their high school teachers considered homosexuality an alternative lifestyle. Moreover, discussion in the classroom never included this topic.

Telljohann and Price (1993) surveyed 120 gays and lesbians ages 14 to 21. Approximately one-third of the students claimed they knew they were gay or lesbian between the ages of 4 and 10, with equal numbers aware of their sexual orientation between 11 and 13 and between 14 and 17 years old. Forty-two percent of the females and 30% of the males indicated their families responded negatively to news of their sexual orientation. Only one-fourth of the students stated they were able to discuss this issue with school counselors. Half of the students said that homosexuality had been discussed in their classes; 50% of the females and 37% of the males claimed it was handled negatively. Less than one in five of the students could identify someone who had been supportive of them.

Sears (1991) reported that 8 out of 10 prospective teachers harbored negative feelings toward gays and lesbians. Prospective teachers pursuing certification in elementary education were more likely to harbor homophobic feelings and express homo-negative attitudes than those planning to teach in the secondary schools. Black prospective teachers expressed more negative attitudes about homosexuality than their white counterparts, but were no more homophobic in their feelings toward gays and lesbians. Less than one-third of the teachers surveyed felt comfortable speaking with a student about his or her same-sex feelings or discussing homosexuality in the classroom. Forty percent of the future teachers surveyed stated they felt it was acceptable to transfer a gay or lesbian student to another class at the request of a homophobic teacher.

Nearly two-thirds of the school counselors in Sears' (1991) study expressed negative attitudes and feelings about homosexuality and homosexual persons. Counselors who worked in administrative areas or in testing and evaluating students were more likely to express homo-negative attitudes than those who devoted more time to counseling students. Less than one-third of the counselors surveyed felt their administrators viewed homosexual concerns as legitimate topics for counselors to discuss with their students. Less than one-fifth of the counselors stated they had participated in any inservice programs to expand their knowledge about homosexuality.

Educators have a significant impact on the feelings and experiences of students. Students look to educators for guidance and exposure to information about attitudes, knowledge, and feelings. Students perceive teacher attitudes and feelings through the teacher's verbal and nonverbal behavior. Gay and lesbian teenagers who are trying to determine teacher acceptance or rejection of homosexuality are particularly attuned to these cues. Teacher attitudes may provide the validation for the student's self-acceptance or self-rejection.

PROFESSIONAL ORGANIZATION GUIDELINES

The National Education Association (NEA, 1994) is committed to justice and human rights. It recommends all school personnel do the following:

Acknowledge the diversity of the student body, including the presence of gay as well as non-gay students.

Address gay and lesbian student needs in programs on self-esteem, adolescent development, human relations, pluralism and diversity, conflict reduction, etc.

Respect the confidentiality of students who confide the fact or suspicion of their homosexual orientation or who ask for assistance in this matter.

Intervene to stop the harassment, including name-calling, of gay and lesbian students.

Include in sex education courses information about risks related to HIV/AIDS and sexually transmitted diseases.

Work to ensure school policy that prevents the harassment of students.

Become involved as volunteers in community programs designed to assist gay and lesbian students.

Work to promote the inclusion of inservice programs that help education employees deal effectively with gay and lesbian youth.

Schools are natural forums for presenting information to students, and homosexuality should be included in the curriculum. Other subjects that affect minority groups are covered, so it seems logical that the subject of homosexuality be addressed. In addition to the usual curriculum, schools throughout the nation are used as forums for teaching about alcohol and drug abuse, race relations, child abuse, automobile safety, voting, gun safety, sex equity, AIDS, world hunger, and many other special interest topics. It is the rare school or community that addresses the needs of the gay and lesbian students.

On July 7, 1988, the NEA adopted a resolution on student sexual orientation that all persons, regardless of sexual orientation, should be afforded equal opportunity within the public education system. The association further believes that every school district should provide counseling for students who are struggling with their sexual/gender orientation (NEA, 1988). In its recommendations to school districts, the NEA (1994) encourages policies and programs that recognize:

the right of all students to attend schools free of verbal and physical harassment;

the right to attend schools where respect and dignity for all is standard;

the right to have access to accurate information about themselves, free of negative judgment, and delivered by trained adults who not only inform them, but affirm them;

the right to positive role models, both in person and the curriculum;

the right to be included in all support programs that exist to help teenagers deal with the difficulties of adolescence;

the right to attend schools where education, not survival, is the priority; and

the right to a heritage free of crippling self-hate and unchallenged discrimination.

Furthermore, the NEA encourages school districts to develop policies and programs for education and counseling. Some of these programs include:

education (awareness training for staff, expansion of the school library, development of a speakers bureau);

school safety (elimination of harassment, training of staff in responding to victims of sexual harassment, and development of systems for reporting harassment);

dropout prevention (sponsoring of rap groups and peer group counseling, inclusion of the gay and lesbian perspective in suicide and substance abuse prevention programs, and sponsoring of positive social programs); and

support services (referrals, hot lines, and accessibility to community resources).

In 1990, the Association for Supervision and Curriculum Development (ASCD) passed a resolution concerning student sexual orientation. The ASCD resolution stated

Recent studies indicate that some students experience discrimination and harassment because of their sexual orientation. ASCD believes that schools should demonstrate respect for the dignity and worth of all students and that all students should be treated equitably. ASCD opposes discrimination and supports policies and programs that promote equity. Therefore, ASCD urges its members to develop policies, curriculum materials, and teaching strategies that do not discriminate on the basis of sexual orientation. ASCD encourages schools to provide staff development training and materials to enable educators to better work with this at-risk student population. Finally, ASCD encourages its members to collaborate with other professional organizations toward this goal. (ASCD, 1990)

In 1990, the American School Health Association (Telljohann & Price, 1993) also passed a resolution stating that sexual orientation should be addressed in the sexuality component of a comprehensive health education curriculum.

SCHOOL-BASED PROGRAMS

During the 1985–1986 school year, an education program developed by Uribe and Harbeck (1991) to address some of the needs of gay and lesbian students was tested in the Los Angeles school system. It is now a model program and is known in the nation's educational circles as Project 10 (see Appendix C for more information). The program focuses on education, suicide prevention, dropout prevention, a safe environment for gay and lesbian students, and precise AIDS education. Uribe and Harbeck found that negative attitudes and stereotypes toward gays, lesbians, and bisexuals could be altered with educational intervention. These findings confirmed the conclusions of Price (1982) in his study of high school students' attitudes toward homosexuality. Furthermore, Uribe and Harbeck found that if they affirm their sexuality, gay and lesbian teachers can have a positive effect on attitudes toward homosexuality for both heterosexual and homosexual students.

Curriculum

Although there has been national educational support for modifying the curriculum and environment for gay and lesbian students, there has been great controversy about what should be taught to students. One of the most publicized cases involved the school chancellor of District 24 in Queens, New York, Dr. Joseph Fernandez, who, in 1990, tried to implement a policy that had been set in place by his predecessor in 1989. This policy had stated that teaching materials be revised to show a greater sensitivity to the city's diversity. A teaching guide entitled "Children of the Rainbow" was devised for implementation beginning with first grade. The so-called Rainbow Curriculum consisted of 443 pages with the objective of teaching elementary school children tolerance toward ethnic groups, gays and lesbians, and people with AIDS. The controversy focused on three pages of the guide that dealt with teaching tolerance of gays and lesbians, and three children's books included on a supplementary book list that were not required reading: *Heather Has Two Mommies*, *Daddy's Roommate*, and *Gloria Goes to Gay Pride*. The school board for District 24, representing 27,000 students, rejected the entire curriculum guide. Four other school boards—Districts 8 and 12 in the Bronx, District 31 on Staten Island, and District 20 in Brooklyn—rejected the part of the guide that dealt with homosexuality.

On November 12, 1992, Mary Cummins, president of the school board of District 24 wrote a letter to Dr. Fernandez stating that the elementary schools in the district would not be using this teaching guide for the first grade because she felt it was inappropriate to teach these issues in the classroom. She stated that if he persisted in using this material he would be taken to court by the district. Parents who supported Ms. Cummins' position held several meetings and demonstrations, and conflict grew among the Central Board of Education members. Ultimately, because of his persistence in including this curriculum, Dr. Fernandez's contract was not renewed (Decter, 1993). Although New York was reluctant to move forward with modifying the school curriculum, Massachusetts was not.

On February 25, 1993, in the state of Massachusetts, an education report entitled *Making Schools Safe for Gay and Lesbian Youth: Breaking the Silence in Schools and in Families* was issued from the Governor's Commission on Gay and Lesbian Youth. This commission was created by Governor Weld in 1992 and was the first of its kind in the United States. The commission made three recommendations to the Department of Education: sponsor training for teachers, families, and students to learn about the problems of gay and lesbian youth; make presentations to school committee associations concerning the problems faced by gay and lesbian youth; and develop and disseminate a yellow pages resource book about gay and lesbian youth, one version each for students, teachers, and families. The commission further recommended to the Executive Office of Education that they focus on policies and research and that they:

1   develop and promote anti-harassment policies and guidelines for protecting gay and lesbian students in schools across the Commonwealth;

2   develop school policies that will guarantee gay and lesbian students equal rights to an education and equal access to school activities; and

3 research the problems of gay and lesbian students and the needs of teachers and families of gay and lesbian youth.

Although there are courses in the secondary curriculum appropriate for discussing the homosexual lifestyle, such as peer counseling, health, and psychology, some teachers are reluctant to facilitate classroom discussions dealing with the subject because they are either academically unprepared or concerned about prejudicial attitudes of parents and school administrators. This omission can cause the self-effacement of gay and lesbian students who are exposed only to information and discussion about the heterosexual lifestyle. The guidelines that follow will help ensure that students do not suffer such self-effacement.

GUIDELINES FOR HELPING STUDENTS

Educators' Self-Assessment

It is important to be aware of one's prejudices and biases. If they are identifiable, efforts can be made to overcome them or work around them. Many individuals are not aware of their prejudices until they are confronted directly with situations that make them uncomfortable. In examining one's feelings regarding gays and lesbians, the following questions are important to answer:

- Do you see yourself as a nonjudgmental person?
- Can you list your social prejudices?
- What experiences helped you develop these prejudices?
- How do you feel about these prejudices?
- How do you deal with them?
- Do you feel you would have any difficulty dealing with gay and lesbian teenagers because of any personal prejudices?
- Can you identify these difficulties?
- What messages did you receive from parents and other significant adults regarding gays or lesbians: as a child, a teenager, an adult?
- Do you think these messages would be influential now in dealing with teenagers?
- Is there someone in your family who is gay or lesbian? How do you feel about this?
- How would you feel if you had a gay or lesbian sister, brother, parent?
- How would you react if you found out your best friend were gay or lesbian? Your child?
- How do you feel about hostile humor such as gay and lesbian jokes?

Once educators have assessed their attitudes and perspectives toward homosexuality, it is easier to become instruments for change. Now we will explore the steps school professionals can take to implement and promote positive attitudes for gays and lesbians.

School Districts

Every institution in our society can, within its own framework, help promote understanding; however, school may be the primary institution for effecting change. School administrators and school board members can help educate and promote understanding and acceptance of the gay and lesbian minority in the schools and help alleviate the personal suffering experienced by the many gay and lesbian students who are in their charge. Educators have an ethical obligation to focus on the needs of these students. To do so, educators need to be prepared to deal with rejection of some of their programs by parents or local communities. School administrators need to move the issue of sexuality from a taboo topic into the mainstream of discussion. Educators must believe and accept that discussing homosexuality in a positive way will not cause teenagers to grow up to become gay and lesbian.

Staff development classes for administrators and school board members are a logical first step toward organizing assistance for gay and lesbian students. Once district leaders are knowledgeable and have a greater sensitivity and understanding of gay and lesbian issues, related policy and curriculum decision making should be easier. These staff development classes should be taught by qualified trainers from within or outside the community.

Next, the school district should provide inservice training for school administrators, teachers, counselors, media specialists, school nurses, and other school-related personnel. The agenda should include:

- General knowledge about homosexuality
- The importance of being nonjudgmental
- Counseling of gay and lesbian children
- How to handle derogatory jokes about and name-calling directed at gay and lesbian students
- Dealing with students who have developed emotional attachments to teachers, counselors, coaches, and other adult personnel
- How to lead nondiscriminatory classroom discussions about homosexuality.

When schools began providing inservice classes for educators regarding the black minority in the 1970s, initially there was much resistance, resentment, and ignorance. Over time, however, educating the educators created understanding and acceptance and dispelled prejudice. Legislation assisted progress in the black community; today, legislation has been proposed to assist gay and lesbian students. School boards, administrators, teachers, and other school personnel have the ethical duty to recognize discrimination against gay and lesbian students and take the appropriate action.

Teachers

Educators who control curriculum development should provide courses in health, human sexuality, the behavioral sciences, and family living that include the concerns of gay and lesbian students. These courses should also be provided in adult education settings. Materials that include the historical contributions of gays and lesbians need to be integrated into the school curricula as well as literature that reflects the experiences and culture of the homosexual community.

Classroom teachers are in a key position to help gay and lesbian students: simply being warm, loving, and accepting to all students and responding in a positive way to the diversities among them. This attitude will promote the trust and communication so vital to the emotional growth of all. A respectful attitude demonstrated by the teacher can be contagious and, in subtle ways, establish desirable student attitudes. Teachers should protect students from prejudicial and discriminatory acts.

Any expression of homophobia in the classroom by the teacher or students can be frightening to gay and lesbian students. It is the same feeling racial and religious minority youngsters experience when derogatory remarks are made about their groups; they feel rejected and unsafe.

Teachers who maintain trust and open communication with their students are likely to precipitate counseling sessions with their gay and lesbian students. Some students may have great difficulty initiating the topic of their sexual orientation. Others may be very direct. In either case, it is important to be nonjudgmental. The students are taking a great risk by making the move to talk with an adult. It is usually a mistake to tell the student "I don't know too much about this, shouldn't you talk with a counselor?" This kind of dismissal is not helpful to the student. It would be more appropriate for the teacher to confer with a counselor for direction, without revealing the student's identity. The main concern would be to provide understanding and support for the student and stay in close touch with a qualified counselor.

Teachers can arrange to invite professional people from the community to lecture in the classroom about homosexuality. Many psychologists and psychiatrists will agree to accept this community service assignment if they are notified several weeks in advance. This lecture would be suitable for biology, health, psychology, sociology, family living, and peer counseling classes.

It is important for all educators to know that most gay and lesbian students do not look or act different from their heterosexual counterparts; they are generally conformists. The sexual orientation of many heterosexual effeminate men and masculine women has been misjudged by people who think sexual orientation is obvious. People around the world were shocked to discover that Greg Louganis, an Olympic gold medal winner, was gay when he came out publicly at the 1994 Gay Games.

An assessment inventory such as the following might be helpful in examining teachers' and students' feelings about their sexuality; both could benefit from thinking about these issues. The inventory is a personal exploration that should be done individually. Parts of it may or may not be shared with others. Whereas some students might have difficulty with such a discussion, others may welcome the opportunity to acquire insights and answers to questions.

- Do you prefer to spend time with people of the same sex or the opposite sex?
- Do you have a crush on someone of the same sex? Opposite sex?
- Who is this person? Peer? Teacher? Coach?
- When did you first become aware of your sexual feelings?
- How did you feel about this?
- Was this okay or did you feel different?
- What physical or emotional signs made you aware of these feelings?
- Do/did these feelings affect your interaction with others? Parents? Siblings? Teachers? Peers?
- Do/did these feelings affect your learning experience in school or your participation in athletics or extracurricular activities?
- What verbal/nonverbal messages did your parents convey regarding sex?
- How comfortable are you with these messages?
- What support do you receive about your sexuality from your parents, family members, and friends?
- How comfortable are you with these messages?
- What problems concerning your sexual experience did you have in elementary school, middle school, and high school?
- Do your feelings of love seem different from or similar to those of your peer group?
- Are you comfortable discussing your sexual feelings with someone? If yes, who?
- How comfortable do you feel discussing your sexuality with your friends?
- Have you had a sexual experience?
- With same or opposite sex?
- Who initiated the experience (you or the other person)?
- Would you feel comfortable being the initiator?
- Was it a positive and satisfying experience?
- Was there a special person in your life who helped make you aware of your sexuality?
- If yes, how did this person influence you?
- Do you think talking with a professional counselor would be helpful?
- Would you be interested in reading material concerning teenage sexual matters?

In raising the issue of sexuality, teachers need to be prepared for some of the responses they may get from their students. Some students will feel embarrassed and uncomfortable whereas others may become hostile. A few outspoken students may question the teacher's sexuality and may make homophobic accusations against other students and/or staff.

McCord and Herzog (1991) surveyed students in three undergraduate college courses and asked them to submit their questions about homosexuality in preparation for panels of speakers from a gay rights group. The questions that were asked covered 13 areas: (1) family of origin relationships and reactions, (2) developmental issues, (3) discrimination, (4) experiential issues, (5) etiology, (6) sexual strategies and techniques, (7) experience with and feelings about heterosexuality, (8) religion, (9) raising children in a homosexual household, (10) AIDS, (11) past experiences and influences, (12) homosexual marriage, and (13) self-satisfaction. Teachers need to be prepared to address issues in the above areas. Questions might include:

- How do people know they are gay?
- How do others react to the gay or lesbian person when told they are gay?
- How are their relationships with others affected?
- At what age do they first learn they are gay?
- Do people who are gay have to hide their sexual orientation?
- What kinds of prejudicial experiences do they encounter?
- How does it feel to be gay?
- Is homosexuality a choice?
- Do gays and lesbians ever have sex with straight people?
- Do gays and lesbians want to have families?
- Can they have kids?
- How would the children be affected?
- Do gays and lesbians wish they were straight?
- If they could change, would gays and lesbians become straight?

Teachers and counselors need to be as relaxed and open about the topic as possible. They need to try to make students feel at ease and convey that the topic of homosexuality is an issue that we explore in the same way as other topics. Teachers may wish to emphasize the importance of understanding various ethnic, religious, and otherwise diverse types of people in a community because it fosters tolerance, cooperation, and interaction. If the teacher is asked directly about his or her sexual orientation, the teacher can respond by asking if it matters whether the teacher is straight or gay and whether it would affect the students' feelings toward him. If teachers identify themselves as straight, they may wish to state that they care very much about gay and lesbian people and what they think, thus providing a positive role model of acceptance. If teachers identify themselves as gay or lesbian, the students will have an opportunity to see that there may be individuals they can like and respect whose sexual orientation might be different from theirs (Lipkin, 1992).

Curriculum Suggestions

Language Arts   Language arts teachers can mention the issue of gays and lesbians in biographical studies of literary figures, inventors, musicians, political leaders, composers, scientists, entertainers, artists, and other renowned contributors to world history (see Appendix D). It is just as important for gay and lesbian students to recognize role models as it is for any other minority. Brick (1991) cites a teacher who developed a course in "Adolescence in Literature," which presented adolescent sexuality within the context of an adolescent's life. The class examined the feelings and actions of various characters; the relationships the characters had with each other, their parents, and other adults; and ideas of masculinity and femininity. Sexuality was explored as an additional search for self-understanding. Another example for study might be comparing the relationship between Romeo and Juliet with the behavior and feelings of today's teens. Course objectives might include students becoming aware of their own sexual values and standards, which may be explored through the various literature and class assignments.

Social Studies   Social studies is an area in which the concept of sexuality can be examined within an historical context. Stereotyping and prejudice as well as sex in culture, history, and politics can be explored. Brick (1991) suggested five essential levels of learning when presenting sex within the curriculum: (1) cognitive; (2) affective, including feelings, attitudes, beliefs, and values; (3) skills, particularly communications, decision making, and assertiveness; (4) critical analysis through examining one's society; and (5) action through planning how one would act in support of one's values. Brick believes that the most compelling reason for including sex education in social studies is the need for critical analysis of media and advertising sex messages. Sexual images are an important part of children's lives. Students need to learn to question and challenge some of those images.

Contributions of known gay and lesbian individuals should be noted wherever it is appropriate in the curriculum. Most courses provide a framework that allows for presentation of the names of famous people whom scholars have identified as having experienced homosexual relationships. Although it may be easier to introduce the topic of sexuality in health, social studies, and literature, it can also be discussed in the context of science, music, art, journalism, drama, peer counseling, sports, business, and foreign language classes that also study cultures.

Gay and lesbian teenagers need to be prepared to deal with the discrimination and prejudice they may encounter in the workplace. Certain business courses in the school curriculum would be effective for introducing this information and helping prepare the gay and lesbian teenager to more effectively deal with the community.

American History and Government   American history and government instructors have numerous opportunities to relate gay and lesbian issues when they discuss subjects such as intolerance during colonial times, the Bill of Rights, the Constitution, the judicial system, political activism, civil rights, public opinion, pressure groups, legislation, presidential powers, states' rights, the military, and the differences among the powers of local, state, and federal governments. As of Fall 1993, President Clinton had appointed 25 openly gay and lesbian men and women to administrative positions (*The Victory Fund,* 1993). American government teachers have the opportunity to raise discussion about the many openly gay and lesbian officials in local, state, and federal governments (e.g., U.S. Congressman Gerry Studds, U.S. Congressman Barney Frank, and Roberta Achtenberg, Assistant Secretary of Fair Housing and Equal Opportunity/Department of Housing and Urban Development).

Courses organized for the study of cultures may include the various attitudes concerning gays and lesbians within the different cultures. Students need to understand cultural differences concerning gays and lesbians in relation to societal acceptance of the sexual orientation, laws regulating sexual behavior, and religious attitudes. Within American cultural minorities there is also the subminority problems of gays and lesbians who belong to other minority groups and therefore must cope with prejudice and discrimination on all counts.

Psychology and Sociology   Teachers of psychology and sociology have opportunities to address many gay and lesbian issues as they guide students through the study of individual and group behavior. In psychology, units on human development, the bases of behavior, motivation and emotion, personality theories, and research can be a catalyst for discussions relative to sexual orientation. Sociology teachers can focus on gay and lesbian concerns as they discuss the motivation and effects of prejudice and discrimination among people. The study of homophobia might be appropriate in this class and be beneficial to both gay and lesbian students and their heterosexual classmates.

Health   Health classes are important to all students, heterosexual, bisexual, and homosexual; all students need competent instruction concerning their sexual orientation. It is important to provide teenagers with information about HIV/ AIDS, safe sex, sexually transmitted diseases, alcohol and substance abuse, psychological and physical health, and where to get help for problems. Local, state, and federal hotline numbers should be made available to students, in addition to information about local physical and psychological health agencies (see Appendix C for listing of national agencies, organizations, and hotlines). Health instructors can collaborate with school media specialists to develop pertinent bibliographies for students. Materials should be provided via handouts and bulletin boards to make this information accessible to all students.

Peer Counseling   Peer counseling classes can play a significant role in helping the gay and lesbian students. In addition to the usual peer counselor training topics (i.e., alcohol and substance abuse, suicide, family relations, dating relationships, school, and work problems), peer counselors should have appropriate training concerning diverse sexual orientations. The peer counselor instructor, his or her counselees, and the guidance staff may be instrumental in setting up a support group for gay, lesbian, and bisexual students (see Appendix C).

Journalism   Journalism teachers who sponsor school newspapers have an opportunity to suggest various gay and lesbian topics to their student writers. Gay Pride Week, homophobia, editorials concerning gays in the military, or an article alerting gay and lesbian students about school media center materials are just a few of the potential pieces.

WARNING SIGNS OF AT-RISK BEHAVIORS

Educators recognize the behaviors that indicate a teenager is at risk. Many warning signs are the same for all teenagers; however, for gay and lesbian teenagers, the confusion or uncertainty regarding their sexuality frequently is not expressed, leading to further isolation due to fear of rejection. Three main indicators that a teenager is at risk are poor self-image and low self-esteem, alienation from the peer group, and hostility toward authority (Walling, 1993).

Low self-esteem can be manifested by: underachievement, failing to see a relationship between effort and achievement, immature behavior, termination of difficult tasks instead of persevering, and lack of participation in discussions. Most gay and lesbian teenagers are isolated because they are reluctant to disclose their feelings to others. They may have few role models and may not have a trusting relationship with peers to serve as confidants. As a result, they begin to withdraw, become mistrusting of others because they feel different, and believe no one understands them. Their peers may respond by becoming more rejecting or openly hostile. Gay and lesbian teenagers who are alienated react by being tardy to class, cutting classes, not participating in class activities, not participating in extracurricular activities, and failing to establish goals for a future career. When people feel that they are being rejected, they often respond by rejecting others and becoming hostile. This hostility may be manifested as disobedience, rebellion, negative attitudes, running away from home, truancy, alcohol or drug abuse, aggression toward other students, or sexual aggression.

Teachers and school counselors need to be aware of the above behaviors and not just consider them typical of troubled youth. Teachers and counselors should be aware that some of this behavior may be due to the teenager's sexual identity confusion. This area could be explored directly with the teenager, but, for this to occur, the teenager must sense a safe and accepting environment. Walling (1993) has identified attitudes that can help gay and lesbian teenagers feel comfortable discussing their feelings. He believes teachers and counselors need to use language that indicates an awareness of sexual diversity and that lets others know they do not assume all teenagers are heterosexual. Teachers need to speak out against harassment and indicate that humor at the expense of gay and lesbians is offensive. By displaying posters and books on the subject of homosexuality, teachers and counselors will indicate they are open to discussing this topic. Counselors need to invite students whom they believe to be wrestling with sexual orientation problems to discuss their feelings.

When students do feel comfortable addressing or disclosing their sexuality with a teacher or counselor the following guidelines might be helpful.

Guidelines for Responding to Students When They Disclose Their Sexuality

1   Do not act surprised when someone comes out to you, telling you he thinks he may be homosexual or bisexual. The person has tested you with a series of "trial balloons" over a period of time and has decided that you can be trusted and helpful. Don't let him down.

2   Deal with the feelings first. Most gay and lesbian teenagers feel alone, afraid, and guilty. You can help by listening, allowing them to unburden uncomfortable feelings and thoughts.

3   Be supportive. Let gay and lesbian teenagers know that they are okay. Explain that many people have struggled with the issue of homosexuality. Acknowledge that dealing with one's sexuality is difficult. Keep the door open for further conversations and assistance.

4   Assess the student's understanding of homosexuality. Replace misinformation with accurate knowledge. Don't assume that gay and lesbian teens know a lot about human sexuality. We have all been exposed to the same myths and stereotypes, so it is helpful to provide clarification.

5   Use nonjudgmental, all-inclusive language in your discussion. Pay attention to verbal and nonverbal cues from students. Do not label or categorize.

6   Respect confidentiality. Gay, lesbian, or bisexual teenagers who share their identity with you have established a sacred trust that must be respected.

7   Anticipate some confusion. Many gay and lesbian teenagers are sure of their sexual orientation by the time they enter high school. Others will be confused and unsure.

8   Examine your own biases. You need to remain a neutral source of information and support.

9   Be informed. Most of us are products of a heterosexist/homophobic society that has been paralyzed by misinformation and fear. You cannot be free of it by just deciding to be free; read reliable resources and talk to qualified persons.

10 Know when and where to seek help. Know the referral agencies and counselors in your area. Gay and lesbian hotlines can provide access to professional persons and agencies that are qualified to help (see Appendix C).

COUNSELORS

Counselors can do a great deal to promote awareness and prevention of emotional disturbances among young gays and lesbians. They need to gather information and present inservice for faculty members, peer counseling programs, and self-help programs for gay and lesbian students and their parents. Many school guidance counseling staffs have successfully organized support groups for drug and alcohol abusers, children of alcoholics, children of divorced parents, overweight students, and others, but few schools arrange support groups for gay and lesbian students.

School guidance offices stock helpful literature for students on an array of topics, but literature on gay and lesbian concerns is usually not available. Literature on the topic of homosexuality needs to be available and displayed in every school guidance office. If school counselors network with school administrators and community agencies, free family counseling services can be provided on school campuses to deal with the issue of homosexuality. Very often gay and lesbian students suffer from other problems such as alcohol and drug abuse caused by persistent fear, ignorance, and/or rejection. These students may need the services of psychiatric social workers, psychologists, or psychiatrists. Family counseling units can arrange these services.

There are some school guidance counselors who prefer not to talk with their counselees about gayness or lesbianism, and when they think a student is about to approach the topic, they redirect the conversation. If the student is courageous enough to be direct and the counselor avoids the discussion, the student receives the message and probably will not initiate the topic again. Sensitive, caring, knowledgeable counselors who are willing to openly discuss gay and lesbian students' concerns can provide the necessary support for these young people to cope with this area of turmoil.

Guidance counselors need to develop a strong referral network within the community to provide additional services for their gay and lesbian students. A list of physicians, both male and female, who work with the gay and lesbian population and are sensitive to their needs should be a basic tool for all counselors.

When a person or family is going through a crisis, medical or otherwise, people often turn to physicians. Because the physician gets to know the family and its history and may have lived through significant events in a family's life, the physician may be someone to whom a teenager or his parents turn. However, because of fear and anxiety, a teenager may not always feel comfortable expressing his feelings or asking for the information. In addition, a physician usually has a little time allotted for each patient, so a teenager's concerns may be overlooked.

Therefore, it is important that the physician be aware of the messages patients are sending. Physicians should feel comfortable discussing a patient's feelings about sexuality and not overlook the possibility that an adolescent patient is struggling with the issue of sexual orientation. Every teenage patient should have some time alone with the physician to provide a private opportunity to ask questions. Physicians should be aware of the messages they are sending to their patients regarding their value system, and they should try to be as accepting and nonjudgmental as possible.

School counselors should also be able to refer students to psychologists and social workers. Students who exhibit at-risk behaviors can often benefit from professional intervention. Like physicians, psychologists and social workers need to be open, supportive, and nonjudgmental. Trust must be developed and confidentiality emphasized. The professional should be aware of his or her own feelings and biases and make sure these are not conveyed to the teenager. If a teenager senses the professional's discomfort, he will not be comfortable disclosing personal emotions. The teenager may feel the professional views sex negatively, which will reinforce his reluctance to discuss the topic. Professionals should include broad questions about a client's sexuality in the initial interview while they are gathering other pertinent historical information.

OTHER SCHOOL PERSONNEL

Although the emphasis so far has been primarily on teachers and counselors, there are many other school-based individuals who are involved with gay and lesbian teenagers on a daily basis: administrators, librarians, nurses, school resource officers, cafeteria personnel, and clerical support staff. They too need to provide attitudes of acceptance that promote positive self-esteem. It is not uncommon for gay and lesbian teenagers to turn to media centers in a private search for information that might help them understand their feelings and provide answers to their questions. Media specialists should have books, pamphlets, videos, and so forth available for both students and teachers. This information should be easily accessible so that gay and lesbian teenagers can access it without feeling self-conscious. Displaying materials in a prominent place in the media center might be helpful. Recognizing Gay Pride Week by a display of materials can facilitate and promote further discussion and exploration of this issue.

School nurses are another resource for homosexual students. They can serve as consultants for teachers, counselors, and students and assist in educating the student population regarding HIV/AIDS, sexually transmitted diseases, and safe sex practices.

The school board should be at the forefront in creating policies that will protect the rights of all minorities for both students and staff. There are many gay and lesbian teachers, counselors, administrators, and other school personnel who expend considerable energy closeting their sexual identity because they fear they would lose their jobs if their sexual orientation were known (Fogarty, 1981; Griffin, 1992; Moses, 1977; Olson, 1986, 1987; Smith, 1985; Woods, 1989). These individuals could serve as positive role models for the gay and lesbian students, but unless there is an atmosphere that promotes acceptance, few gay and lesbian administrators, teachers, counselors, media specialists, coaches, nurses, and other school personnel will be willing to take the risks involved. Consequently, these educators also feel isolated in terms of their relationships with colleagues, students, and parents. School boards and district administrators need to encourage programs that will combat homophobia and heterosexism.

Parents are usually the last to know about their gay and lesbian children, particularly parents who do not have open communication with their children or who have somehow communicated a nonaccepting attitude concerning the gay and lesbian lifestyle. The school and its personnel can be at the forefront in assisting parents to develop more positive and accepting attitudes toward their children. School personnel should be educated in this field so that they will be in a better position to assist gay and lesbian students and their families.

FAMILIES

Since the Gay Liberation movement began, more young gays and lesbians have learned the advantages of taking the risk of confronting their parents with their sexual orientation. When this disclosure takes place, parents can do a lot to help themselves and their children. Knowledge of the gay and lesbian lifestyle is essential for parents. Open communication with a gay son or lesbian daughter will provide much of the necessary information for understanding. When the disclosure occurs, parents often want to blame their own parenting for their son's or daughter's sexual orientation. The parents may need the support of a professional counselor who may refer them to a local support group of parents of gay and lesbian children. These groups are available throughout the nation (see Appendix C). Educating other family members is often the responsibility of the parents, and the knowledge and understanding provided by a support group can be of enormous assistance in this task. Once family members have been made aware of the situation, it is easier for the gay or lesbian son or daughter to once again participate as an active family member as the mystery, anxiety, deceit, and agony are replaced by understanding and acceptance.

We summarize here guidelines for parents to help gay and lesbian teenagers and young adults:

Be aware of the messages you are sending to others regarding your belief system and values. Make sure they are consistent. Examine your own beliefs and feel comfortable with your own sexuality.

Try to provide a forum for trust and acceptance. This will encourage your teenagers to communicate.

Try to be nonjudgmental. Accept the individual as a total human being—do not limit your interest to his or her sexual orientation. Let the teenager know he or she is loved and respected as an individual.

Don't expect to have all the answers. It is okay to say "I do not know." Try to get the questions answered and the feelings addressed.

Obtain as much information as possible through films, books, movies, magazines, workshops, organizations, and so forth (see Appendix C). Develop a good referral base.

Locate the support groups in the community and utilize them.

Educators can take a leading role in assisting gay and lesbian students to feel comfortable about their sexual orientation. Many of the nation's gay, lesbian, and bisexual students are at risk; breaking the silence in the school systems concerning homosexuality is essential to preventing suicide, alcohol and drug abuse, AIDS, violence, poor academic achievement, loss of human potential, and violation of human rights. The indifference that prevails in the majority of the nation's schools is the result of ignorance, fear of controversy, and homophobia. A positive change can occur through a major commitment by state departments of education, school boards, administrators, teachers, counselors, school psychologists, social workers, media specialists, curriculum directors, human resource development staffs, and all other school-related personnel to take the necessary steps to serve gay, lesbian, and bisexual students.

References

Acanfora v. Board of Education of Montgomery County, 359 F. Supp. 846 (District Court, Montgomery County, MD, 1974).

Adam, B. D. (1986). Age, structure, and sexuality: Reflections on the anthropological evidence of homosexual relations. In E. Blackwood (Ed.), *Anthropology and homosexual behavior* (pp. 19–33). New York: The Haworth Press.

Allen, L. S., Hines, M., Shryne, J. E., & Gorski, R. A. (1986). Two sexually dimorphic cell groups in the human brain. *Endocrinology* (Suppl.), *118,* 633.

Allport, G. W. (1983). *ABC's of scapegoating.* New York: Anti-Defamation League of B'nai B'rith.

American Psychological Association. (1975). Proceedings of the American Psychological Association for the year 1974. *American Psychologist, 30,* 620–651.

Anderson, D. (1987). Family and peer relations of gay adolescents. *Adolescent Psychiatry, 14,* 165–178.

Association for Supervision and Curriculum Development. (1990). Student sexual orientation. *Resolutions 1990* [Flyer]. Alexandria, VA: Author.

Attempts to cure homosexuality could mean litigation. (1994, June 13). *Mental Health Weekly, 4*(23), 1–2.

Bailey, J. M. (1993). Heritable factors influence sexual orientation in women. *Archives of General Psychiatry, 50,* 217–223.

Bailey, J. M., & Pillard, R. A. (1991, December). Genetic study of male sexual orientation. *Archives of General Psychiatry, 48,* 1089–1096.

Bawer, B. (1993). *A place at the table.* New York: Poseidon Press.

Bell, R. Q., & Harper, L. (1977). *Child effects on adults.* Hillsdale, NJ: Lawrence Erlbaum.

Bell, A. P., & Weinberg, M. S. (1978). *Homosexualities: A study of diversity among men and women.* New York: Simon & Schuster.

Bell, A. P., Weinberg, M. S., & Hammersmith, S. K. (1981). *Sexual preference: Its development in men and women.* Bloomington, IN: Indiana University Press.

Bem, S. L. (1974). The measurement of psychological androgyny. *Journal of Consulting and Counseling Psychology, 42,* 155–162.

Bem, S. L. (1975). Sex-role adaptability: One consequence of psychological androgyny. *Journal of Personality and Social Psychology, 31,* 634–643.

Berger, G., Hank, L., Rauzi, T., & Simkins, L. (1987). Detection of sexual orientation by heterosexuals and homosexuals. *Journal of Homosexuality, 13*(4), 83–100.

Berger, R. M. (1982). *Gay and gray: The older homosexual man*. Urbana, IL: University of Illinois Press.

Bérubé. A. (1990). *Coming out under fire: The history of gay men and women in World War Two*. New York: Free Press.

Blackwood, E. (1985). Breaking the mirror: The construction of lesbianism and the anthropological discourse on homosexuality. In E. Blackwood (Ed.), *Anthropology and homosexual behavior* (pp. 1–17). New York: Haworth Press.

Block, J. H. (1973). Conceptions of sex role: Some cross-cultural and longitudinal perspectives. *American Psychologist, 28*, 512–526.

Blumenfeld, W. J., & Raymond, D. (1993). *Looking at gay and lesbian life* (2nd ed.). Boston: Beacon Press.

Blumstein, P. W., & Schwartz, P. (1977). Bisexuality: Some social psychological issues. *Journal of Social Issues, 33*, 30–45.

Bode, J. (1976). *View from another closet. Exploring bisexuality in women*. New York: Hawthorne Books.

Boswell, J. (1980). *Christianity, social tolerance and homosexuality: Gay people in Western Europe from the beginning of the Christian era to the fourteenth century*. Chicago: University of Chicago Press.

Boxer, A. M., & Cohler, B. J. (1989). The life course of gay and lesbian youth: An immodest proposal for the study of lives. *Journal of Homosexuality, 17*, 315–355.

Boxer, A. M., Cook, J. A., & Cohler, B. J. (1986). Grandfathers, fathers, and sons: Intergenerational relations among men. In K. Pillemer & R. Wolf (Eds.), *Elder abuse: Conflict in the family* (pp. 93–121). Dover, MA: Auburn House.

Bozett, F. W. (1980). Gay fathers: How and why they disclose their homosexuality to their children. *Family Relations: Journal of Applied Family & Child Studies, 29*, 173–179.

Bozett, F. W. (1981). Gay fathers: Identity conflict resolution through integrative sanctioning. *Alternative Lifestyles, 4*, 90–107.

Bozett, F. W. (1982). Heterogenous couples in heterosexual marriages: Gay men and straight women. *Journal of Marital and Family Therapy, 8*, 81–89.

Bozett, F. W. (Ed.). (1987). *Gay and lesbian parents*. New York: Praeger.

Bray, A. (1982). *Homosexuality in Renaissance England*. London: Gay Men's Press.

Brick, P. (1991). Fostering positive sexuality. *Educational Leadership, 49*(1), 51–53.

Bull, C. (1992, May 5). Conservative Jews face growing rift over gay issues. *The Advocate, 602*, 24.

Bullough, V. L. (1979). *Homosexuality: A history from ancient Greece to gay liberation*. New York: New American Library.

Byne, W. (1994, May). The biological evidence challenged. *Scientific American, 270*, 50–55.

Califia, P. (1979). Lesbian sexuality. *Journal of Homosexuality, 4*, 255–266.

Cass, V. C. (1979). Homosexual identity formation: A theoretical model. *Journal of Homosexuality, 4*, 219–235.

Cass, V. C. (1984). Homosexual identity formation: Testing a theoretical model. *Journal of Sex Research, 20*, 143–167.

Clausen, J. A. (1975). The social meaning of differential physical and sexual maturation. In S. Dragastin & G. H. Elder (Eds.), *Adolescence in the life cycle* (pp. 25–47). Washington, DC: Hemisphere.

Cohler, B. J., & Geyer, E. S. (1982). Psychological autonomy and interdependence within the family. In F. Walsh (Ed.), *Normal family process* (pp. 196–288). New York: Guilford Press.

Coleman, E. (1982a). Changing approaches to the treatment of homosexuality: A review. *American Behavioral Scientist, 25*, 397–405.

Coleman, E. (1982b). Developmental stages of the coming-out process. In W. Paul, J. D. Weinrich, J. C. Gonsiorek, & M. E. Hotvedt (Eds.), *Homosexuality: Social, psychological and biological issues* (pp. 149–158). Beverly Hills, CA: Sage.

Coles, R., & Stokes, J. (1985). *Sex and the American teenager.* New York: Rolling Stone Press.

Comstock, G. D. (1991). *Violence against lesbians and gay men.* New York: Columbia University Press.

Cook, J. A. (1988). Who mothers the chronically mentally ill. *Family Relations, 37,* 42–49.

Cranston, K. (1991). HIV education for gay, lesbian and bisexual youth: Personal risk, personal power, and the community of conscience. *Journal of Homosexuality, 22,* 247–259.

Crompton, L. (1978). Gay genocide: From Leviticus to Hitler. In L. Crew (Ed.), *The gay academic.* Palm Springs, CA: ETC Publications.

Dank, B. (1971). Coming out in the gay world. *Psychiatry, 34,* 180–197.

Day, D. (1980). *The evolution of love.* New York: Dial Press.

Decter, M. (1993). Homosexuality and the schools. *Commentary, 95,* 19–25.

deMonteflores, C., & Schultz, S. J. (1978). Coming out: Similarities and differences for lesbians and gay men. *Journal of Social Issues, 34,* 59–72.

DeVries, R. (1969). Constancy of generic identity in the years three to six. *Monographs of the Society for Research in Child Development, 34*(3, Serial No. 127).

Dickemann, M. (1993). Reproductive strategies and gender construction: An evolutionary view of homosexualities. *Journal of Homosexuality, 24,* 55–71.

Dover, K. J. (1980). *Greek homosexuality.* New York: Vintage Books.

Dynes, W. R. (Ed.). (1990). *Encyclopedia of homosexuality.* New York: Garland.

Elliott, S. (1994, June 16). A sharper view of gay consumers. *New York Times,* pp. D1, D19.

Ellis, H. (1936). *Sexual inversion: Studies in the psychology of sex.* New York: Random House.

Fairchild, B., & Hayward, N. (1979). *Now that you know.* New York: Harcourt Brace Jovanovich.

Feldman, D. A. (1989). Gay youth and AIDS. *Journal of Homosexuality, 17,* 185–193.

Fletcher, L. Y. (1992). *The first gay pope and other records.* Boston: Alyson.

Fogarty, E. (1981). Passing as straight: A phenomenological analysis of the experience of the lesbian who is professionally employed (Doctoral dissertation, University of Pittsburgh, 1980). *Dissertation Abstracts International, 41*(6), 2384B.

Freud, S. (1953). Three essays on the theory of sexuality. In J. Strachey (Ed. and Trans.), *The standard edition of the complete psychological works of Sigmund Freud* (Vol. 7, pp. 125–245). London: Hogarth Press. (Original work published 1901)

Freud, S. (1963a). A case of homosexuality in a woman. In *Sexuality and the psychology of love* (pp. 123–149). New York: Collier.

Freud, S. (1963b). Certain neurotic mechanisms. In *Sexuality and the psychology of love* (pp. 150–160). New York: Collier.

Freund, K., Langevin, R., Cibiri, S., & Zajac, Y. (1973). Heterosexual aversion in homosexual males. *British Journal of Psychiatry, 122,* 163–169.

Fricke, A. (1981). *Reflections of a rock lobster: A story about growing up gay.* Boston: Alyson.

Gadamer, H. G. (1965). *Truth & method.* New York: Crossroad.

Gagnon, J. H., & Simon, W. (1973). *Sexual conduct: The social sources of human sexuality.* Chicago: Aldine.

Gay men's health crisis. (1993, August). *GMHC facts* [Brochure]. New York: Author.

Gay yellowpages. New York: Renaissance.

Gebhard, P. H. (1965). Situational factors affecting human sexual behavior. In F. A. Beach (Ed.), *Sex and behavior* (pp. 65–78). New York: Wiley.

Gibson, P. (1989). Gay male and lesbian youth suicide. In M. R. Feinleib (Ed.), *Report of the secretary's task force on youth suicide: Prevention and interventions in youth suicide* (Vol. 3, pp. 110–142). Washington, DC: U.S. Department of Health and Human Services.

Gilbert, A. (1976). Buggery and the British Navy, 1700–1861. *Journal of Social History, 10,* 72–98.

Goldstein, R. (1986). The gay family. *Voice, 11*(27), 19–29.

Golombok, S., Spencer, A., & Rutter, M. (1983). Children in lesbian and single parent households: Psycho–sexual and psychiatric appraisal. *Journal of Child Psychology & Psychiatry, 24*(4), 551–572.

Goode, E. (1984). *Deviant behavior.* Englewood Cliffs, NJ: Prentice Hall.

Goodman, B. (1973). The lesbian mother. *American Journal of Orthopsychiatry, 43,* 283–284.

Gorski, R. A., Gordon, J. H., Shryne, J. E., & Southam, A. M. (1978). Evidence for a morphological sex difference within the medial preoptic area of the rat brain. *Brain Research, 148,* 333–346.

Governor's Commission on Gay and Lesbian Youth. (1993, February 25). *Making schools safe for gay and lesbian youth: Breaking the silence in schools and in families.* Publication #17296-60-500-2/93-C.R. Boston, MA: State House.

Green, R. (1978). Sexual identity of 37 children raised by homosexual or transsexual parents. *American Journal of Psychiatry, 135*(6), 692–697.

Green, R. (1987). *The "Sissy Boy Syndrome" and the development of homosexuality.* New Haven, CT: Yale University Press.

Griffin, P. (1992). From hiding out to coming out: Empowering lesbian and gay educators. *Journal of Homosexuality, 22,* 167–196.

Groth, A. N., & Birnbaum, H. J. (1978). Adult sexual orientation and attraction to underage children. *Archives of Sexual Behavior, 7,* 175–181.

Hagestad, G. O. (1981). Problems and promises in the social psychology of intergenerational relations. In R. W. Fogel, E. Hatfield, S. B. Keisler, & E. Shanas (Eds.), *Stability and change in the family* (pp. 11–46). New York: Academic Press.

Hamer, D., Hu, S., Magnuson, V., Hu, N., & Pattatucci, A. (1993, July 16). A linkage between DNA markers on the X chromosome and male sexual orientation. *Science, 261,* 321–327.

Harbeck, K. M. (1991). Gay and lesbian educators: Past history/future prospects. *Journal of Homosexuality, 22,* 121–139.

Harbeck, K. M. (Ed.). (1992).*Coming out of the classroom closet: Gay and lesbian students, teachers and curricula.* New York: Harrington Park Press.

Harding, R. (1991, January 1). Minneapolis panel: Catholic officials violated bias law. *The Advocate, 567,* 20.

Harris, M. B., & Turner, P. H. (1986). Gay and lesbian parents. *Journal of Homosexuality, 12,* 101–113.

Harry, J. (1982). *Gay children grown up: Gender culture and gender deviance.* New York: Praeger.

Harry, J., & DeVall, W. B. (1978). *The social organization of gay males.* New York: Praeger.

Hecker, C. E. (1994, April 21). Gay writer "comes out," loses fear of evangelists. *Miami Herald,* p. 3G.

Heilbrun, A. B. (1976). The measurement of masculine and feminine sex role identities as independent dimensions. *Journal of Consulting and Clinical Psychology, 44,* 183–190.

Henry, W. A. III (1994, June 27). Pride and prejudice. *Time,* 53–59.

Herdt, G. (1989). Introduction: Gay and lesbian youth, emergent identities, and cultural scenes at home and abroad. *Journal of Homosexuality, 17,* 1–42.

Herek, G. (1985). Beyond "homophobia": A social psychological perspective on attitudes toward lesbians and gay men. In J. D'Emilio (Ed.), *Bashers, baiters, and bigots: Homophobia in American society* (pp. 1–21). New York: Harrington Park Press.

Herek, G. M., & Berrill, K. T. (1992). *Hate crimes: Confronting violence against lesbians and gay men.* Newbury Park, CA: Sage.

Hetrick, E. S., & Martin, A. D. (1987). Developmental issues and their resolution for gay and lesbian adolescents. *Journal of Homosexuality, 2*(1/2), 25–43.

Hidalgo, H. A., & Christensen, E. H. (1976–77). The Puerto Rican lesbian and the Puerto Rican community. *Journal of Homosexuality, 2,* 109–121.

Hoebel, E. A. (1960). *The Cheyennes: Indians of the Great Plains* (p. 77). New York: Holt, Rinehart & Winston.

Hoeffer, B. (1981). Children's acquisition of sex-role behavior in lesbian-mother families. *American Journal of Orthopsychiatry, 51*(31), 536–543.

Hotvedt, M., & Mandel, J. (1982). Children of lesbian mothers. In W. Paul, J. D. Weinrich, J. C. Gonsiorek, & M. E. Hotvedt (Eds.), *Homosexuality: Social, psychological and biological issues* (pp. 275–285). Beverly Hills, CA: Sage.

Hunter, N. D., Michaelson, S. E., & Stoddard, T. B. (1992). *The rights of lesbians and gay men: The basic ACLU guide to a gay person's rights.* Carbondale, IL: Southern Illinois University Press.

Icard, L. (1986). Black gay men and conflicting social identities: Sexual orientation versus racial identity. *Journal of Social Work and Human Sexuality, 4*, 83–93.

Isay, R. A. (1985). On the analytic therapy of homosexual men. *Psychoanalytic Study of the Child, 40*, 235–254.

Isay, R. A. (1986). The development of sexual identity in homosexual men. *Psychoanalytic Study of the Child, 41*, 467–489.

Isay, R. A. (1987). Fathers and their homosexually inclined sons in childhood. *Psychoanalytic Study of the Child, 42*, 275–294.

Johns Committee. (1964). *Homosexuality and citizenship in Florida* [Pamphlet]. Tallahassee, FL: Author.

Judge orders that lesbian be reinstated into military. (1994, June 2). *Miami Herald*, p. 3A.

Kagan, J., & Moss, H. A. (1962). *Birth to maturity.* New York: Wiley.

Katz, J. (1976). *Gay American history: Lesbians and gay men in the U.S.A.* New York: Avon Books.

Kinsey, A. C., Pomeroy, W. B., & Martin, C. E. (1948). *Sexual behavior in the human male.* Philadelphia: W.B. Saunders.

Kirkpatrick, M., Smith, C., & Roy, R. (1981). Lesbian mothers and their children: A comparative study. *American Journal of Orthopsychiatry, 51*(3), 545–551.

Klein, F. (1978). *The bisexual option.* New York: Arbor House.

Kooden, H. D., Morin, S. F., Riddle, D. L., Rogers, M., Strang, B. E., & Strassburger, F. (1979). *Removing the stigma: Final report of the Board of Social and Ethical Responsibility for Psychology's Task Force on the Status of Lesbian and Gay Male Psychologists.* Washington, DC: American Psychological Association.

Lambda Legal Defense and Educational Fund Inc. (1993). New York: Author. (Available from the Lambda Legal Defense and Educational Fund Inc., 666 Broadway, New York, NY 10012)

Landers, P. (1993, February 21). God's word on gays? Believers disagree. *Miami Herald*, p. 5J.

Lea, H. C. (1907). *A history of the inquisition of Spain.* New York: Macmillan.

Lee, J. A. (1977). Going public: A study in the sociology of homosexual liberation. *Journal of Homosexuality, 3*, 49–78.

LeVay, S. (1991, August 30). A difference in hypothalamic structure between heterosexual and homosexual men. *Science, 253*, 1034–1037.

LeVay, S., & Hamer, D. H. (1994, May). Evidence for a biological influence in male homosexuality. *Scientific American, 270*, 44–49.

Lewin, T. (1994, April 30). A killing in a small town becomes a chastening lesson in intolerance. *New York Times*, p. L8.

Lewin, E., & Lyons, T. A. (1982). Everything in its place: The coexistence of lesbianism and motherhood. In W. Paul, J. D. Weinrich, J. C. Gonsiorek, & M. E. Hotvedt, (Eds.), *Homosexuality: Social, psychological and biological issues* (pp. 249–273). Beverly Hills, CA: Sage.

Lipkin, A. (1992, Fall). Project 10: Gay and lesbian students find acceptance in their school community. *Teaching Tolerance*, 25–27.

Lofland, J. (1969). *Deviance and identity.* Englewood Cliffs, NJ: Prentice Hall.

Long, P. (1994, June 26). "The witch hunts" go on. *Miami Herald*, p. B6.

MacInnes, C. (1973). *Loving them both: A study in bisexuality and bisexuals.* London: Martin Bran & O'Keefe.

Martin, L. (1994, June 19). Stonewall, 1969: Where fight for gay rights began. *Miami Herald*, p. 1A.

Martin, N. S. (1994, November 21). Mourners pay tribute to AIDS activist Zamora. *Sun-Sentinel*, pp. A1, A8.

Mason, R. (1994, June 30). Orthodox, conservative, reform and reconstructionist speak out on gays. *Broward Jewish Journal*, pp. A8, A10.

Masters, W. H., & Johnson, V. E. (1979). *Homosexuality in perspective*. Boston: Little, Brown.

Mathis, J. L. (1972). *Clear thinking about sexual deviations*. Chicago: Nelson-Hall.

McCord, D. M., & Herzog, H. A. (1991). What undergraduates want to know about homosexuality. *Teaching of Psychology, 18*, 243–244.

McDonald, G. J. (1982). Individual differences in the coming out process for gay men: Implications for theoretical models. *Journal of Homosexuality, 8*, 47–60.

McGarrahan, E. (1991, December 8). Florida's secret shame. *Miami Herald*, pp. 9–18.

Melton, J. G. (1991). *The churches speak on homosexuality*. Detroit: Gale Research.

Mickens, E. (1994, April 9). Waging war on Wall Street. *The Advocate*, 40–45.

Miller, B. (1978). About sexual resocialization: Adjustments toward a stigmatized identity. *Alternative Lifestyles, 1*, 207–234.

Miller, B. (1979). Gay fathers and their children. *The Family Coordinator, 28*, 544–552.

Miller, J. A., Mucklow, B. M., Jacobsen, R. B., & Bigner, J. J. (1980). Comparison of family relationships: Homosexual versus heterosexual women. *Psychological Reports, 46*, 1127–1132.

Money, J. (1970). Sexual dimorphism and homosexual gender identity. *Psychological Bulletin, 74*, 425–440.

Money, J. (1988). *Gay, straight and in-between*. New York: Oxford Press.

Money, J., & Ehrhardt, A. (1972). *Man and woman, boy and girl: The differentiation and dimorphism of gender identity from conception to maturity*. Baltimore: Johns Hopkins University Press.

Money, J., & Tucker, P. (1975). *Sexual signatures: On being a man or a woman*. Boston: Little, Brown.

Morin, S. F., & Schultz, S. J. (1978). The gay movement and the rights of children. *Journal of Social Issues, 34*(2), 137–148.

Moses, A. (1977). Playing it straight: A study of identity management in a sample of lesbian women (Doctoral dissertation, University of California, Berkeley, 1977). *Dissertation Abstracts International, 39*(2), 1149A.

Mussen, P. H. (1969). Early sex-role development. In D. A. Goslin (Ed.), *Handbook of socialization theory and research*. Chicago: Rand McNally.

National Education Association. (1974). *1974–1975 Book of resolutions*. Washington, DC: Author.

National Education Association. (1994). Teaching and counseling gay and lesbian students. *Human and civil rights action sheet*. Washington, DC: Author.

National Education Association. (1988, July 7). Student sexual orientation. *National Education Association Resolution C–11*. Adopted by NEA in 1988 at NEA convention, New Orleans.

National Gay and Lesbian Task Force. (1993). *National Gay and Lesbian Task Force Policy Institute. Anti-gay/lesbian violence, victimization and defamation in 1992*. Washington, DC: Author.

Neergaard, L. (1993, October 28). New indicators show AIDS #1 killer of men 25–44. *Associated Press*.

Newman, B. S., & Muzzonigro, P. G. (1993). The effects of traditional family values on the coming out process of gay male adolescents. *Adolescence, 28*, 213–226.

Nurius, P. S. (1983). Mental health implications of sexual orientation. *Journal of Sex Research, 19*, 119–136.

Olson, M. (1986). *From closet to classroom: A perspective on gay and lesbian individuals in U.S. schools*. Grand Forks, ND: University of North Dakota Bookstore.

Olson, M. (1987). A study of gay and lesbian teachers. *Journal of Homosexuality, 13*, 73–81.

Oprah Winfrey Show. (1986, November 13). *Homophobia*. Transcript #8639. New York: Journal Graphics.

Oprah Winfrey Show. (1994, October 24). *Schools for gay teens.* Burrelles Transcripts.

Ostling, R. N. (1992, March 16). Christians spar in Harvard yard. *Time,* p. 49.

Pagelow, M. (1980). Heterosexual and lesbian single mothers: A comparison of problems coping and solutions. *Journal of Homosexuality, 5,* 189–205.

Patterson, C. J. (1992). Children of lesbian and gay parents. *Child Development, 14,* 177–196.

Paul, J. P. (1985). Bisexuality: Reassessing our paradigms of sexuality. In F. Klein & T. J. Wolf (Eds.), *Two lives to lead: Bisexuality in men and women* (pp. 21–34). New York: Harrington Park Press.

Paul, W., Weinrich, J. D., Gonsiorek, J. C. & Hotvedt, M. E. (Eds.). (1982). *Homosexuality: Social, psychological and biological issues.* Beverly Hills, CA: Sage.

Pennington, S. B. (1987). Children of lesbian mothers. In F. W. Bozett (Ed.), *Gay and lesbian parents* (pp. 58–74). New York: Praeger.

People For the American Way. (1993). *Hostile climate: A state by state report on anti–gay activities.* New York: Author.

Peplau, L. A. (1983/1984). What homosexuals want. In *Human sexuality* (pp. 201–207). Guilford, CT: Dushkin Publishing.

Peterson, A. C., & Crockett, L. (1985). Pubertal timing and grade effects. *Journal of Youth and Adolescence, 14,* 191–206.

Peterson, N. (1984, April 30). Coming to terms with gay parents. *USA Today,* p. 30.

Pillard, E., & Weinrich, J. (1986). Evidence of familial nature of male homosexuality. *Archives of General Psychiatry, 43,* 808–812.

Plant, R. (1986). *The pink triangle: The Nazi war against homosexuals.* New York: Holt.

Pool, R. (1993). Evidence for homosexuality gene. *Science, 261,* 291–292.

Price, J. (1982). High school students' attitudes toward homosexuality. *Journal of School Health, 52,* 469–474.

Remafedi, G. (1987). Male homosexuality: The adolescent's perspective. *Pediatrics, 79,* 326–330.

Remafedi, G., Farrow, J. A., & Deisher, R. W. (1991, June). Risk factors for attempted suicide in gay and bisexual youth. *Pediatrics, 87*(6), 869–875.

Riddle, D. (1978). Relating to children: Gays as role models. *Journal of Social Issues, 34*(3), 38–58.

Riddle, D. (1985). In K. Obear (Writer). *Opening doors to understanding and acceptance: A facilitator's guide for presenting workshops on lesbians and gay issues* (p. 14). Chicago: Campaign to End Homophobia.

Riddle, D. I., & Morin, S. F. (1977, November). Removing the stigma: Data from individuals. *APA Monitor, 16,* 28.

Roane, K. R. (1994, May 22). Two white sport coats, two pink carnations: One couple for a prom. *New York Times,* p. Y12.

Rochlin, M. (1992). Heterosexual questionnaire. In W. J. Blumenfeld (Ed.), *Homophobia: How we all pay the price* (pp. 203–204). Boston: Beacon Press.

Rofes, E. (1989). Opening up the classroom closet: Responding to the educational needs of gay and lesbian youth. *Harvard Educational Review, 59,* 443–453.

Rubenstein, W. B. (Ed.). (1993). *Lesbians, gay men and the law.* New York: The New Press.

Ruggerio, G. (1975). Sexual criminality in the early renaissance. *Journal of Social History, 8,* 18–37.

Saghir, M. T., & Robbins, E. (1973). *Male and female homosexuality: A comprehensive investigation.* Baltimore: Williams & Wilkins.

Savin-Williams, R. C. (1988, March). Theoretical perspectives accounting for adolescent homosexuality. *Journal of Adolescent Health Care, 9*(2), 95–104.

Savin-Williams, R. C. (1990). *Gay and lesbian youth: Expressions of identity.* New York: Hemisphere.

Schafer, S. (1976). Sexual and social problems among lesbians. *Journal of Sex Research, 12,* 50–69.

Schulenburg, J. A. (1985). *Gay parenting: A complete guide for gay men and lesbians with children.* Garden City, NY: Anchor Books.

Scott, J. (pseud.). (1978). *Wives who love women.* New York: Walker.

Sears, J. T. (1991). Educators, homosexuality and homosexual students: Are personal feelings related to professional beliefs? *Journal of Homosexuality, 22,* 29–79.

Shilts, R. (1993). *Conduct unbecoming: Gays and lesbians in the U.S. military.* New York: St. Martin's Press.

Shurtleff, W. (Ed.). (1898). *Records of the Colony of New Plymouth in New England.* Boston: William White.

Slaby, R. G., & Frey, K. S. (1975). Development of gender constancy and selective attention to same-sex models. *Child Development, 46,* 849–856.

Smith, D. (1985). An ethnographic study of homosexual teachers' perspectives (Doctoral dissertation, State University of New York, Albany, 1985). *Dissertation Abstracts International, 46,* A66.

Smith, S. (1994, April 10). Gays meet to compare their ordinary lives. *Miami Herald,* p. B2.

Sophie, J. (1985/1986). A critical examination of stage theories of lesbian identity development. *Journal of Homosexuality, 12,* 39–51.

Spence, J. T., & Helmreich, R. L. (1978). *Masculinity and femininity: Their psychological dimensions, correlates, and antecedents.* Austin, TX: University of Texas Press.

Stewart, T. A. (1991, December 16). Gay in corporate America. *Fortune,* 42–55.

Stoller, M. (1972). Sexual orientation and self-perception. In K. R. Pilner, M. Blanstein, I. M. Spiegel, T. Alloway, & L. Krames (Eds.), *Advances in the study of communication and affect: Perception of emotion in self and others* (Vol. 5). New York: Plenum.

Taylor, C. L., Jr. (1978). *El ambiente: Male homosexual social life in Mexico City.* Unpublished doctoral dissertation, University of California, Berkeley.

Telljohann, S. K., & Price, J. H. (1993). A qualitative examination of adolescent homosexuals' life experiences: Ramifications for secondary school personnel. *Journal of Homosexuality, 26,* 41–56.

Thornton, R., & Nardi, P. M. (1975). The dynamics of role acquisition. *American Journal of Sociology, 46,* 339–347.

Thou shalt not lie. (1994, April 27). *TWN (The Weekly News),* p. 14.

Tierney, L. M., Jr., McPhee, S. J., & Papadakis, M. A. (1995). *Current medical diagnosis and treatment 1995.* Norwalk, CT: Appleton & Lange.

Tinney, J. S. (1983). Interconnections. In *Interracial books for children bulletin* (Vol. 14, pp. 3–4). New York: Council on Interracial Books for Children.

Tremble, B., Schneider, M., & Appathurai, C. (1989). Growing up gay or lesbian in a multicultural context. *Journal of Homosexuality, 17*(3/4), 253–267.

Tripp, C. A. (1987). *The homosexual matrix* (2nd ed.). New York: Meridian.

Troiden, R. R. (1979). Becoming homosexual: A model for gay identity acquisition. *Psychiatry, 42,* 362–373.

Troiden, R. R. (1989). The formation of homosexual identities. *Journal of Homosexuality, 17*(1–2), 43–73.

Turner, P. H., Scadden, L., & Harris, M. B. (1985, March). *Parenting in gay and lesbian families.* Paper presented at the first meeting of the Future of Parenting Symposium, Chicago, IL.

Uribe, V., & Harbeck, K. M. (1991). Addressing the needs of lesbian, gay and bisexual youth. *Journal of Homosexuality, 22,* 9–28.

U.S. Department of Health and Human Services. (1989). *Report on the secretary's task force on youth suicide.* Washington, DC: Author.

U.S. Department of Justice. National Institute of Justice. (1987). *The response of the criminal justice system to bias crime: An exploratory review.* Washington, DC: Author.

The Victory Fund. (1993). Washington, DC: Author.

Wagner, G., Serafini, J., Rabin, J., Remien, R., & Williams, J. (1994). Integration of one's religion and homosexuality: A weapon against internalized homophobia? *Journal of Homosexuality, 26*(4), 91–110.

Wallechinsky, D., Wallace, I., & Wallace, A. (1977). *The book of lists* (pp. 336–338). New York: William Morrow.

Walling, D. R. (1993). Gay teens at risk. *Fastback series of Phi Delta Kappa Educational Foundation* (p. 371). Bloomington, IN: Phi Delta Kappa Educational Foundation.

Weeks, R. B., Derdeyn, A., & Langman, M. (1975). Two cases of children of homosexuals. *Child Psychology and Human Development, 6*, 26–32.

Weiner, H. (1994, March 22). The buzz about bisexuality: Celebs raising its visibility in the 90's culture. *Miami Herald*, pp. E1, E5.

Wendell, D., Onorato, I., Allen, D., McCray, E., Sweeney, P., & state and local health departments. (1990). *HIV seroprevalence among adolescents and young adults in selected clinic settings, United States, 1988–1990.* Paper presented at the sixth International Conference on AIDS, San Francisco, CA.

Will all the homophobes please stand up? (1994, June 20). *New York*, 40–45.

Wilson, P. M. (1986). Black culture and sexuality. *Journal of Social Work and Human Sexuality, 4*(3), 29–46.

Woods, S. (1989). The contextual realities of being a lesbian physical education teacher: Living in two worlds (Doctoral dissertation, University of Massachusetts, Amherst, 1989). *Dissertation Abstracts International, 51*(3), 788.

Wurzel, J. (1986). The functions and forms of prejudice. In *A world of difference: Resource guide for reduction of prejudice.* Boston: Anti-Defamation League of B'nai B'rith and Facing History and Ourselves National Foundation, Inc.

Wyers, N. L. (1984). *Lesbian and gay spouses and parents: Homosexuality in the family.* Portland, OR: School of Social Work, Portland State University.

Zinik, G. (1985). Identity conflict or adaptive flexibility? Bisexuality reconsidered. In F. Klein & T. J. Wolf (Eds.), *Two lives to lead: Bisexuality in men and women* (pp. 7–17). New York: Harrington Park Press.

Appendix A: Further Reading

The following bibliography of books and periodicals has been selected for educators and other professionals who help students of different sexual orientations and their families. Books are available through bookstores, libraries, and publishers.

(Reader code: E = educators and other professionals, Y = younger readers, T = teenagers, P = parents, F = fiction, N = nonfiction)

BOOKS

Abelove, H., Barale, M. A., & Halperin, D. (1993). *The lesbian and gay studies reader*. New York: Routledge. (EN)

Allport, G. (1954). *The nature of prejudice*. Reading, MA: Addison-Wesley. (EN)

Alpert, H. (1988). *We are everywhere: Writings by and about lesbian parents*. Marshall, MN: Crossing Press. (PEN)

Altman, D. (1983). *The homosexualization of America: The Americanization of the homosexual*. Boston: Beacon Press. (EN)

Alyson, S. (Ed.). (1991). *Young, gay, & proud!* Boston: Alyson. (TN)

Andrews, N. (1994). *Family: A portrait of gay and lesbian America*. New York: HarperCollins. (PTEN)

Atkinson, D. R., Morten, G., & Sue, D. W. (1979). *Counseling American Minorities*. Dubuque, IA: Brown. (EN)

Balka, C., & Rose, A. (Eds.). (1991). *Twice blessed: On being lesbian or gay and Jewish*. Boston: Beacon Press. (TN)

Barrett, M. B. (1990). *Invisible lives: The truth about millions of women—loving women*. New York: Perennial Lib. (EN)

Bawer, B. (1993). *A place at the table: The gay individual in American society*. New York: Poseidon Press. (TEN)

Beck, E. T., (Ed.). (1989). *Nice Jewish girls: A lesbian anthology*. Boston: Beacon Press. (TEN)

Benkov, L. (1994). *Reinventing the family*. New York: Crown Publishers. (PEN)

Bérubé, A. (1990). *Coming out under fire: The history of gay men and women in World War Two*. New York: Free Press. (EN)

Berzon, B. (Ed.). (1992). *Positively gay: New approaches to gay and lesbian life*. Berkeley, CA: Celestial Arts. (PTEN)

Blumenfeld, W. J. (Ed.). (1992). *Homophobia: How we all pay the price*. Boston: Beacon Press. (EN)

Blumenfeld, W. J., & Raymond, D. (1993). *Looking at gay and lesbian life* (2nd ed.). Boston: Beacon Press. (EN)

Borhek, M. V. (1984). *My son Eric*. Cleveland, OH: Pilgrim Press. (PEN)

Borhek, M. V. (1993). *Coming out to parents*. Cleveland, OH: Pilgrim Press. (PTEN)

Boswell, J. (1980). *Christianity, social tolerance and homosexuality: Gay people in Western Europe from the beginning of the Christian era to the fourteenth century*. Chicago: University of Chicago Press. (EN)

Bozett, F. W. (Ed.). (1987). *Gay and lesbian parents*. New York: Praeger. (PEN)

Bozett, F. W., & Sussman, M. B. (Eds.). (1990). *Homosexuality and family relations*. Binghamton, NY: Haworth Press. (EN)

Brown, H. (1989). *Familiar faces, hidden lives*. Orlando, FL: Harcourt, Brace, Jovanovich. (EN)

Brown, R. M. (1988). *Rubyfruit jungle*. New York: Bantam. (TF)

Buxton, A. P. (1994). *The coming-out crisis for straight spouses and families*. New York: John Wiley & Sons. (PEN)

Clark, D. (1992). *The new loving someone gay*. Berkeley, CA: Celestial Arts. (TEN)

Coffin, W. S. (1982). *The courage to love*. New York: Harper & Row. (TEN)

Cohen, S., & Cohen, D. (1992). *When someone you know is gay*. New York: Dell. (TEN)

Coles, R., & Stokes, J. (1985). *Sex and the American teenager*. New York: Rolling Stone Press. (EN)

Comstock, G. D. (1991). *Violence against lesbians and gay men*. New York: Columbia University Press. (EN)

Corley, A. (1990). *The final closet*. Miami, FL: Editech Press. (EN)

Cowan, T. D. (1988). *Gay men and women who enriched the world*. New Canaan, CT: Mulvey Books. (TEN)

Curb, R., & Manahan, N. (Eds.). (1986). *Lesbian nuns: Breaking silence*. New York: Warner Books. (EN)

Curtis, W. (Ed.). (1988). *Revelations: A collection of gay male coming out stories*. Boston: Alyson. (TEN)

DeCecco, J. (Ed.). (1987). *Gay relationships*. New York: Harrington Park Press. (EN)

D'Emilio, J. (1983). *Sexual politics, sexual communities: The making of a homosexual minority in the United States, 1940–1970*. Chicago: University of Chicago Press. (EN)

D'Emilio, J. (1985). *Bashers, baiters and bigots: Homophobia in American society*. New York: Harrington Park Press. (EN)

Denman, R. M. (1990). *Let my people in: A lesbian minister tells of her struggles to live openly and maintain her ministry*. New York: Morrow. (PEN)

Dew, R. F. (1994). *The family heart: A memoir of when our son came out*. New York: Addison-Wesley. (PEN)

Dietz, S. D., & Hicks, M. J. P. (1992). *Take these broken wings and learn to fly: The AIDS support book for patients, families and friends*. Tucson, AZ: Harbinger House. (EN)

Doaghe, R. E. (1989). *Common sons*. Austin, TX: Edward William. (TEN)

Donovan, J. (1969). *I'll get there: It better be worth the trip*. New York: HarperCollins Children's Books. (Y)

Duberman, M. (1993). *Stonewall*. New York: Dutton. (EN)

Dudley, W. (Ed.). (1993). *Homosexuality: Opposing viewpoints*. San Diego, CA: Greenhaven Press. (EN)

Dyer, K. (1990). *Gays in uniform*. Boston: Alyson. (EN)

Eichberg, R. (1991). *Coming out: An act of love*. New York: Plume. (TEN)

Faderman, L. (1991). *Odd girls and twilight lovers: A history of lesbian life in twentieth-century America*. New York: Penguin. (EN)

Fairchild, B., & Hayward, N. (1989). *Now that you know: What every parent should know about homosexuality*. San Diego: Harcourt, Brace, Jovanovich. (PEN)

Fricke, A. (1981). *Reflections of a rock lobster: A story about growing up gay*. Boston: Alyson. (TEN)

Fuss, D. (Ed.). (1991). *Inside/out: Lesbian theories—gay theories*. New York: Routledge. (EN)

Garden, N. (1992). *Annie on my mind*. New York: Farrar, Straus & Giroux. (TF)

Geller, T. (Ed.). (1990). *Bisexuality: A reader and sourcebook*. Ojai, CA: Times Change. (EN)

Grahn, J. (1991). *Another mother tongue: Gay words, gay worlds*. Boston: Beacon. (EN)

Green, R. (1987). *The "sissy boy syndrome" and the development of homosexuality*. New Haven, CT: Yale University Press. (EN)

Griffin, C., & Wirth, M. A. (1990). *Beyond acceptance*. New York: St. Martin's Press. (EN)

Hall, R. (1992). *The well of loneliness*. Cutchoque, NY: Buccaneer Books. (TF)

Hanckel, F., & Cunningham, J. (1979). *A way of love, a way of life: A young person's introduction to what it means to be gay*. New York: Lothrop, Lee & Shepard. (TEN)

Harbeck, K. M. (Ed.). (1992).*Coming out of the classroom closet: Gay and lesbian students, teachers and curricula*. New York: Harrington Park Press. (EN)

Hein, K. (1989). *AIDS: Trading fears for facts—a guide for teens*. Mount Vernon, NY: Consumers Union. (TEN)

Herdt, G. (Ed.). (1989). *Gay and lesbian youth*. New York: Harrington Park Press. (EN)

Herek, G. (1984). *Beyond "homophobia": A social psychological perspective on attitudes toward lesbians and gay men*. Binghamton, NY: Haworth Press. (EN)

Heron, A. (Ed.). (1983). *One teenager in ten*. Boston: Alyson. (PTEN)

Heron, A. (Ed.). (1994). *Two teenagers in twenty: Writings by gay and lesbian youth*. Boston: Alyson. (PTEN)

Hippler, M. (1989). *Matlovich: The good soldier*. Boston: Alyson. (EN)

Holmes, S. (Ed.). (1994). *Testimonies: A collection of lesbian coming out stories*. Boston: Alyson. (PEN)

Holobaugh, J., & Hale, K. (1992). *Torn allegiances: The story of a gay cadet*. Boston: Alyson. (TEN)

Homes, A. M. (1989). *Jack*. New York: Macmillan Child Group. (YF)

Hunter, N., Michaelson, S., & Stoddard, T. (1992). *The rights of lesbians and gay men: The basic ACLU guide to a gay person's rights*. Carbondale, IL: Southern Illinois University Press. (EN)

Hutchins, L., & Kaahumanu, L. (Eds.). (1991). *Bi any other name: Bisexual people speak out*. Boston: Alyson. (EN)

Isay, R. (1989). *Being homosexual: Gay men and their development*. New York: Farrar, Straus & Giroux. (EN)

James, J. S. (1992). *AIDS treatment news* (Issues 76–125, Vol. 2). Berkeley, CA: Celestial Arts. (EN)

Jennings, K. (Ed.). (1994). *Becoming visible: A reader in gay and lesbian history for high school and college students*. Boston: Alyson. (TEN)

Jennings, K. (Ed.). (1994). *One teacher in ten: Lesbian and gay educators tell their stories*. Boston: Alyson. (EN)

Kenan, R. (1994). *James Baldwin*. New York: Chelsea House. (TEN)

Khayatt, M. D. (1992). *Lesbian teachers: An invisible presence*. Albany, NY: State University of New York Press. (EN)

Kinsey, A. C., Pomeroy, W. B., & Martin, C. E. (1948). *Sexual behavior in the human male*. Philadelphia: W.B. Saunders. (EN)

Kinsey, A. C., Pomeroy, W., Martin, C. E., & Gebhard, R. (1953). *Sexual behavior in the human female*. Philadelphia: W.B. Saunders. (EN)

Klein, F., & Wolf, T. J. (Eds.). (1985). *Two lives to lead: Bisexuality in men and women*. New York: Harrington Park Press. (EN)

Kramer, L. (1989). *Reports from the Holocaust: The making of an AIDS activist*. New York: St. Martin's Press. (EN)

Landau, E. (1986). *Different drummer: Homosexuality in America*. New York: J. Messner. (TEN)

Leinen, S. (1993). *Gay cops*. New Brunswick, NJ: Rutgers University Press. (EN)

Leming, D. (1994). *James Baldwin*. New York: Knopf. (EN)

Lewes, K. (1988). *The psychoanalytic theory of male homosexuality*. New York: Simon & Schuster. (EN)

Likosky, S. (Ed.). (1992). *Coming out: An anthology of international gay and lesbian writings*. New York: Pantheon Books. (EN)

Louganis, G. (1995). *Breaking the surface*. New York: Random House. (TEN)

MacPike, L. (Ed.). (1989). *There's something I've been meaning to tell you*. Tallahassee, FL: Naiad Press. (PTEN)

Marcus, E. (1992). *Making history: The struggle for gay and lesbian equal rights*. New York: HarperCollins. (EN)

Marcus, E. (1993). *Is it a choice?* New York: HarperCollins. (PTEN)

Martin, A. (1993). *The lesbian and gay parenting handbook: Creating and raising our families*. New York: HarperCollins. (PEN)

McNaught, B. (1989). *On being gay*. New York: St. Martin's Press. (PTEN)

McNaught, B. (1993). *Gay issues in the workplace*. New York: St. Martin's Press. (TEN)

McNeill, J. J. (1988). *The church and the homosexual* (3rd ed.). Boston: Beacon Press. (EN)

Mickens, E. (1994). *The 100 best companies for gay men and lesbians*. New York: Pocketbooks. (EN)

Miller, A. (1984). *Thou shalt not be aware: Society's betrayal of the child*. New York: Farrar, Straus & Giroux. (EN)

Miller, N. (1989). *In search of gay America*. New York: Atlantic Monthly Press. (EN)

Mohr, R. D. (1988). *Gays/justice: A study of ethics, society and law*. New York: Columbia University Press. (EN)

Mohr, R. D. (1994). *A more perfect union: Why straight America must stand up for gay rights*. Boston: Beacon. (EN)

Monette, P. (1988). *Borrowed time: An AIDS memoir*. New York: Avon. (EN)

Monette, P. (1992). *Becoming a man: Half a life's story*. New York: Harcourt, Brace, Jovanovich. (EN)

Morales, A. L. (1986). *Getting home alive*. Ithaca, NY: Firebrand Books. (EN)

Morales, E. S. (1992). Counseling Latino gays and Latina lesbians. In S. H. Dworkin, & F. J. Guiterrez (Eds.). *Counseling gay men and lesbians: Journey to the end of the rainbow*. Alexandria, VA: American Association for Counseling & Development. (EN)

Morse, C., & Larkin, J. (Eds.). (1988). *Gay and lesbian poetry of our time: An anthology*. New York: St. Martin's Press. (EN)

Muller, A. (1987). *Parents matter*. Tallahassee, FL: Naiad Press. (PEN)

Nardi, P. M., Sanders, D., & Marmor, J. (1994). *Growing up before stonewall*. New York: Routledge. (EN)

Nava, M., & Dawidoff, R. (1994). *Created equal: Why gay rights matter to America*. New York: St. Martin's Press. (EN)

O'Brien, S. (1995). *Lives of notable gays and lesbians: Willa Cather*. New York: Chelsea House. (PTEN)

Olson, M. R. (1986). *From closet to classroom: A perspective on gay and lesbian individuals in U.S. schools*. Grand Forks, ND: University of North Dakota Bookstore. (EN)

Pallone, D., & Steinberg, A. (1991). *Behind the mask: My double life in baseball*. New York: Dutton. (TEN)

Paul, W., Weinrich, J. D., Gonsiorek, J. C., & Hofvedt, M. E. (Eds.). (1982). *Homosexuality: Social, psychological and biological issues*. Beverly Hills, CA: Sage. (EN)

Penelope, J., & Wolfe, S. J. (Eds.). (1993). *Lesbian culture: An anthology*. Freedom, CA: Crossing Press. (EN)

Pharr, S. (1988). *Homophobia: A weapon of sexism*. Inverness, CA: Chardon Press. (EN)

Plant, R. (1986). *The pink triangle: The Nazi war against homosexuals*. New York: Holt. (EN)

Preston, J. (Ed.). (1994). *A member of the family*. New York: Plume. (EN)

Rafkin, L. (Ed.). (1987) *Different daughters: A book by mothers of lesbians*. Pittsburgh, PA: Cleis Press. (PTEN)

Rafkin, L. (Ed.). (1990). *Different mothers: Sons and daughters of lesbians talk about their lives.* Pittsburgh, PA: Cleis Press. (PTEN)

Ramos, J. (Ed.). (1987). *Companeras. Latina lesbians: An anthology*. New York: Latina Lesbian History Project. (EN)

Ratti, R. (Ed.). (1993). *A lotus of another color: An unfolding of the South Asian gay and lesbian experience*. Boston: Alyson. (EN)

Reid, J. (1993). *The best little boy in the world: The true and moving story of coming to terms with being gay*. New York: Ballantine. (PTEN)

Remafedi, G. *Death by denial*. (1994). Boston: Alyson. (PTEN)

Reynolds, M. (Ed.). (1993). *The Penguin book of lesbian short stories*. New York: Viking. (EN)

Roscoe, W. (1989). *Living the spirit: A gay native American anthology*. New York: St. Martin's Press. (EN)

Rubenstein, W. B. (Ed.). (1993). *Lesbians, gay men and the law*. New York: The New Press. (EN)

Savin-Williams, R. C. (1990). *Gay and lesbian youth: Expressions of identity*. New York: Hemisphere. (EN)

Schulenburg, J. (1985). *Gay parenting: A complete guide for gay men and lesbians with children*. Garden City, NY: Anchor Books. (PEN)

Schulman, S. (1994). *My American history: Lesbian and gay life during the Reagan/Bush years*. New York: Routledge. (EN)

Sears, J. T. (1991). *Growing up gay in the South: Race, gender and journeys of the spirit*. New York: Haworth Press. (TEN)

Sherman, P., & Bernstein, S. (Eds.) (1994). *Uncommon heroes: A celebration of heroes and role models for gay and lesbian Americans*. New York: Fletcher Press. (PTEN)

Shilts, R. (1982). *The mayor of Castro Street: The life and times of Harvey Milk*. New York: St. Martin's Press. (EN)

Shilts, R. (1987). *And the band played on: People, politics, and the AIDS epidemic*. New York: St. Martin's Press. (EN)

Shilts, R. (Ed.). (1992). *Sexuality and the curriculum*. New York: Columbia University Press. (EN)

Shilts, R. (1993). *Conduct unbecoming: Gays and lesbians in the U.S. military*. New York: St. Martin's Press. (EN)

Siegel, S., & Lowe, E., Jr. (1994). *Uncharted lives: The psychological journey of gay men*. New York: Dutton. (EN)

Silverstein, C. (1977). *A family matter: A parents' guide to homosexuality*. New York: McGraw-Hill. (PEN)

Singer, B. L. (1994). *Growing up lesbian*. New York: The New Press. (EN)

Singer, B. L., & Deschamps, D. (Eds.). (1994). *Gay and lesbian stats: A pocket guide of facts and figures*. New York: The New Press. (EN)

Skidelsky, R. (1986). *John Maynard Keynes: Hopes betrayed, 1883–1920*. New York: Viking. (EN)

Spoto, D. (1985). *The kindness of strangers: The life of Tennessee Williams*. Boston: Little, Brown. (EN)

Steffan, J. (1993). *Honor bound*. New York: Avon. (TEN)

Toder, N. (1991). *Choices*. Boston: Alyson. (EN)

Tripp, C. A. (1987). *The homosexual matrix* (2nd ed.). New York: Meridian. (EN)

Vaid, U. (1995). *Margin to center: The mainstreaming of gay and lesbian liberation*. New York: Anchor Books. (EN)

Wallechinsky, D., Wallace, I., & Wallace, A. (1978). *The book of lists*. New York: Bantam Books. (EN)

Walters, A. L. (1992). *Talking Indian: Reflections on survival and writing*. Ithaca, NY: Firebrand Books. (EN)

Waugh, E. (1982). *Brideshead revisited.* New York: Little. (TEF)

Webster, H. (1991). *Family secrets: How telling and not telling affects our children, our relationships and our lives.* New York: Addison-Wesley. (PEN)

Weinberg, M. S., Williams, C. J., & Pryor, D. W. (1994). *Dual attraction: Understanding bisexuality.* New York: Oxford University Press. (EN)

Weinrich, J. D. (1987). *Sexual landscapes: Why we are what we are, why we love whom we love.* New York: Scribner's. (EN)

Weston, K. (1991). *Families we choose: Lesbians, gays, kinship.* New York: Columbia University Press. (EN)

White, E. (Ed.). (1992). *Gay short fiction.* Boston: Faber & Faber. (EF)

White, M. (1994). *Stranger at the gate: To be gay and Christian in America.* New York: Simon & Schuster. (EN)

Whitlock, K. (1989). *Bridges of respect: Creating support for lesbian and gay youth.* Philadelphia: American Friends Service Committee. (EN)

Wilde, O. (1990). *The picture of Dorian Gray.* Cutchoque, NY: Buccaneer Books. (TEF)

Williams, W. (1987). *The spirit and the flesh: Sexual diversity in American Indian culture.* New York: Harper & Row. (EN)

Wolff, C. G. (1986). *Emily Dickinson.* New York: Knopf. (EN)

Woodman, N. J. (Ed.). (1992). *Lesbian and gay lifestyles: A guide for counseling and education.* New York: Irvington. (EN)

Woods, J. D., & Lucas, J. H. (1993). *The corporate closet: The professional lives of gay men in America*: New York: The Free Press. (EN)

Zanotti, B. (Ed.). (1986). *A faith of one's own: Explorations by Catholic lesbians.* Marshall, MN: Crossing Press. (EN)

PERIODICALS

Angier, N. (1993, March 12). Study suggests strong genetic role in lesbianism. *New York Times*, p. A8 (N), p. A11 (L). (EN)

Angier, N. (1993, July 18). Research on sex orientation doesn't neatly fit the mold. *New York Times*, p. 13. (EN)

Association for Supervision & Curriculum Development (ASCD). (1992, March). At-risk kids schools ignore. *Executive Educator* (Newsletter), *14*(3), 28–31. (EN)

Berkhan, W. (1990). *Guide to curriculum planning in suicide prevention.* Madison, WI: Wisconsin Department of Public Instruction. (EN)

Bernstein, R. A. (1988, February 24). My daughter is a lesbian. *New York Times*, p. A27. (PN)

Bidwell, R. J. (1988). The gay and lesbian teen: A case of denied adolescence. *Journal of Pediatric Health Care, 2*, 3–8. (EN)

Brownworth, V. A. (1992, March 24). America's worst kept secret: AIDS is devastating the nation's teenagers, and gay kids are dying by the thousands. *The Advocate, 602*, 38–46. (EN)

Burr, C. (1993, August 2). Genes vs. hormones. *New York Times*, p. A11 (N), p. A15 (L). (EN)

Burr, C. (1993, March). Homosexuality and biology. *The Atlantic*, pp. 47–60. (EN)

Cage, M. C. (1993, March 10). Openly gay students face harassment and physical assaults on some campuses. *Chronicle of Higher Education, 39*(27), A22. (EN)

Caywood, C. (1993, April). Reaching out to gay teens: Library materials that offer support to gay and lesbian teens can save lives. *School Library Journal*, 50. (EN)

Chan, C. S. (1989). Issues of identity development among Asian-American lesbians and gay men. *Journal of Counseling & Development, 68*, 16–20. (EN)

Cohen, E. (1993, September 30). A house with no closets: Delta Lambda Phi is the first gay frat. *Rolling Stone*, p. 87. (TEN)

D'Augelli, A. R. (1992, September). Lesbian and gay male undergraduates' experiences of harassment and fear on campus. *Journal of Interpersonal Violence, 7*(3), 383. (EN)

Dennis, D. I., & Harlow, R. E. (1986). Gay youth and the right to education. *Yale Law & Policy Review, 4*(2), 446–478. (EN)

Dougherty, J. W. (1990). *Effective programs for at-risk adolescents.* Fastback 308. Bloomington, IN: Phi Delta Kappa Educational Foundation. (EN)

Fejes, F., & Petrich, K. (1993, December). Invisibility, homophobia and heterosexism: Lesbians, gays and the media. *Critical Studies in Mass Communication, 10*(4), 396. (EN)

Friend, R. A. (1993, February). Undoing homophobia in schools. *Education Digest,* 62–68. (EN)

Gelman, D. (1993, November 8). Tune in and come out: Growing acceptance of gays and bisexuals in high schools. *Newsweek,* pp. 70–71. (TEN)

Gibson, P. (1989). Gay male and lesbian youth suicide. In *Report of the secretary's task force on youth suicide: Prevention and interventions in youth suicide.* Washington, DC: U.S. Department of Health and Human Services. (EN)

Governor Weld offers aid to gay pupils: All schools in Massachusetts will be asked to promote more tolerant climate. (1993, July 4). *New York Times,* p. 11. (EN)

Green, J. (1993, June 13). Out and organized: As the national gay movement shies away from the subject of homosexuality among the young, some gay teen-agers are determined to open the subject up. *New York Times,* p. V1. (TEN)

Grossman, A. H. (1992). Inclusion not exclusion: Recreation service delivery to lesbian, gay and bisexual youth. *Journal of Physical Education, Recreation and Dance, 63*(4), 45–47. (EN)

Gurney, R. (1993, March). Looking for a safe haven: Helping students struggling with their sexual identity. *NEA Today, 11,* 7, 27. (EN)

Harlan, H. (1992, April 5). Books help children of gay parents. *New York Times,* sec. 4A, p. ED8. (PEN)

High school council passes a gay ban on leaders. (1993, May 16). *New York Times,* sec. 1, p. 17. (TEN)

Hoffman, M. (1993, September). Teaching "Torch Song": Gay literature in the classroom ("Torch Song Trilogy" by Harvey Fierstein). *English Journal, 82*(5), 55–58. (EN)

Humm, A. J. (1982). Homosexuality: The new frontier in sexuality education. *Family Life Educator, 10*(3), 13–18. (EN)

Hunter, J. (1990). Violence against lesbian and gay male youths. *Journal of Interpersonal Violence, 5*(3), 295–300. (EN)

Hunter, J., & Schaecher, R. (1987). Stresses on lesbian and gay adolescents in schools. *Social Work in Education, 9,* 180–184. (EN)

Kournay, R. F. (1987). Suicide among homosexual adolescents. *Journal of Homosexuality, 13*(4), 111–117. (EN)

Krysiak, G. J. (1987, March). Needs of gay students for acceptance and support. *School Counselor, 34,* 304–307. (EN)

Mallon, G. (1992, November/December) Gay and no place to go: Assessing the needs of gay and lesbian adolescents in out-of-home care settings. *Child Welfare, 71*(6), 547. (EN)

Martin, A. D., & Hetrick, E. S. (1988). The stigmatization of the gay and lesbian adolescent. *Journal of Homosexuality, 15*(1/2), 163–183. (EN)

Masello, D. (1994, January 2). In my father's house. *New York Times Magazine,* p. 13. (TEN)

McFarland, W. P. (1993, September). A developmental approach to gay and lesbian youth. *Journal of Humanistic Education and Development, 32*(1), 17–29. (EN)

Mestel, R. (1994, January). X marks the spot. *Discover,* p. 71. (EN)

New book series for gay teen-agers. (1992, November 24). *New York Times,* p. B3. (TEN)

Newman, B. S., & Muzzonigro, P. G. (1993). The effects of traditional family values on the coming out process of gay male adolescents. *Adolescence, 28,* 213–226. (EN)

O'Connor, J. J. (1991, May 19). Gay's images: TV's mixed signals. *New York Times,* p. H1. (EN)

Pfeifer, J. K. (1986). *Teenage suicide: What can the schools do?* Fastback 234. Bloomington, IN: Phi Delta Kappa Educational Foundation. (EN)

Pool, R. (1993, July 26). Evidence for homosexuality gene. *Science, 261,* 291–292. (EN)

Remafedi, G. (1987). Homosexual youth: A challenge to contemporary society. *Journal of the American Medical Association, 258,* 222–225. (EN)

Remafedi, G. (1987). Male homosexuality: The adolescent's perspective. *Pediatrics, 79,* 326–330. (EN)

Remafedi, G. (1993, March). The impact of training on school professionals' knowledge, beliefs, and behaviors regarding HIV/AIDS and adolescent homosexuality. *Journal of School Health, 63,* 3. (EN)

Remafedi, G., Farrow, J. A., & Deisher, R. W. (1991, June). Risk factors for attempted suicide in gay and bisexual youth. *Pediatrics, 87*(6), 869–875. (EN)

Rimer, S. (1993, December 12). Massachusetts movement: Rights for gay students in public school. *New York Times,* p. E2. (TEN)

Rofes, E. (1989). Opening up the classroom closet: Responding to the educational needs of gay and lesbian youth. *Harvard Educational Review, 59,* 443–453. (EN)

Rudolph, J. (1988, November). Counselors' attitudes toward homosexuality: A selective review of the literature. *Journal of Counseling & Development, 67*(3), 165–168. (EN)

Schaecher, R. (1989, Winter). Reducing homophobia among educators and students. *Independent School, 48,* 29–35. (EN)

Schneider, S. G., Farberow, N. L., & Nikruks, G. N. (1989, Winter). Suicidal behavior in adolescent and young adult gay men. *Suicide and Life-Threatening Behavior, 19*(4), 381. (EN)

School district allows gay students to meet. (1994, January 15). *New York Times,* p. 8. (TEN)

Sears, J. T. (1987). Peering into the well of loneliness: The responsibility of educators to gay and lesbian youth. In A. Molnar (Ed.), *Social issues and education: Challenge and responsibility.* Alexandria, VA: Association for Supervision and Curriculum Development. (EN)

Sears, J. T. (1991, September). Helping students understand and accept sexual diversity. *Educational Leadership, 49*(1), 54–56. (EN)

Sherrill, J. M. (1994). *The gay, lesbian, and bisexual students' guide to colleges, universities and graduate schools.* New York: New York University Press. (TEN)

Stover, D. (1992, May). The at-risk students schools continue to ignore. *Education Digest, 57,* 9, 36. (EN)

Tartagni, D. (1978). Counseling gays in a school setting. *School Counselor, 26,* 26–32. (EN)

Treadway, L., & Yakum, J. (1992, September). Creating a safer school environment for lesbian and gay students. *Journal of School Health, 62,* 7, 352. (EN)

Tremble, B., Schneider, M., & Appathurai, C. (1989). Growing up gay or lesbian in a multicultural context. *Journal of Homosexuality, 17*(3/4), 253–267. (EN)

Virginia school board prohibits anti-gay harassment by students. (1992, July 27). *New York Times,* p. A7. (EN)

Williams, R. F. (1993, Spring). Gays and lesbian teenagers: A reading ladder for students, media specialists and parents. *ALAN Review, 20*(3), 12–17. (EN)

Willis, S. (1991, March). Teaching gay students. *ASCD Update, 33,* 3. (EN)

Winerip, M. (1994, February 23). A high school club for gay students has gained a foothold, though not everyone may feel secure. *New York Times,* p. B7. (TEN)

Yarber, W. L. (1987). *AIDS education: Curriculum and health policy.* Fastback 265. Bloomington, IN: Phi Delta Kappa Educational Foundation. (EN)

Zera, D. (1992, Winter). Coming of age in a heterosexist world: The development of gay and lesbian adolescents. *Adolescence, 27,* 108, 849–854. (EN)

Appendix B: A Model Workshop on Homophobia for Educators

INTRODUCTION

One of the initial steps in helping gay and lesbian students is to establish an awareness of sexual diversity and homophobia among school personnel, with whom gay and lesbian students spend at least 11 years of their lives. All school employees have the ability to create a positive educational atmosphere of acceptance and understanding, or an atmosphere of rejection and discrimination that may result in intimidation, isolation, desperation, violence, or death.

The gay and lesbian school population includes students from all cultures, races, religions, economic levels, and disability groups. Therefore, many of them must cope with the problems associated with belonging to two or three minority groups.

Homophobia is institutionalized within our society and the best strategy for change is through education of school personnel, who are in the best position to make a difference in attitudes and beliefs based on facts rather than myths.

This workshop has been designed to involve 20 volunteer participants led by an experienced facilitator and co-facilitator to promote awareness and commitment to change. The workshop may be adapted for fewer or more participants. Although the model has been designed for educators, it can easily be tailored for other groups associated with school systems.

The workshop requires experienced and knowledgeable trainers because the workshop participants will have varying levels of knowledge and individual biases concerning homosexuality and homophobia. Facilitators must create a safe climate for discussion, acceptance of diverse opinions, and prevention of personal attacks. Empathetic participants who have an understanding and acceptance of people who are different from themselves will be helpful in the small group activities and general discussion. The estimated time for completing the workshop is 6 1/4 hours.

PREPARING FOR THE WORKSHOP

Checklist of Materials and Equipment

☐ Order ONE of the following videotapes. Preview the chosen videotape and prepare several questions that can be used to generate discussion in Activity J.

Homosexuality: The Adolescent's Perspective (30 minutes; 1987)
Six teenagers describe their lives to adolescent viewers, parents, and educators. [University of Minnesota, Media Distribution, Box 734 Mayo, 420 Delaware St. S.E., Minneapolis, MN 55455. Telephone: (612) 624-7906]

Pink Triangles: A Study of Prejudice Against Lesbians and Gay Men (35 minutes; 1982)
An award-winning documentary on homophobia. [Cambridge Documentary Films, Inc., P.O. Box 385, Cambridge, MA 02139. Telephone: (617) 354-3677 / (617) 492-7653]

Sexual Orientation: Reading Between the Labels (30 minutes; 1991)
Personal accounts from gay and lesbian teens interspersed with input from youth workers, medical experts, and parents of gays and lesbians. [NEWIST/CESA #7 Telecommunications, IS 1110, University of Wisconsin, Green Bay, WI 54311. Telephone: (414) 465-2599]

Reunion: One Family Overcomes Religious Homophobia (30 minutes)
This video features Dr. Carter Heyward, a lesbian ordained Episcopal priest, author, and professor of theology. Dr. Heyward and her family discuss their process of reconciling religious beliefs about homosexuality with their love for each other. (21st Century News Human Rights Video Series, 21st Century News, Inc., P.O. Box 42286, Tucson, AZ 85733)

☐ VCR, color monitor, and stand
☐ Overhead projector (with extra bulb)
☐ Table for overhead projector
☐ Screen
☐ Refreshment table
☐ Two chart easels
☐ Four chart pads
☐ Two extension cords with three-prong adapters
☐ Ten inexpensive prizes for winners of the icebreaker
☐ Name tags, prepared in advance with the name of each participant and a color-coded "X" (5 sets of 4 tags with different colors). Include name tags for the facilitators.
☐ Two rolls of masking tape
☐ 20 Felt markers (4 per table)
☐ 125 Sheets of blank paper for distribution among the tables
☐ Pens and pencils for each table

☐ 25 #10 Business envelopes
☐ Refreshments for agenda breaks
☐ 100 3 × 5 index cards

Facility Requirements

• A room large enough to accommodate 6 tables (5 for participants and 1 for the facilitators).
• Four chairs set at each of the 5 tables; 2 chairs for facilitators' table.
• Furniture arrangements that allow participants to focus on facilitator leadership.
• Adequate wall space for hanging chart paper.
• Window treatments and lighting that allow for room darkening.

As Participants Arrive

• Co-facilitator registers participants and distributes name tags and agendas.
• Facilitator greets participants and invites them to the refreshment table.
• When all participants are present, the facilitator asks them to locate the other three people who share the same name tag color code and be seated at the same table.

Prepared Handouts

1 Agenda (25 copies)
2 20 3 × 5 cards for icebreaker (see Activity A, pp. 138–139, for list of names—each card should bear a name and title from the list)
3 Four sets of "read arounds" (total of 14 different readings) (Activities D, F, I, and L)
4 Questionnaire: Fact or Myth? (10 copies) (Activity C)
5 Facts and Figures About Gays and Lesbians: (7 copies) + (20 copies*) (Activity E)
6 Defining Homophobia (25 copies) (Activity G)
7 Evaluation forms (25 copies) (Activity O)
8 Testimonial read aloud by facilitator (25 copies*) (Activity P)
9 Information compiled by facilitators from Appendix C (pp. 155–161) of Besner, H., & Spungin, C. (1995). *Gay and lesbian students: Understanding their needs* (25 copies*)
10 List of famous gays and lesbians from Appendix D (pp. 163–166) of Besner, H., & Spungin, C. (1995). *Gay and lesbian students: Understanding their needs* (25 copies*)
11 A selected list of readings compiled by facilitators from Appendix A (pp. 125–132) of Besner, H., & Spungin, C. (1995). *Gay and lesbian students: Understanding their needs* (25 copies*)

* To be assembled as part of a packet for distribution to participants at the end of the workshop.

12 Educator Behaviors That Signal Safety (25 copies*) (Activity M)

13 Heterosexual Questionnaire from pp. 33–34 of Besner, H., & Spungin, C. (1995). *Gay and lesbian students: Understanding their needs* (25 copies*)

14 Guidelines for Responding to Students When They Disclose Their Sexuality from pp. 110–111 of Besner, H., & Spungin, C. (1995). *Gay and lesbian students: Understanding their needs* (25 copies*)

Chart Preparation

Workshop Goals (Activity B)

Transparencies

Educator Behaviors That Signal Safety (Activity M)
Use three transparencies—two indicators on each transparency

WORKSHOP: HOMOPHOBIA

(Location of Workshop)

(Date of Workshop)

(Name of Facilitator)
(Name of Co-Facilitator)

AGENDA

Welcome
Introduction
Agenda Review
Activity A: Icebreaker
Activity B: Presentation of Workshop Goals
Activity C: Fact or Myth?
Activity D: Read Around #1 and Discussion
Activity E: Facts and Figures
Activity F: Read Around #2 and Discussion
(Break)
Activity G: What Is Homophobia?
Activity H: Effects of Homophobia
Activity I: Read Around #3 and Discussion
(Lunch)
Activity J: Videotape and Discussion
Activity K: Action Steps
(Break)
Activity L: Read Around #4 and Discussion

* To be assembled as part of a packet for distribution to participants at the end of the workshop.

Activity M: Educator Behaviors That Signal Safety
Activity N: Personal Action Steps
Activity O: Workshop Evaluation
Activity P: Ending Testimonial and Closing Remarks
Activity Q: Distribution of Information Packets

SUGGESTED TIME SCHEDULE

Activity	**Estimated number of minutes**
Welcome, introduction, agenda review	10
A: Icebreaker	20
B: Workshop goals	10
C: Questionnaire—Fact or myth?	30
D: Read around #1	10
E: Facts and figures	30
F: Read around #2	10
Break	15
G: What is homophobia?	25
H: Effects of homophobia	25
I: Read around #3	10
Lunch	60
J: Videotape	40
K: Action steps	20
Break	10
L: Read around #4	10
M: Educator behaviors that signal safety	10
N: Personal action steps	10
O: Workshop evaluation	10
P: Testimonial and closing remarks	5
Q: Distribution of information packets	5
TOTAL:	6 1/4 hours

ACTIVITY A
ICEBREAKER: WHAT'S MY NAME?

Objectives:

1   To help each participant learn the names of other participants
2   To stimulate interaction among participants
3   To help participants relax
4   To create an awareness of some famous gays and lesbians (*Do not reveal this objective until the end of the activity*)

Estimated time: 20 minutes

Directions for Facilitators

1 Without revealing the name on the card to the participant, tape one of the prepared 3 × 5 cards to the back of each participant. Each card should bear a name and title from the list of names of famous gays and lesbians (below).

2 Ask participants not to reveal the card names to the wearers.

3 Announce that there will be a prize for each person who guesses the name of the person he or she represents.

Instructions to Participants

1 The objective of this activity is to guess the name of the person you represent.

2 Circulate around the room, introduce yourself to individual participants, and ask them questions that will help you guess whom you represent (e.g., "Am I an American" "Am I living" "Am I male/female" "Am I an historical figure?").

3 When you have determined the correct name, report it to a facilitator and continue trying to help others guess by answering their questions.

4 Time will be called after 20 minutes.

Note to Facilitators

At the end of the activity, ask participants to be seated. Distribute prizes to those who guessed correctly. After each member of the group has announced the person he/she represented reveal that all of the names on the cards belonged to famous gays and lesbians. Discussion may or may not follow.

NAMES OF FAMOUS GAYS AND LESBIANS

1 Martina Navratilova, tennis champion

2 W. Somerset Maugham, British author

3 Virginia Woolf, British author

4 Gore Vidal, American author

5 James Baldwin, American author

6 Janis Joplin, American singer

7 Elton John, British composer/singer

8 k.d. lang, singer

9 Roberta Achtenberg, Assistant Director of U.S. Housing & Urban Development (HUD)

10 Lewis Carroll, author and mathematician

11 A.E. Housman, British poet

12 Walt Whitman, American poet

13 Gertrude Stein, American author

14 Willa Cather, American novelist

15 Janis Ian, singer/songwriter

16 Edward Albee, American playwright

17 Andy Warhol, American artist
18 Leonardo da Vinci, Italian painter, inventor, scientist
19 Oscar Wilde, British playwright and author
20 Cole Porter, composer

ACTIVITY B
WORKSHOP GOALS (TRANSPARENCIES)
Note to Facilitators

Present these goals using the overhead projector. Participants may wish to add their own goals to the list.

1 To define homophobia and promote awareness of the effects it has on the lives of gay and lesbian students
2 To examine personal active and passive homophobic attitudes toward gay and lesbian students
3 To examine active and passive homophobic attitudes towards gays and lesbians that prevail within school systems
4 To provide participants with factual information concerning gay and lesbian students
5 To promote awareness of personal and institutional action steps that can be taken to improve the quality of life for gay and lesbian students

ACTIVITY C
FACT OR MYTH?

Objective: To help participants think about, identify, and discuss some of the common myths about homosexuality that exist in society
Estimated time: 30 minutes

Directions for Facilitators

Distribute one copy of the "Questionnaire: Fact or Myth?" to each table. Instruct participants to choose one person at each table to read each statement aloud and lead the group through discussion to a consensus for each statement. After all groups have completed the questionnaire, review the answers by calling on each group leader to report three or four responses until all statements have been discussed. When possible, encourage participants to substantiate their answers. The facilitators should be prepared to provide supporting evidence for correct responses. (See Chapter 2 of Besner, H., & Spungin, C. (1995). *Gay and lesbian students: Understanding their needs* for substantiation for questionnaire statements.) (#15 is based on Kinsey's 10% statistic; #16 is substantiated by testimonials of gays and lesbians who reported on their experiences as teenagers)

(Correct responses: 1–10, 13, & 14 = Myth; 11, 12, & 15–17 = Fact)

QUESTIONNAIRE: FACT OR MYTH?

Directions: Read each statement and circle "F" for fact and "M" for myth, based on group consensus.

   1 Most gays and lesbians can be identified by their mannerisms, dress, and/or appearance.   F M

   2 In homosexual relationships, one partner is always "male" and the other is "female."   F M

   3 Homosexuality is an emotional illness.   F M

   4 Gays and lesbians can change to become heterosexuals.   F M

   5 Acting like a sissy or a tomboy causes homosexuality.   F M

   6 Gays and lesbians are oversexed and indiscriminately promiscuous.   F M

   7 Gay men and lesbians gravitate only to certain occupations.   F M

   8 Gays and lesbians tend to hang out in seedy bars and restaurants, and gay men frequent bath houses.   F M

   9 Gay and lesbian parents will raise gay and lesbian children.   F M

  10 Gays and lesbians have abandoned organized religion.   F M

  11 Homosexuality has existed in the world for centuries.   F M

  12 The majority of child molesters are heterosexual men whose victims are young girls.   F M

  13 Homosexual teachers can cause students to become homosexuals.   F M

  14 The American Psychiatric Association considers homosexuality a mental illness.   F M

  15 One American family in four has a gay or lesbian member in the immediate family.   F M

  16 Many gay and lesbian adolescents force themselves to be sexually active with the opposite sex to prove they are "straight." This results in many teenage pregnancies.   F M

  17 Homophobia hurts *everyone*, not just gays and lesbians.   F M

ACTIVITY D
READ AROUND #1 AND DISCUSSION (4 Readings)

Objective: To provide supportive information regarding the workshop content through anecdotes, articles from the press, and testimonials

Estimated time: 10 minutes

Directions for Facilitators

There are four read arounds in the workshop (Activities D, F, I, and L). Activities D, F, and I involve four read arounds each; activity L consists of two. For each activity, distribute the number of prepared readings to volunteer participants and ask them to read their selections to the entire group. Facilitators should encourage discussions after each reading.

1 "Some busybody at church told my mother there was a rumor going around that I was a lesbian. My mother confronted me and I decided there's no time like the present, so I admitted it. It happened in January of my senior year in high school. She said I was grounded until my June graduation and if I made any telephone calls, they had to be in front of her. I made it through my 18th birthday in March and ran away. I missed all the senior graduation activities and messed up my education." (a 19-year-old woman)

2 It is the duty of school administrators to provide a safe environment for all students and when they do not protect gay and lesbian students from physical or verbal harassment they are not fulfilling their duty. The source of an administrator's responsibility to ensure a safe environment for all students is the compulsory education law. The students are legally entrusted to the care of school officials and if they do not take action when gay and lesbian students are verbally or physically harassed, they are neglecting their lawful duty. [Dennis, D., & Harlow, R. E., (1986). Gay youth and the right to education. *Yale Law & Policy Review*, 4(2), 451.]

3 "People hate and fear what they don't know or understand. Most of what we know about gay and lesbian people is based on misinformation and/or stereotypes. We use disrespectful terms like *fag*, *dyke*, *queer*, *fairy*, *pansy*, *lezzie*, *homo*, *fruit*, *sissy* without thinking of the people behind the names and how they are hurt by name-calling." (a school psychologist)

4 "Some of my best friends are straight. In fact, my entire immediate family—mom, dad, my two brothers—all of them are straight, except me; I am gay. There are an estimated 25 million men and women in this country who are gay and lesbian. So, I'm not surprised that some of *you* have met some of *them*." (an alumnus of a high school, currently a university professor, speaking to an audience of parents)

ACTIVITY E
FACTS AND FIGURES ABOUT GAYS AND LESBIANS

Objective: To acquaint participants with statistics pertaining to gays and lesbians and to consider their significance relative to educational systems
Estimated time: 30 minutes

Directions for Facilitators

1 Distribute one copy of the handout "Facts and Figures About Gays and Lesbians" to each table.

2 To each of three tables, assign four of the statistical statements. To the remaining two tables, assign three statements each.

Instructions to Participants

1 After careful consideration of the assigned statistical statements, reach a consensus and write at least one specific recommendation for each statement that

could be made to a school, a school district, or state department of education for changes in the curriculum, policies, or the ways schools operate.

2 Write the recommendations on chart paper.

3 Choose one member of the group to present the assigned statistical statements and the recommendations. The presenter should be prepared to explain the recommendations.

FACTS AND FIGURES ABOUT GAYS AND LESBIANS*

1 There are currently between 1 and 5 million lesbian mothers in the United States and between 1 and 3 million gay fathers. (1)

2 An estimated 6–14 million children have a lesbian or gay parent. (1)

3 51% of college freshmen surveyed in 1991 said they think gays and lesbians should try to be heterosexual. (2)

4 55% of Americans would object to having a gay or lesbian elementary school teacher. (3)

5 As many as 7.2 million Americans under age 20 are gay or lesbian. (4)

6 In a 1992 study of gay and lesbian youths in Chicago, 64% of the males and 50% of the females said their self-esteem was affected positively by "coming out." (5)

7 The average age at which lesbians "come out" is between 16 and 19; the average age for males is between 14 and 16. (6)

8 Half of all gay and lesbian youths interviewed in a 1987 study report that their parents rejected them for being gay. (6)

9 1 in 4 gay and lesbian youths are forced to leave home because of conflicts with their families about their sexual orientation. (6)

10 Gay and lesbian youths constitute up to 25% of all youths living on the streets in the United States. (7)

11 80% of gay and lesbian youths who took part in a 1987 study reported severe isolation. (6)

12 Gay and lesbian youths account for 30% of all completed suicides among youths. (7)

13 In 1993 52% of Americans surveyed opposed teaching about gay and lesbian orientation in sex-education classes in public schools. (8)

14 Using Kinsey's findings, there are an estimated 360,000 gay and lesbian teachers in the United States. (9)

15 45% of gay males and 20% of lesbians experience physical or verbal assault in high school. 28% of these young people feel forced to drop out of school because of harassment based on sexual orientation. (6)

16 As of 1993, there were more than 100 gay and lesbian support groups in American high schools. (10)

17 In 1993, Massachusetts became the first and only state in the United States to outlaw discrimination against gay and lesbian students in public schools. (11)

* From *Gay and lesbian stats: A pocket guide of facts and figures* by Bennett L. Singer and David Deschamps (eds.). Copyright © 1994 by Bennett L. Singer and David Deschamps. Reprinted by permission of The New Press.

18   In surveys from 1985 to 1989 at five major American universities, between 45% and 76% of gay and lesbian students said they were verbally threatened or harassed. An average of 90% of these incidents were unreported. (9)

SOURCES

(1)   Patterson, Charlotte. Children of lesbian and gay parents. *Child Development*, 63, 1992.
(2)   Comstock, Gary D. *Violence against Lesbians and Gay Men*. NY: Columbia University Press, 1991.
(3)   Schmalz, J. Poll finds even split on homosexuality's cause. *New York Times*, March 5, 1993.
(4)   *Statistical Abstract of the United States*. Washington, DC: U.S. Bureau of Census, 1992; and Kinsey estimates.
(5)   Herdt, Gilbert & Boxer, Andrew. *Children of Horizons*. Boston: Beacon Press, 1993.
(6)   "*Factfile: Lesbian, Gay & Bisexual Youth*". NY: Hetrick-Martin Institute, 1992.
(7)   United States Department of Health & Human Services. *Report of the Secretary's Task Force on Youth Suicide*, 1989.
(8)   Shapiro, Joseph P. et al. Straight talk about gays. *U.S. News & World Report*, July 5, 1993.
(9)   Harbeck, Karen M. (Ed.) *Coming Out of the Classroom Closet: Gay and Lesbian Students, Teachers and Curricula*. Binghamton, NY: Harrington Park Press, 1992.
(10) Dorning, Mike. Schools support groups helping gay teens to cope. *Chicago Tribune*, November 30, 1993.
(11) Rimer, Sara. Rights for gay students in public schools. *New York Times*, December 12, 1993.

ACTIVITY F
READ AROUND #2 AND DISCUSSION (4 Readings)

Objective: To provide supportive information regarding the workshop content through anecdotes, articles from the press, and testimonials
Estimated time: 10 minutes

Directions for Facilitators

Distribute the prepared readings to volunteer participants and ask them to read their selections to the entire group. Facilitators should encourage discussions after each reading.

1   "Last year at my high school there was an incident which shocked everyone. Two female students were standing in the hall with their arms around each other. Students began to encircle them and yell profanities until a group of about thirty kids surrounded them." (Zoe Hart, 17-year-old student testifying at the public hearings, Massachusetts, Governor's Commission on Gay and Lesbian Youth, 1992)

2   The National Network of Runaway & Youth Services estimates that any-where from a quarter to a half million lesbian, gay, and bisexual youth in the United States run away or are forced out of their homes *annually.*

3   When children reach puberty many of them have learned to tease one another by using the words *fag, queer,* or *pervert.* During these early adoles-cent years boys and girls feel the pressure to adapt to heterosexuality and prepare themselves for married life. We have taught them well; we have taught them if they deviate from society's standards they will be made to conform. [Pharr, S. (1988). *Homophobia: A weapon of sexism.* Inverness, CA: Chardon Press.]

4   A gay male high school student was beaten up by several students, sprayed with a fire extinguisher, and locked in a gym closet. The boy passed out and was discovered several hours later by a custodian. The students who attacked him were expelled from school.

ACTIVITY G
WHAT IS HOMOPHOBIA?

Objective: To define homophobia and its various aspects and to give participants the opportunity to discuss how homophobia is manifested within the school environment
Estimated time: 25 minutes

Directions for Facilitators

1   Distribute the handout "Defining Homophobia" to all participants. Ask them to read it and follow the instructions noted at the end of the handout.

2   As each group leader presents, facilitators should stimulate discussion.

3   If participants overlook certain examples of institutional homophobia, the facilitators should initiate discussion that includes the following:

- the lack of support services for gay and lesbian students
- the lack of positive role models for gay and lesbian students
- the silence of teachers when derogatory terms are used by students
- the absence of honest discussions of homosexuality in health and sex education classes
- subtle discrimination against gay and lesbian educational personnel
- not acknowledging famous gays and lesbians in various curriculum areas
- the absence of appropriate gay and lesbian fiction and nonfiction mate-rials in school media
- the lack of training for school personnel concerning how to meet the needs of gay and lesbian students
- the lack of school policies protecting gay and lesbian students from harassment, violence, and discrimination
- the lack of support for families of gay and lesbian students

DEFINING HOMOPHOBIA

Homophobia is defined as an intense fear or hatred of gays and lesbians that includes various levels of prejudice, discrimination, or aggression.

Prejudice is a rigid, inflexible attitude in a closed mind that fails to stand the test of logical scrutiny. If it is kept to oneself and not acted out, it does no great *social* harm, but when it is expressed it can lead to discrimination and/or aggression.

Discrimination is an act of exclusion based on a label, branding the victim as a member of a discredited group. It means forcibly and unjustly separating a person against whom we are prejudiced from our social institutions simply because the person bears the unsavory label.

Aggression includes harassment, verbal abuse, and physical abuse.

Homophobia can be expressed personally, interpersonally, or through various social institutions such as schools, businesses, religious organizations, or government.

Personal homophobia involves the personal belief that gays and lesbians are inferior to heterosexuals, mentally ill, sinners, immoral, and unacceptable in society. Sometimes it involves the fear of being considered gay or lesbian, regardless of one's sexual orientation, and thus being subjected to stereotyping and hostility.

Interpersonal homophobia involves a fear or hatred of people believed to be gay or lesbian. This fear or hatred may be expressed through discrimination or various degrees of aggression.

Institutional homophobia involves the ways that social institutions, such as government, religious organizations, businesses, and schools discriminate against people (sometimes in subtle ways) on the basis of sexual orientation.

Instructions to Participants

Create two lists on chart paper:

   1 Specific examples of *interpersonal* homophobia expressed by individuals within the school setting.
   2 Specific examples of *institutional* homophobia, expressed or unexpressed, within the school setting. Select a person from the group to post the lists and report to the entire group.

ACTIVITY H
EFFECTS OF HOMOPHOBIA

Objective: To create an awareness and sensitivity among participants regarding the effects of homophobia in the educational system on gay and lesbian students
Estimated time: 25 minutes

Directions for Facilitators

Elicit answers and lead an open discussion on the following question: "How does homophobia affect gay and lesbian students?" Co-facilitator should list participant responses on chart paper. Make sure all of the responses listed below are included:

- loneliness and isolation
- low self-esteem
- suicide and suicide attempts
- drug/alcohol abuse
- low academic achievement
- nonparticipation in school activities
- fighting
- dropping out of school
- self-hatred
- inability to participate in academic classes
- fearful
- feelings of guilt
- feel like an outsider
- lack accurate and unbiased information relative to sexual orientation
- irresponsible sexual activity
- victims of verbal and physical abuse
- alienation from the family
- homelessness
- unaware of their civil rights

ACTIVITY I
READ AROUND #3 AND DISCUSSION (4 Readings)

Objective: To provide supportive information regarding the workshop content through anecdotes, articles from the press, and testimonials
Estimated time: 10 minutes

Directions for Facilitators

Distribute the prepared readings to volunteer participants and ask them to read their selections to the entire group. Facilitators should encourage discussions after each reading.

   1   "One night after a basketball game when I was a junior in high school, three guys followed my friend and me on the way home. We didn't realize they were following us until we exited the highway and they drove right up close behind us. They ran us off the road. Two of them grabbed us out of the car and held us while

the other one spray-painted 'fag' all over my car. They stole my tape deck. Dad had the car repainted and told me not to report the incident to the school or the police; he was afraid of retaliation." (gay college freshman)

2 "If not for the support I found from openly gay teachers at my high school, I would be dead today. I hope to God that future teachers have the courage to come out for their students." (Sharon Bergman, 18 year old, testifying at the public hearings, Massachusetts, Governor's Commission on Gay and Lesbian Youth, 1992)

3 "It seems that almost every day, either in the teachers' lounge or at the faculty lunch table, someone either tells a hostile 'joke' about gays and lesbians or uses a derogatory word describing us. The laughter always reminds me I'm in enemy territory. I would like to believe these people don't intend their remarks to hurt anyone, but somehow I think educated people should know better. When it happens, I always wonder if these teachers talk this way in their classrooms and, if they do, what damage they are doing to their gay and lesbian students. Ever since fourth grade I have wanted to be a teacher, but now I'm beginning to wonder how long I can survive the prejudice. If I object or disclose myself, I could lose my job. Right now I'm hiding behind the fact that I was married, divorced and have a two-year-old son." (a middle school teacher)

4 "I dropped out of school when I was 16. I had lousy grades and I knew I wouldn't graduate. My teachers and the guidance counselor did everything they could to make me stay in school, but I was messed up about being gay, I just wanted out. Education is important to my mom and dad because neither of them graduated from high school and they wanted me to graduate. They were so mad they threw me out of the house. They didn't know I was gay and they still don't. A friend of mine was a carpenter and gave me a job helping in construction. I worked for him until I was 18 and moved to the city. I lived with a gay friend of mine. He belonged to a gay support group and asked me to go with him one night. They were the ones who helped me get my GED. You can't get anywhere without a diploma. Now I'm working and going to school to learn how to repair air conditioners. My parents are still mad and I haven't seen them since they threw me out." (a 20-year-old gay man)

ACTIVITY J
VIDEOTAPE

Objective: To give participants the opportunity to reinforce what they have learned about homophobia and to hear remarks by gays, lesbians, professionals, and parents regarding the effects of homophobia
Estimated time: 40 minutes

Directions for Facilitators

After viewing the videotape, initiate and guide open discussion. (The questions asked to generate discussion will depend on the videotape chosen for this activity.)

ACTIVITY K
ACTION STEPS

Objective: To help participants articulate action steps based on what they have learned about gay and lesbian students, homophobia, and its effects
Estimated time: 20 minutes

Directions for Facilitators

Assign each group of participants one of the following questions to discuss. Each group will write *specific* recommendations on chart paper, post them, and share them with the entire group. Encourage discussion after each group presents.

   1   What can *teachers* do to help reduce homophobia and assist gay and lesbian students?
   2   What can *counselors* do to support gay and lesbian students?
   3   What can *media specialists* do to help gay and lesbian students?
   4   How can *school and district administrators* reduce homophobia and help gay and lesbian students?
   5   What can *school boards* do to help gay and lesbian students and school personnel?

ACTIVITY L
READ AROUND #4 AND DISCUSSION (2 Readings)

Objective: To provide supportive information regarding the workshop content through anecdotes, articles from the press, and testimonials
Estimated time: 10 minutes

Directions for Facilitators

Distribute the prepared readings to volunteer participants and ask them to read their selections to the entire group. Facilitators should encourage discussions after each reading.

   1   "I was a star student in elementary school, but middle school was a nightmare. I was harassed almost every day by other boys. I hated school, my grades dropped to a 'D' average and I gave up participating in school activities. My parents had no idea what was happening to me or how I felt and I was afraid to tell them. They decided to send me away to a boarding school known for disciplining 'academic failures' where my life was absolute hell. I ran away when I turned 16 and lived on the streets of New York for two years." (a 19-year-old gay man)
   2   "While I was growing up, I had heard my parents and their friends express their attitudes about gays and lesbians by telling 'jokes' and using derogatory words to describe us, so I knew, when I realized at 14 I was a lesbian, I could never

talk to them about it. All through high school they hassled me about dating boys. I was so miserable I started drinking, and one night, while I was drunk, I tried to commit suicide by taking some of my mom's sleeping pills. They found me passed out on the bathroom floor and called the paramedics. When I got to the hospital they pumped my stomach. I wound up seeing a psychiatrist, but I never told him why I did it." (a 20-year-old lesbian)

ACTIVITY M
EDUCATOR BEHAVIORS THAT SIGNAL SAFETY (Transparencies)

Objective: To provide a list of behaviors that indicate to gay and lesbian students that they are safe with educators and can ask for help or talk about their sexual orientation
Estimated time: 10 minutes

Directions for Facilitators

1   Mention that this information is contained in the packet of information to be distributed at the end of the workshop.
2   Review the following indicators with participants, using the overhead projector. Encourage discussion.

ATTITUDE INDICATORS*

1   When educators indicate by what they say that they are aware of different sexual orientations and do not assume all teenagers are heterosexual.
2   When educators do not tolerate harassment of gay and lesbian students.
3   When educators do not tolerate offensive "humor" involving gays and lesbians and take a stand against it.
4   When teachers recognize famous gays and lesbians as they are studied in the curriculum and talk openly about their contributions.
5   When educators display materials in their classrooms, media centers, and guidance offices that indicate they are open to discussing the subject of homosexuality.
6   When guidance counselors initiate discussion with students they believe are struggling with their sexual orientation, or do not dismiss the subject when it is initiated by counselees.

ACTIVITY N
PERSONAL ACTION STEPS TO REDUCE HOMOPHOBIA IN SCHOOLS

Objective: To encourage personal commitment to reduce homophobia in educational settings
Estimated time: 10 minutes

---

* From Walling, D. R. (1993). Gay teens at risk. *Fastback series of Phi Delta Kappa Educational Foundation* (#357). Bloomington, IN: Phi Delta Kappa Educational Foundation.

Directions for Facilitators

Distribute envelopes to all participants. Instruct them to write four specific positive actions they are willing to take within their workplaces during the next two months that will contribute to the reduction of homophobia. Ask them to seal their written statements in the envelope, address it to themselves, and return it to the facilitators for mailing at the end of two months.

ACTIVITY O
WORKSHOP EVALUATION

Objective: To provide facilitators with feedback on their preparation; presentation skills; appropriateness of material and activities; and how participants were affected by the content of the workshop
Estimated time: 10 minutes

Directions for Facilitators

- Post the workshop goals
- Distribute copies of the evaluation form
- Collect all evaluations

WORKSHOP: HOMOPHOBIA
EVALUATION FORM

Date: _____

Directions: Please rate by placing a check mark in the appropriate column.

Facilitators':	Excellent	Good	Fair	Poor
Overall presentation	_____	_____	_____	_____
Preparation	_____	_____	_____	_____
Accomplishment of workshop goals	_____	_____	_____	_____
Skills in promoting discussion	_____	_____	_____	_____
Organizational skills	_____	_____	_____	_____
Knowledge of content	_____	_____	_____	_____

Please complete the following:

1 Three things I learned about myself as a result of this workshop are: _____

_____

_____

_____

2 As a result of this workshop, now I believe _____

_____

_____

_____

3 Before this workshop, I believed _____

_____

_____

_____

4 What suggestions would you recommend to improve this workshop? _____

_____

_____

_____

5 What additional comments or observations would you like to make? _____

_____

_____

_____

Thank you for completing this evaluation.

ACTIVITY P
ENDING TESTIMONIAL AND CLOSING REMARKS

Objective: To end the workshop with a positive activity to re-emphasize the importance of helping gay and lesbian students
Estimated time: 5 minutes

Directions for Facilitators

Read the following testimonial to the participants:

> I knew I was gay in middle school and realized I had better keep it a secret from everyone, including my mom, dad and two sisters. I was on the baseball team and heard all the rotten talk and the jokes about gays in the locker room, so I wasn't taking any chances. I hid who I really was from everyone. It was pretty easy to do, because I didn't fit the so-called gay stereotype; I was tall, strong, a good athlete and popular with the girls. When I got to high school, I was miserable and felt I didn't belong. I stopped studying and was satisfied with mediocre grades. I had a terrific science teacher in my sophomore year who included me in a weekend science field trip. She and her husband were kind, loving people. On that trip she asked me why I wasn't doing better in school. I felt I could trust her and told her what was bothering me. She didn't seem shocked and we had a long talk. She told me she had a gay stepson in engineering school who also had a difficult time in high school from hiding who he really was. We talked about how she and her husband felt when their son admitted he was gay and how much closer the family has been since he included them in his life. Anyway, to make a long story short, she mentored me through the rest of high school, guided me through 'coming out' to my family and, even though my grades were average in my freshman year and part of my sophomore year, I recovered and graduated with honors, received a scholarship to a university and now I'm in the last year of my pediatric residency. I love that teacher and always will for helping me through one of the most difficult times of my life. I hate to think what could have happened to me without her; I believe she saved my life. (testimonial by a gay M.D.)

Note to Facilitators

Conclude the workshop with closing remarks of appreciation and mention that packets of information will be distributed to participants as they leave the room.

ACTIVITY Q
DISTRIBUTION OF INFORMATION PACKETS

Objective: To provide participants with reference material
Estimated time: 5 minutes

Directions for Facilitators

Stand at the door, hand each participant a packet of information, and thank him/
her for attending the workshop. Each packet should contain the following items:

   1   Facts and Figures (from Activity E)
   2   Information compiled by facilitators from Appendix C of Besner, H., &
Spungin, C. (1995). *Gay and lesbian students: Understanding their needs.*
   3   List of famous gays and lesbians from Appendix D of Besner, H., &
Spungin, C. (1995). *Gay and lesbian students: Understanding their needs.*
   4   Educator Behaviors That Signal Safety (from Activity M)
   5   Selected list of readings compiled by facilitators from Appendix A of
Besner, H., & Spungin, C. (1995). *Gay and lesbian students: Understanding their
needs.*
   6   End-of-workshop testimonial (from Activity P)
   7   Heterosexual Questionnaire from pp. 33–34 of Besner, H., & Spungin, C.
(1995). *Gay and lesbian students: Understanding their needs.*
   8   Guidelines for Responding to Students When They Disclose Their Sexuality from pp. 110–111 of Besner, H., & Spungin, C. (1995). *Gay and lesbian
students: Understanding their needs.*

Reminder to Facilitators

Remember to mail the envelopes two months from the workshop date (see
Activity N).

Appendix C: Resources

The organizations, videos, and hotlines listed here are valuable resources for educators and other professionals who work with gay, lesbian, and bisexual youth and their families or who are responsible for staff development.

ORGANIZATIONS

AMERICAN ASSOCIATION OF SEX
EDUCATORS, COUNSELORS AND
THERAPISTS (AASECT)
435 North Michigan Avenue, Suite 1717
Chicago, IL 60611-4067
(312) 644-0828

AMERICAN CIVIL LIBERTIES UNION
(ACLU) NATIONAL GAY AND
LESBIAN RIGHTS PROJECT
132 West 43rd Street
New York, NY 10036
(212) 944-9800 (ext. 545)

AMERICAN FOUNDATION FOR AIDS
RESEARCH (AMFAR)
733 Third Avenue, 12th Floor
New York, NY 10017
(212) 682-7440

AMERICAN PSYCHOLOGICAL
ASSOCIATION COMMITTEE ON
LESBIAN AND GAY CONCERNS
750 First Street, NE
Washington, DC 20002-4241
(202) 336-6052

ASSOCIATION FOR SUPERVISION &
CURRICULUM DEVELOPMENT
(ASCD)
1250 North Pitt Street
Alexandria, VA 22314-1403
(703) 549-9110

BLACK GAY & LESBIAN
LEADERSHIP FORUM
3924 West Sunset Boulevard, Suite 2
Los Angeles, CA 90026
(213) 666-5495

CAMPAIGN TO END HOMOPHOBIA
P.O. Box 819
Cambridge, MA 02139
(617) 868-8280
OR
P.O. Box 438316
Chicago, IL 60643-8316

The purpose of this organization is to build and support a network of people working together to end homophobia and heterosexism through education. Write for their publications list.

FRIENDS OF PROJECT 10, INC.
Virginia Uribe, Ph.D.
7850 Melrose Avenue
Los Angeles, CA 90046
(213) 651-5200

Project 10 is a dropout prevention program offering emotional support, information, and resources to young people who identify themselves as lesbian, gay, or bisexual or who want information about sexual orientation. Project 10 was the first school-based program to address the needs of these students. It is being used as a model in other school districts. Write or call for the *Project 10 Handbook: Addressing Lesbian and Gay Issues in Our Schools.*

GAY AND LESBIAN ADVOCATES
AND DEFENDERS (GLAD)
P.O. Box 218
Boston, MA 02112
(617) 426-1350

GAY AND LESBIAN ARABIC
SOCIETY
P.O. Box 4971
Washington, DC 20008

This organization provides a support network for gays and lesbians of Arabic origin or descent.

GAY AND LESBIAN PARENTS
COALITION INTERNATIONAL
P.O. Box 50360
Washington, DC 20091
(202) 583-8029

GAY TASK FORCE OF THE SOCIAL
RESPONSIBILITIES TASK FORCE OF
THE AMERICAN LIBRARY
ASSOCIATION
50 East Huron
Chicago, IL 60611

GOVERNOR'S COMMISSION ON
GAY AND LESBIAN YOUTH
State House, Room 111
Boston, MA 02133

Write for *Making Schools Safe for Gay and Lesbian Youth: Breaking the Silence in Schools and in Families*, Publication #17296-60-500-2/93-C.R., 1993. Massachusetts was the first state to pass legislation protecting public school students from antigay/antilesbian discrimination.

THE HETRICK-MARTIN INSTITUTE,
INC., FOR LESBIAN & GAY YOUTH
2 Astor Place
New York, NY 10003-6998
(212) 674-2400
(212) 674-8650 (FAX)
(212) 674-8695 (TTY)

A social service, education, and advocacy organization. Write for *You Are Not Alone: A National Lesbian, Gay & Bisexual Youth Organization Directory*. (Listings are by state, with supplements for Canada, national organizations, scholarships, and toll-free numbers.)

LAMBDA LEGAL DEFENSE AND
EDUCATION FUND
666 Broadway,12th Floor
New York, NY 10012
(212) 995-8585

NATIONAL AIDS INFORMATION
CLEARING HOUSE
P.O. Box 6003
Rockville, MD 20849-6003
(800) 458-5231

NATIONAL CENTER FOR LESBIAN
RIGHTS
1663 Mission Street, Suite 550
San Francisco, CA 94103
(415) 621-0674

NATIONAL COALITION OF BLACK
LESBIANS & GAYS (NCBLG)
P.O. Box 19248
Washington, DC 200366
(202) 265-4725

A national civil rights organization that
has as its focus the concerns of black
lesbians and gays.

NATIONAL EDUCATION
ASSOCIATION (NEA)
GAY & LESBIAN CAUCUS
P.O. Box 314
Roosevelt, NJ 08555
(609) 448-5215

The NEA has developed a training
course to help teachers discuss homosexuality.

NATIONAL GAY & LESBIAN
CAUCUS OF THE AMERICAN
FEDERATION OF TEACHERS
P.O. Box 19856
Cincinnatti, OH 45219

NATIONAL GAY AND LESBIAN
TASK FORCE
2320 17th Street, NW
Washington, DC 20009
(202) 332-6483
(202) 332-0207 (FAX)
(202) 332-6219 (TTY)

Write for their publications list and a
sample newsletter.

NATIONAL LESBIAN AND GAY LAW
ASSOCIATION
Box 77130
National Capital Station
Washington, DC 20014
(202) 389-0161

NATIONAL NETWORK OF
RUNAWAY AND YOUTH
SERVICES
Suite 330
1400 I Street, NW
Washington, DC 20005
(202) 682-4114

PARENTS AND FRIENDS OF
LESBIANS AND GAYS (P-FLAG)
P.O. Box 27605
Washington, DC 20038-7605
(202) 638-4200

A national support group for family
members and friends of gays and
lesbians. There are 340 affiliate groups
nationwide. Call 1-800-4-FAMILY for
the group serving your area. Their
quarterly publication, *P-FLAGpole,* is
available from P-FLAG, 1012 14th St.,
NW, Suite 700, Washington, DC
20005.

SEX INFORMATION & EDUCATION
COUNCIL OF THE UNITED STATES
(SIECUS)
32 Washington Place, 5th Floor
New York, NY 10003
(212) 673-3850

THE TEACHERS' GROUP
P.O. Box 280346
Lakewood, CO 80228-0346
(303) 232-3789

A national organization of gays and lesbians
working in education. Write for information
about training programs on gay and lesbian
youth issues for professionals and a
comprehensive bibliography of materials on
homosexuality, homophobia, and gay and
lesbian youth issues.

AUDIOVISUALS

Audiotape

Accepting Your Gay or Lesbian Child: Parents Share Their Stories
Sounds True
735 Walnut Street
Boulder, CO 80302

Videotapes

Before Stonewall: The Making of a Gay and Lesbian Community (87 minutes; color; 1984)
This video portrays the history of homosexual experience in America from the 1920s to recent times. It traces the social, political, and cultural development of the lesbian and gay community and a period of remarkable social change in America.

The Cinema Guild
1697 Broadway, Suite 506
New York, NY 10019-5904
(212) 246-5522
(212) 246-5525 (FAX)
(800) 723-5522 (orders only)
Also available in many public library video collections.

Gay Issues in the Workplace
Gay, lesbian, and bisexual employees speak for themselves.

TRB Productions
P.O. Box 2362
Boston, MA 02107
(617) 236-7800

Homosexuality: The Adolescent's Perspective (30 minutes; 1987)
Produced by Gary Remafedi, M.D., M.P.H. Six teenagers describe their lives to adolescent viewers, parents, and educators.

University of Minnesota
Media Distribution
Box 734 Mayo
420 Delaware Street, S.E.
Minneapolis, MN 55455
(612) 624-7906

Not All Parents Are Straight (58 minutes; 1986)
This video examines the dynamics of the parent–child relationship within several different households where children are being raised by gay and lesbian parents.

The Cinema Guild
1697 Broadway, Suite 506
New York, NY 10019-5904
(212) 246-5522
(800) 723-5522 (orders only)
(212) 246-5525 (FAX)

On Being Gay: A Conversation with Brian McNaught (80 minutes)

TRB Productions
P.O. Box 2362
Boston, MA 02107
(617) 236-7800

Pink Triangles: A Study of Prejudice Against Lesbians and Gay Men (35 minutes;
color)
This award-winning documentary on homophobia was produced by a group of
health workers, teachers, social workers, mental health workers, historians, and
photographers.

Cambridge Documentary Films, Inc.
P.O. Box 385
Cambridge, MA 02139
(617) 354-3677
(617) 492-7653

Running Gay (20 minutes; color; 1991)
This video examines the participation of lesbians and gay men in sports, focusing
on the homophobia they confront in mainstream sporting events and their recent
efforts to organize the annual International Gay Games. The video highlights the
3rd annual International Gay Games held in Vancouver in August 1990, in which
7,300 athletes participated.

The Cinema Guild
1697 Broadway, Suite 506
New York, NY 10019-5904
(212) 246-5522
(212) 246-5525 (FAX)
(800) 723-5522 (orders only)

Sexual Orientation: Reading Between the Labels (30 minutes; color; 1991)
Personal accounts from lesbian and gay teens are interspersed with input from
youth workers, medical experts, and parents of lesbian and gay youth. Young
people describe damaging labels, rejection, and support found through friends,
family, and counseling.

NEWIST/CESA #7 Telecommunications
IS 1110, University of Wisconsin
Green Bay, WI 54311
(414) 465-2599

21st Century News Human Rights Video Series
This series is being used by schools and counselors to increase awareness, promote discussion, and help eradicate homophobia in our society.

The following six videotapes are available from:

21st Century News, Inc.
P.O. Box 42286
Tucson, AZ 85733

Another Side of the Closet (30 minutes)
Three former spouses of gay men discuss the process of when their husbands acknowledged their homosexuality. Their honest sharing provides insight and hope for others in similar situations.

Be True to Yourself (28 minutes)
Authors and human rights activists Bob and Rod Jackson-Paris talk with ten teenagers about growing up gay, self-esteem, and the courage to be true to yourself.

Families Come Out (30 minutes)
This program offers insight and support to the one in four families with a gay, lesbian, or bisexual person in the immediate family. Families share their experiences in dealing with a son or daughter, sister, brother, or parent coming out of the closet.

Family AIDS Support (25 minutes)
Parents and siblings talk about their experiences having a family member with AIDS.

Reunion: One Family Overcomes Religious Homophobia (30 minutes)
This video features Dr. Carter Heyward, a lesbian ordained Episcopal priest, author, and professor of theology. Dr. Heyward and her family discuss their process of reconciling religious beliefs about homosexuality with their love for each other.

Teens Speak Out (45 minutes)
A young lesbian and two gay men discuss their lives and their process of coming out. Two black participants discuss what it is like to be part of a double minority.

Who's Afraid of Project 10? (23 minutes; 1990)
A debate over counseling services for gay and lesbian youth in the Los Angeles public schools. Contact Scott Greene for availability: (213) 656-7327.

HOTLINES

DEAF COMMUNITY AIDS HOTLINE
(TTY/TDD)
800-243-7889
Monday through Friday

IYG GAY/LESBIAN/BISEXUAL
YOUTH HOTLINE
800-347-8336
Thursday through Sunday
Peer counseling and information for youth
under 21 years of age.

LINEA NACIONAL DE SIDA
(SPANISH AIDS HOTLINE)
800-344-7432
Daily

NATIONAL AIDS HOTLINE
800-342-AIDS (24-hour service)
800-AIDS-TTY (hearing impaired)

NATIONAL GAY & LESBIAN
CRISISLINE
800-767-4297
Crisis intervention, information, and
referral.

NATIONAL RUNAWAY
SWITCHBOARD
800-621-4000 (seven days a week, 24
hours)
Hotline for runaway/homeless youth and
their families.

UNITED STATES JUSTICE
DEPARTMENT NATIONAL HATE
CRIME REPORTING NUMBER
800-347-HATE

Appendix D: Famous Gays and Lesbians

As gay and lesbian youth attempt to understand themselves, it is important that they are presented with role models in educational curricula that will help promote self-acceptance. Recognition and discussion of notable gay and lesbian people in society can help reduce homophobia. When students recognize the contributions gays and lesbians have made to literature, history, science, math, the fine arts, and other aspects of life throughout world history and modern society they can begin to accept this aspect of themselves or others.

The following lists contain the names of prominent historical and modern gays, lesbians, and bisexuals, the majority of whom have made major contributions that have enriched the world. The first list, compiled in *The Book of Lists* (Wallechinsky, Wallace, & Wallace, 1977, pp. 336–338), includes many names from early world history and a few from modern times. The second list contains names of additional modern representatives and was compiled from scholarly biographical sources and from public announcements made by the persons themselves.

GAYS, LESBIANS, AND BISEXUALS FROM EARLY WORLD HISTORY AND MODERN TIMES

1 Sappho (flourished c. 600 B.C.), Greek poet
2 Christina (1626–1689), Swedish queen
3 Madame de Staël (1766–1817), French author
4 Charlotte Cushman (1816–1876), U.S. actress
5 Gertrude Stein (1874–1946), U.S. author
6 Alice B. Toklas (1877–1967), U.S. author, cook
7 Virginia Woolf (1882–1941), British author
8 Victoria Sackville-West (1892–1962), British author
9 Bessie Smith (1894–1937), U.S. singer
10 Kate Millett (b. 1934), U.S. author

11 Janis Joplin (1943–1970), U.S. singer
12 Zeno of Elea (fifth century B.C.), Greek philosopher
13 Sophocles (496?–406 B.C.), Greek playwright
14 Euripides (480? – 406? B.C.), Greek dramatist
15 Socrates (470?–399 B.C.), Greek philosopher
16 Aristotle (384–322 B.C.), Greek philosopher
17 Alexander the Great (356–323 B.C.), Macedonian ruler
18 Julius Ceasar (100–44 B.C.), Roman emperor
19 Hadrian (76–138 A.D.), Roman emperor
20 Richard the Lion-Hearted (1157–1199), British king
21 Richard II (1367–1400), British king
22 Sandro Botticelli (1444?–1510), Italian painter
23 Leonardo da Vinci (1452–1519), Italian painter, scientist
24 Julius III (1487–1555), Italian pope
25 Benvenuto Cellini (1500–1571) Italian goldsmith
26 Francis Bacon (1561–1626), British philosopher, statesman
27 Christopher Marlowe (1564–1593), British playwright
28 James I (1566–1625), British king
29 John Milton (1608–1674), British author
30 Jean-Baptiste Lully (1632–1687), French composer
31 Peter the Great (1672–1725), Russian czar
32 Frederick the Great (1712–1786), Prussian king
33 Gustavus III (1746–1792), Swedish king
34 Alexander von Humboldt (1769–1859), German naturalist
35 George Gordon, Lord Byron (1788–1824), British poet
36 Hans Christian Andersen (1805–1875), Danish author
37 Walt Whitman (1819–1892), U.S. poet
38 Horatio Alger (1832–1899), U.S. author
39 Samuel Butler (1835–1902), British author
40 Algernon Swinburne (1837–1909), British poet
41 Piotr Ilich Tchaikovsky (1840–1893), Russian composer
42 Paul Verlaine (1844–1896), French poet
43 Arthur Rimbaud (1854–1891), French poet
44 Oscar Wilde (1854–1900), British playwright
45 Frederick Rolfe (Baron Corvo) (1860–1913), British author
46 Andre Gide (1869–1951), French author
47 Marcel Proust (1871–1922), French author
48 E.M. Forster (1879–1970), British author
49 John Maynard Keynes (1883–1946), British economist
50 Harold Nicholson (1886–1968), British author, diplomat
51 Ernst Rohm (1887–1934), German nazi leader
52 T.E. Lawrence (1888–1935), British soldier, author
53 Jean Cocteau (1889–1963), French author
54 Waslaw Nijinsky (1890–1950), Russian ballet dancer
55 Bill Tilden (1893–1953), U.S. tennis player
56 Christopher Isherwood (b. 1904), British author
57 Dag Hammarskjöld (1905–1961), Swedish U.N. secretary-general

58 W.H. Auden (1907–1973), British–U.S. poet
59 Jean Genet (b. 1910), French playwright
60 Tennessee Williams (b. 1911), U.S. playwright
61 Merle Miller (b. 1919), U.S. author
62 Pier Paolo Pasolini (1922–1975), Italian film director
63 Brendan Behan (1923–1964), Irish author
64 Malcolm Boyd (b. 1923), U.S. theologian
65 Allan Ginsberg (b. 1926), U.S. poet
66 David Bowie (b. 1947), British singer
67 Elton John (b. 1947), British singer

ADDITIONAL FAMOUS GAYS AND LESBIANS

1 Gore Vidal, author
2 Benjamin Britton, composer
3 Samuel Barber, composer
4 Cole Porter, composer
5 k.d. lang, singer
6 Andy Warhol, artist
7 Alan Turing, mathematical–computer genius
8 Barney Frank, U.S. Congressman (Massachusetts)
9 Gerry Studds, U.S. Congressman (Massachusetts)
10 George Cukor, film director
11 Martina Navratilova, tennis champion
12 Greg Louganis, Olympic diving gold medalist
13 Roberta Achtenberg, attorney/Assistant Director of U.S. Housing & Urban Development
14 Urvashi Vaid, attorney and former Executive Director of the National Gay and Lesbian Task Force
15 Colonel Margarethe Cammermeyer, U.S. National Guard
16 Rita Mae Brown, author
17 James Baldwin, author
18 Truman Capote, author
19 Edward Albee, playwright
20 Willa Cather, author
21 W. Somerset Maugham, author
22 A.E. Housman, poet
23 Lewis Carroll, author and mathematician
24 David B. Mixner, political consultant
25 Denise L. Eger, rabbi
26 David Kopay, professional football player
27 Audre Lorde, poet
28 Karen Clark, state legislator (Minnesota)
29 Marion Riggs, filmmaker
30 Alison Bechdel, cartoonist
31 Bruce Hayes, Olympic gold medal swimmer

32 Suzanne Westenhofer, commedienne
33 Reverend Troy Perry, spiritual leader
34 Richard C. Failla, New York Supreme Court justice
35 Amanda Bearse, actress
36 Harvey Fierstein, playwright/actor
37 Janis Ian, singer/songwriter
38 Debra A. Batts, federal judge
39 Melissa Etheridge, musician
40 Marvin Schwam, founder—Gay Entertainment Television
41 Susan Love, physician, breast cancer activist

Index

Author Index